AMERICAN HUCKSTER

AMERICAN HUCKSTER

**HOW CHUCK BLAZER GOT RICH FROM—AND SOLD OUT—
THE MOST POWERFUL CABAL IN WORLD SPORTS**

MARY PAPENFUSS
AND TERI THOMPSON

HARPER

An Imprint of HarperCollinsPublishers
www.harpercollins.com

HarperCollins books may be purchased for educational, business, or sales promotional use. For information, please e-mail the Special Markets Department at SPsales@harpercollins.com.

FIRST EDITION

Library of Congress Cataloging-in-Publication Data has been applied for.

ISBN: 978-0-06-244967-2

16 17 18 19 20   DIX/RRD   10 9 8 7 6 5 4 3 2 1

For ML, who lived it.

CONTENTS

INTRODUCTION

EARLY ON A NOVEMBER EVENING IN 2011, AN EXTRAVAGANTLY BEARDED MAN EXITED HIS apartment in Manhattan's Trump Tower. He was seated on a mobility scooter—he weighed an immobile 450 pounds—and was accompanied by his longtime partner, former actress Mary Lynn Blanks, and an elderly lawyer friend, Al Rosenstein. They left the chrome-and-marble lobby through a glass door under a gold-plated awning onto East Fifty-Sixth Street. Then they turned right and headed toward Fifth Avenue, bound for a neighborhood steakhouse called Uncle Jack's.

They had gone only a few feet before someone called out behind them: "Mr. Blazer, may we have a word with you, please?"

The voice belonged to a federal agent. There were two of them, one from the Federal Bureau of Investigation, the other from the Internal Revenue Service. They escorted Chuck Blazer back to the Trump Tower public atrium a few yards away. There, sitting at a table among tourists and bamboo trees, the three cut a deal that would ultimately dismantle the world's most powerful sports organization: the Switzerland-based Fédération Internationale de Football Association, or as it is known to soccer fans, FIFA.

The deal also signaled the end of Blazer's improbable rise from Westchester County soccer dad to the uppermost reaches of FIFA, and the culture of corruption in international soccer that would make him ever fatter and richer.

For seventeen years, Blazer was one of twenty-four members of a formidable but secretive cabal, the FIFA executive committee, Ex-Co, who had unqualified control of the world's most popular sport and its most prestigious tournament, the World Cup. The selection of the host nation for the tournament, as well as the assignment of global television rights, is worth billions of dollars and is the source of an unending amount of intrigue surrounding FIFA and its then president, Sepp Blatter. Incredibly, in 2010 the Ex-Co selected Qatar—a desert nation with no suitable stadiums—to host the 2022 World Cup. Despite this and other sordid dealings uncovered by European investigators and journalists, and even by FIFA itself, the Ex-Co power structure seemed as impervious as one of Zurich's bank vaults.

That all changed when the agents intercepted Blazer. As general secretary of CONCACAF, the regional soccer federation representing the Caribbean and Central and North America, Blazer and Trinidad and Tobago's Jack Warner—CONCACAF's president and a fellow Ex-Co member—had helped themselves to millions in kickbacks and bribes tied to World Cup bids, as well as to marketing rights to a variety of regional tournaments. Blazer stashed his take in secret offshore bank accounts, safe-deposit boxes in Zurich, and in file cabinets in his Trump Tower lair. He often carried bundles of cash through airports in thin packs bound by a paper strip—never more than $9,900 per trip, to avoid customs restrictions. To protect his illegal lucre, he hadn't filed a US tax return in at least two decades, an omission that would prove his undoing.

The agents needed less than an hour to flip him.

Once confronted, Blazer agreed to a broad array of onerous conditions. He would cooperate with the agents, the FBI's Jared Randall and IRS investigator Steve Berryman, and inform on the men he had spent so many years cultivating. He would use a miniature device hidden in his key chain—he was too obese to be fitted for a wire—to record them at endless lavish dinners and Ex-Co meetings, exploiting their contacts and access to the world's power brokers. He would pass along their e-mail addresses and mobile phone numbers and tape their calls to his home. He would make a list of those he had done business with or had contact with, including his girlfriend Blanks and her two children. He would even record conversations while he was attending the 2012 Olympics in London, tossing down his key fob as he talked business at the exclusive May Fair Hotel, or at Ciro's Pomodoro in Knightsbridge, or the Ivy, near Cambridge Circus, his other posh hangouts.

"They've got me for RICO," Blazer would tell Blanks later that evening. "Racketeering, embezzlement, fraud, income tax." RICO, the federal Racketeer Influenced and Corrupt Organizations Act, was passed in 1970 to help lawmen bring down the Mafia. Now they were using it against the self-described godfather of American soccer to help them topple the game's kingpins.

Blazer's cooperation with the feds, uncovered in November 2014 by the New York *Daily News* sports investigative team, which includes this book's coauthors, gave US Department of Justice investigators a window on the corruption permeating the sport's finances—and readers a voyeuristic glimpse at Blazer's outlandish lifestyle. There was the $288,000 annual rent for his three-bedroom Trump Tower apartment and an adjacent one-bedroom flat for his two leaky cats. There was his $29 million in American Express charges over seven years, homes in Miami and the Bahamas, offshore accounts funding countless five-figure meals in the world's finest restaurants, and a parade of strippers and mistresses. What wasn't paid for by FIFA was covered by CONCACAF: the Confederation of North, Central American and Caribbean Association Football.

The information that Blazer divulged would result in one of the most remarkable press conferences in the history of sport. On the morning of May 27, 2015, almost three and a half years after the two agents had interrupted Blazer's dinner plans, US Attorney General Loretta Lynch unsealed a 161-page indictment in Brooklyn federal court containing forty-seven counts of racketeering, wire fraud, and money laundering against fourteen defendants. The list included nine current or former high-ranking FIFA officials and five sports marketing executives charged with "conspiring to solicit and receive well over $150 million in bribes and kickbacks." A second indictment, unsealed on December 3, 2015, added sixteen more defendants to the roster on similar charges.

Blazer himself had secretly pled guilty two years before in the United States District Court for the Eastern District of New York to ten counts of racketeering, wire fraud, money laundering, income tax evasion, and failure to report foreign bank and financial accounts.

Some eleven hours before Lynch's press conference, soccer fans had watched news coverage in utter amazement as Swiss cops rounded up seven members of the executive committee in a daybreak raid at the five-star hotel Baur au Lac, on the shores of Lake Zurich near FIFA headquarters. The Ex-Co big shots were arrested and escorted out of their plush digs, their perp walks hidden by a veil of white bed linens held aloft by hotel staff to shield them from the press and the public.

The indictment list included two men not present at the Baur au Lac: Argentinian marketing executive Alejandro Burzaco, who was staying at another Zurich hotel and who fled immediately to Italy once the commotion began; and Blazer's buddy Jack Warner, who had been ousted from the Ex-Co and the presidency of CONCACAF in 2011 and was ensconced in extradition-averse Trinidad. Warner loudly proclaimed his innocence. But four others allied with him had earlier pled guilty and began cooperating, including Blazer, the Brazilian marketing king Jose Hawilla, and, curiously enough, Warner's own sons, Darryl and Daryan Warner. The latter once flew to Paris, packed multiple $10,000 stacks of cash in a briefcase, and delivered the money to his father in Port of Spain. All in a day's time. The indictment covered schemes arranged by Blazer, referred to as "coconspirator number 1," and Warner, whose bizarre, often comical battle to avoid extradition would make headlines through the winter of 2015.

Significantly absent on the indictment list was Sepp Blatter, FIFA's imperious Swiss president. Unindicted but not unnoticed. After Blazer's cooperation became known, an alarmed Blatter put the United States on his personal no-fly list, apparently fearful that he'd be apprehended. He chose to skip the biggest FIFA tournament of 2015: the Women's World Cup, held too close for comfort in Canada. Blatter retained noted US white-collar-criminal specialist Richard Cullen to handle matters with the Department of Justice, but his real legal exposure came in Zurich in October 2015, when Swiss attorney general Michael Lauber started a criminal investigation over a $2 million payment FIFA made to European federation president Michel Platini—a former star player and Blatter's presumed successor—reportedly in exchange for Platini's supporting Blatter in the 2011 FIFA presidential election.

Lauber questioned Blatter as a suspect for "criminal mismanagement" and "appropriation" of funds. Blatter said that the payment was for services rendered FIFA by Platini. The two men were provisionally suspended for ninety days by the FIFA ethics committee amid a range of inquiries following questionable payments and the controversial Ex-Co vote to hand the World Cup to Russia in 2018 and to Qatar in 2022. They appealed, and lost, and as 2016 approached, both were hit with eight-year bans, guilty of "disloyal payment surrounding the sport." Both planned to appeal to the Court of Arbitration for Sport (CAS), in Lausanne, Switzerland, formed in 1981 to resolved sports-related legal disputes.

For soccer fans who had long despaired that FIFA would ever be held accountable to anyone, the scope of the Justice Department's indictment was extraordinary. Just as it had unraveled the secretive Swiss banking industry years earlier, exposing billions of illegally cached dollars, the feds used an informant to build a case steadily with tentacles in a foreign country. Blazer, a US citizen conducting FIFA business on American soil, was the legal wedge into the organization's bolted Swiss door.

Thousands of miles beyond the Brooklyn courtroom, it would become clear that Blatter was finished, and perhaps lucky to have avoided jail. The Ex-Co itself was in disarray, the result of the raft of suspensions by the ethics committee's probe, which had been led quietly by former Department of Justice attorney William Burck, a partner in the Washington, DC–based firm Quinn Emanuel Urquhart & Sullivan. Burck was reported by the *Wall Street Journal* to be taking "unprecedented measures to compel testimony from dozens of current and former top officials and seize documents and electronic records that go back more than a decade." The reason for the unusual demand for cooperation from the secretive board: to protect the organization itself from becoming a target of the US probe. If FIFA were indicted, its assets would be frozen; its very existence put in jeopardy.

On the day that Lynch's indictment was unsealed, Blazer lay ill with cancer in a New Jersey medical facility, breathing with the aid of a machine and fighting infections from the treatment. But by then, the world had come to understand how an overweight overachiever from the working-class New York City borough of Queens had toppled the game's regency. Fans worldwide reveled that it had taken a snitch, a tough, ambitious prosecutor, and the boy scouts of the FBI and IRS from soccer-come-lately America to once and for all shine the light on FIFA corruption.

"If the Americans end up laying a glove on those powerful men long alleged to have fleeced the world in the name of sport," wrote columnist Marina Hyde of Britain's *Guardian*, employing the newspaper's sarcastic terminology for American soccer, "let no one ever be sniffy about their involvement in soccerball again."

ONE

TEETERING AT THE TOP

CHUCK BLAZER WAS PALE, BREATHING HARD, SITTING HUNCHED ON THE EDGE OF HIS bed, the force of his weight compressing the mattress. The shrewd sports administrator who had helped bring soccer to millions of Americans had just heard news that could destroy him—and the empire he had helped create.

Despite his momentary distress on May 10, 2011, Blazer felt safe. He had a few days to sort things out, time to plan his next move. Blazer considered his $18,000-a-month apartment in Midtown Manhattan a refuge. The crow's-nest home on the forty-ninth floor of the iconic Trump Tower offered a respite from the constant demands of the business of soccer, with a calming, panoramic view north of Central Park to the horizon, and vistas south over the Empire State Building. To Blazer, his address was also a reassuringly sublime perch befitting a borough-bred hustler who reinvented himself as a top-of-the-food-chain man of substance. The home had an elegant décor, with royal-green walls and furniture inspired by the Far East. The living room was dominated by a Chinese lacquer screen featuring a bas-relief of the Forbidden City speckled with gems, which Blazer had quietly acquired in Beijing while hunting for bargain artifacts appropriated during China's Cultural Revolution of the late 1960s. The apartment was so high that it wasn't unusual for visitors to become light-headed standing next to one of the floor-to-ceiling windows if they peered at the relentless waves of pedestrians and traffic far below. But it wasn't vertigo, exactly, that Blazer was experiencing just then.

The source of Blazer's panic that moment was a spotty phone call he had just concluded with a soccer official in the Bahamas that revealed a $1 million payoff and an attempted coup in the international association that controlled global soccer. Now the suddenly rattled Blazer could imagine himself busted down to what he once told a confidant he knew himself to be: just a fat crook from Queens. He was acutely aware of how far he had risen—and how far he could plummet from prestige and power back to the modest beginnings that, as a young man, Blazer couldn't escape fast enough. What he didn't know—what he couldn't have predicted—was that the chain of events begun this day would result four years later in a spectacular crackdown on FIFA corruption by the US Justice Department—with the help of Chuck Blazer.

It would also expose Blazer's unique place in history as a sports organization megaswindler who secretly collected millions of dollars in bribes, kickbacks, and a flood of unauthorized expense money even as he helped breathe life into the US soccer market.

For Blazer, it had been a compulsive, grasping climb to his Fifth Avenue aerie from his childhood home, a clone of the other bland, white clapboard-and-brick two-story houses on his block on 193rd Street in Flushing in a borough he was loath to mention: Queens. He often boasted that his grandfather Max had *washed* windows in Midtown Manhattan; now he dwelled in one of the most expensive high-rises in the neighborhood. Blazer had been living large in every sense of the word since 1991. He had a prodigious appetite for food, as well as for money, power, adulation—and women. Despite his gargantuan size, he could be a captivating, even seductive character, with a penetrating, brown-eyed gaze and a voice he described as "liquid chocolate," which he believed women found irresistible. Against the odds, he had leveraged his scrappy cunning and surprising charisma to hoist his way doggedly from volunteering in suburban youth sports organizations to the very pinnacle of international soccer power. He gamed, and gained, a seat on the exalted executive committee of FIFA, the richest, mightiest, and most corrupt sports organization in the world. He wasn't even a big soccer fan.

Blazer's longtime lover, Mary Lynn Blanks, was in the bedroom when the unnerving phone call came. The petite blonde, a former soap-opera actress who had also worked as a public relations and video production assistant for the Ringling Bros. and Barnum & Bailey Circus, served as Blazer's de facto wife, accompanying him on the FIFA circuit beginning in 2002. Well read, attentive to Blazer, and gracious, Blanks moved comfortably among the old-school European power brokers and their elegant wives during the sumptuous dinners in the five-star hotels, palaces, and museum galleries where the Ex-Co members were feted.

Blanks could sense Blazer's agitation the instant the call began. His huge head with its leonine cloud of thick, dark curls threaded with gray was tipped forward as he clutched the phone to his ear. "Absolutely not," Blazer was saying to the soccer official. "The cash didn't come from us." He rubbed a hand over his salt-and-pepper beard. "Uh-huh," he said, nodding, after a few seconds. "Does anyone else know?"

Blanks paced the room as Blazer spoke, straining to hear his side of the conversation over the blaring fifty-inch Sony flat-screen TV at the foot of the bed that Blazer kept on day and night. The TV was seldom tuned to soccer games. Blazer preferred programs about the subjects dearest to him: business and stock advice on Fox and CNBC. He liked to brag to underlings about his stock-picking prowess. Now CNBC's loudmouth market wag, Jim Cramer, was shouting on *Mad Money*, and Blanks struggled to make out what Chuck was saying. Finally, Blazer tossed his cell phone angrily across the bed. Blanks stopped pacing.

"It's Jack," Blazer said. "He's really done it now."

Jack was Jack Warner, Blazer's putative boss at CONCACAF. Blazer had helped elevate Warner, a brash, raw-boned Trinidadian, to the presidency of CONCACAF twenty-one years earlier, and Chuck had worked as his general secretary ever since. The two contrived in tandem to transform the once-negligible CONCACAF into a regional powerhouse that raked in tens of millions of dollars annually in soccer tournaments, TV rights, and sponsorship fees. Along the way, the friends became multimillionaires through a clandestine system of backroom deals.

What Jack had "done" was to try to seize the FIFA presidency from longtime boss Sepp Blatter and deliver it to Mohamed bin Hammam, a billionaire Qatari construction magnate who served on the Ex-Co with Warner and Blazer and headed the Asian Football Confederation, another of FIFA's global associations. It was a gutsy, even foolhardy, maneuver, but one that could position Warner within a heartbeat of the presidency. The key? Money: brown envelopes stuffed with $40,000 in cash—four $10,000 stacks of $100 bills—to buy twenty-five votes at a special meeting convened in Port of Spain, Trinidad. The tally from the Caribbean Football Union (CFU), the largest organization of CONCACAF, could very likely boost bin Hammam to FIFA's highest office.

An infuriated Blazer had just learned that the money had already changed hands; it was too late to reel in the cash. The phone call came from the boss of a stunned Bahamian whistle-blower who had witnessed the payoffs. The whistle-blower had accepted one of the envelopes, reported the bribe to his association president, and then photographed the bundled bills before returning them. Warner and bin Hammam's scheme was the kind of outlandish plot that cynical soccer fans around the world had long assumed occurred regularly in the meeting rooms of FIFA and its member associations, and feared would never be exposed. Now someone from the inside was talking, threatening to lay bare FIFA's secrets. The next move was up to Blazer.

Weeks earlier, Blazer had pleaded desperately with Warner not to go through with the Port of Spain meeting. He initially learned of the plan shortly after bin Hammam had declared his candidacy for the FIFA presidency that March, three months after FIFA's controversial decision to make Qatar, inhumanly hot in summer, host of the 2022 World Cup. "Dear Brother," bin Hammam wrote Warner on April 1, "I will really appreciate if you can kindly organize a special congress for my brothers at CONCACAF before your congress in May. I count a lot on your support for both of us to achieve our common goals for the future." Warner responded within minutes, vowing in an e-mail, "I will do my utmost to assist you," while informing the Qatari that he would have to pick up the bill for everyone's travel.

"I hope this is an April Fool's joke," a perturbed Blazer fired off in an angry e-mail to Warner that same day after his boss had copied him on the e-mail. "I regret the need to address this issue after the fact and that you didn't see fit to talk with me prior to your response to Mohamed." Blazer reminded Warner that it was the worst time of the year to summon CONCACAF members to any special meeting. CONCACAF's annual Ordinary Congress was scheduled in Miami on May 3, 2011, an obligatory gathering for association officers. CONCACAF would mark its milestone fiftieth anniversary then, and members would also be finishing up complicated planning for the biennial Gold Cup tournament beginning the following month in eleven cities. Bin Hammam's planned April meeting would also fall on the Passover holiday as well as during the first leg of the Champions League tournament in Mexico City.

"Our offices in New York, Guatemala, and Miami are working around the clock," Blazer wrote. "I can clearly say that we have never had a period of activity as intense as now. Mohamed's request, while convenient for him, is really quite impossible."

Blazer suggested that instead of going to Port of Spain, bin Hammam come to the Miami congress and promote his candidacy at a forum of the forty-one CONCACAF member associations. He pointed out that bin Hammam would be relatively close on May 1, in Paraguay, where he would be attending meetings with the Confederación Sudamericana de Fútbol (CONMEBOL), FIFA's South American Football Confederation. FIFA president Blatter would also be attending the CONCACAF Congress to urge members to reelect him. (Blatter would offer his own monetary inducement for votes: a promise to allocate $1.5 million in FIFA funds to CONCACAF territory.)

If Warner and bin Hammam insisted on their strategy, Blazer told Warner in the carefully worded e-mail, there were better—and more circumspect—ways to carry out their plan. He urged Warner not to capitulate to bin Hammam's demands and jeopardize a system that had served them both so well. "At a number of levels, the request that he is making is not practical, while other solutions for his purpose are available," Blazer wrote. "If you would like to discuss alternatives to find a way to give Mohamed an audience with our members, I am happy to do that. But, please, do not destroy the work that needs to be done by rushing into decisions which cause problems for us." In a subsequent e-mail, Blazer warned Warner about the "ethical issue" of bin Hammam "paying for a meeting and bringing in delegates."

Warner was annoyed by Blazer's patronizing tone, especially the "April Fool's" line. "I do find it offensive," he wrote. "All I said was that I would like to make it happen . . . and I get this long response in a very incredulous tone that suggests something is wrong." Despite Blazer's warning to call off the meeting, Warner reached out to CONCACAF special events planner Jill Fracisco, who worked for the association in New York, to ask her to arrange a special congress for bin Hammam. An angry Blazer called Fracisco into his office to tell her "No fucking way," and yanked her off the project.

Blazer also warned Warner that hit reading of the North and Central American members of CONCACAF indicated that they preferred

Sepp Blatter remain as president, and wouldn't support bin Hammam. Warner finally told Blazer flatly that bin Hammam did not want to attend the Miami congress, adding: "and, in some ways, neither do I wish for him to do so," offering no further explanation. He would instead arrange a meeting for bin Hammam with the members of the CFU, representing twenty-five of CONCACAF's thirty-five votes. Blazer stopped arguing and responded simply: "Acknowledged." The Warner family travel agency arranged all the trips for the Caribbean representatives to the meeting, with bin Hammam covering costs. A Warner aide would testify later that staffers were told to calculate all costs—and then bill bin Hammam twice the amount. According to the December Eastern District indictments, by the end of April, bin Hammam transferred $364,000 via a New York City bank to a CFU account in Trinidad controlled by Warner and in July bin Hammam would transfer an additional $1.2 million to an account in Warner's name in Trinidad.

After the meeting was over, and the cash had been exchanged, Blazer was confronted with a treacherous choice. He was furious but also reluctant to turn in Warner to FIFA officials, even though they increasingly bickered about Warner's ever-more-reckless demands for money over the years. But how could Blazer ignore the Bahamian whistle-blower without jeopardizing his own position and raising suspicions about his possible role in the scandal? Warner and Blazer had enjoyed a long, lucrative run heading up CONCACAF and serving together on the Ex-Co. The two apparently anomalous personalities bonded in part because they were both outlaws—and outcasts. Blazer sometimes felt like a chubby, clownish American fraud among the snooty European soccer administrators, and Warner considered himself persecuted and misunderstood because he grew up poor and black in Trinidad.

The two CONCACAF leaders now stood on opposite sides of a critical FIFA power showdown. Warner and his Caribbean nations were aligning themselves with bin Hammam and his increasingly powerful Asian Football Confederation in the wake of Qatar's successful

World Cup campaign. Blazer opted to throw his support behind Blatter and the rest of the FIFA old guard by turning in his friend with a call to FIFA. What he didn't realize was that his actions would inexorably lead US authorities right back to him and light the fuse to take down FIFA.

Three days after the first tip-off phone call from the Bahamas—on Friday, May 13, 2011—Blazer hesitated before ringing Zurich to report Warner for a suspected ethics violation to FIFA General Secretary Jérôme Valcke. Though he had no conception of what he was about to unleash, Blazer was worried about the fallout. He and Warner had operated with impunity for more than two decades. They knew the intricacies of scams that could get them both bounced from their prestigious positions—and even land them in prison. Warner was a volatile, vengeful man when people crossed him. Blazer realized that reporting the bin Hammam meeting to FIFA would sunder their relationship, and Warner would no doubt seek payback. On the other side of the equation was Sepp Blatter. Though FIFA's president at times appeared to be a slightly addled grandfather, he was, in fact, a ruthless despot who viciously punished Ex-Co officials who challenged or criticized him.

Blazer stared into the distance, phone in hand, again slouched on the edge of his bed, frown lines creasing his forehead. Blanks was nearby, sitting at her desk in their bedroom, convinced that Blazer was torn about betraying Warner and concerned about the consequences for himself. She tried to console him. "There's really no choice, Chuck," she said. "You have to report Jack."

Blazer shook his head as he hit the speed dial for Valcke. "You don't understand, Mel," said Blazer, using his pet name for Blanks. "Everything I know about Jack, he knows about me.

"This isn't going to end well."

TWO

ON THE HUSTLE

MARY LYNN BLANKS WAS STUNNED TO RECEIVE A LETTER OUT OF THE CLEAR BLUE FROM long-ago lover Chuck Blazer offering sunny birthday greetings when she turned fifty. Blazer boasted in the October 2002 note that he had achieved "most of my goals, both professional and personally." He expressed the hope that she was enjoying a good life too.

The last time Blanks had seen Blazer, to her great relief, was twenty-five years earlier, as he stomped out of their bedroom in the East Side Manhattan condo they shared. She was left trembling and spattered with her own blood. Moments before, Blazer had bellowed at her to clean the apartment; she was making a protein shake in the kitchen and yelled back that the place didn't need it. Furious, Blazer grabbed her by her hair and arm, dragged her into the bedroom, threw her on the bed, and punched her, hard, in the face, shattering her glasses and cutting her cheek. He stopped only when she was able to wriggle free from his grip.

His rage apparently spent, Blazer left, slamming the apartment door behind him. Blanks quickly contacted a friend for protection and to help her pack. "She was in bad shape," recalled her pal Cynthia Georgeson. "She was bloody and frightened. Her cheek was cut and swollen, her eye closing up and turning black." Georgeson urged her friend to call the police, but Blanks—hurt, scared, and embarrassed—wanted to put the ugly confrontation behind her as quickly as possible. She moved back into her old apartment on the Upper West Side and resumed her former life. Aside from a short note from Blazer, blaming her for the violence, and an odd phone call years later to say hello after her marriage to another man, Blanks hadn't heard from Chuck—until now. She had no idea where he lived or what he did for work.

"In my mind's eye you will always be captured as the exuberant and beautiful 25-year-old beginning a career and, ultimately, what I hope has been a very good life," Blazer wrote in the birthday letter, as if the two had parted the best of friends. "My running off on Saturdays to coach the kids' soccer games ultimately moved me into a new professional forum and facilitated the pursuit of a political career in sports. I now, as the only American in history, have a key leadership role on the world body of soccer, FIFA and the World Cup. I have dined with kings and presidents while averaging over 200,000 miles a year globetrotting and having fun. It has been a great ride."

Soon Blanks would be along—again—for the Blazer ride. But first, he'd have to sell her on the idea. And Chuck Blazer was very good at selling.

BLAZER WAS TWENTY-EIGHT WHEN HE FIRST MET BLANKS IN 1973. HE WAS A RAKISH, six-foot, two-hundred-pound marketing consultant on the move. Blanks, a Florida native living in Manhattan, was a twenty-one-year-old aspiring actress who worked between auditions as a cocktail waitress, model, and at trade show gigs. She would have a unique view into the personality and early days of the future master of the soccer universe.

They met while she was modeling for a print ad for the Seagram's liquor company, one of Blazer's clients at the time. She was to pose in a bikini next to a giant inflatable whiskey bottle; the shoot took place at a studio in Chelsea. Before the session, the photographer called Chuck and urged him to meet Blanks because "I think you'll like her." So Blazer arrived and leaned against the doorway of Blanks's dressing room, chatting with her as she sat with a bathrobe over her bikini. "I told him I moved to New York to be an actress, but was mostly waiting tables at night, handing out cosmetic samples, and spraying shoppers with Norell perfume in department stores, and working at trade shows," Blanks recalled. "He told me about his businesses. He was fascinating. That beautiful voice, those eyes—only a few pounds overweight then. He wasn't the kind of guy I was typically attracted to, but his voice got to me. And he asked me a lot of questions; he was interested in me, in my life." He was also married, with a wife and two young kids at home in Westchester. "I was living with my boyfriend, and I had no intention of cheating on him," said Blanks.

Over the next few years, Blazer continued to seek out Blanks at trade shows in Manhattan's old New York Coliseum, a squat, tan brick building at Columbus Circle that then served as New York's convention center. Blazer was there plugging products, keeping an eye on the competition, and drumming up new business. He worked primarily in corporate incentives marketing. His Cavalier Production Company sold motivational giveaways used by businesses to reward salespeople, such as golf balls bearing the slogan "Thank You, Paine Webber" for stockbrokers, or branded beach towels for agents selling Holland America cruises. He also did product promotions for Hula Hoop creator Wham-O, Kentucky Fried Chicken, and Kodak. He arranged "fly-ins" with local radio stations to distribute free Frisbees at events. In one cross-marketing scheme, Blazer used Frisbees as covers on buckets of Kentucky Fried Chicken; in others, he shrink-wrapped Coppertone tanning lotion or rolls of Kodak film with Frisbees.

Blanks worked as a model and spokeswoman at the Coliseum during car and boat shows, as well as technology and medical supply exhibitions. She was a regular at General Aniline and Film (GAF) booths, hawking the company's toy View-Master, dressed as a fortune-teller. She also showed off GAF's film cassettes used in X-rays, dressed, far more popularly, as a nurse. GAF and Blazer client Kodak frequently shared exhibition space, and Chuck took those opportunities, and others, to cozy up to Blanks. "He always said hello, asked me how I was doing. He focused on me," recalled Blanks. "He could cast a spell."

It was the same gift that made Blazer a sales wizard. "Chuck could sell ice in Alaska in the middle of winter," said a longtime CONCACAF employee. He first acquired the sales bug as a preteen working at his family's businesses, including Blazer's Spa Luncheonette on Queens Boulevard, a street crowded with mom-and-pop stores. The Blazer shop, in the Forest Hills neighborhood, was an odd mix of café, candy store, and drugstore items. By age twelve, Chuck was traveling to work from the family home in Flushing that he shared with big brother Barry, his mother, Edna, and his father, Abe. He ran the cash register at the luncheonette, flipped burgers, and chatted up the customers. He also helped out at the counter at Blazer's Stationery & Gifts in Rego Park. "He was incredibly personable," recalled Madison Avenue lawyer Sherwood "Woody" Salvan, who lived next door to the stationery store as a boy and was a high school classmate of Blazer's. "He was outgoing, always friendly."

"He was a boy entrepreneur," said express delivery manager Kirby Sales, who knew Chuck when they were junior high school students. "He didn't run with my crew. He was a loner. But he was a hard worker and go-getter. He was thinking business while the rest of us were hanging out."

After junior high, Chuck landed a treasured spot in the Bronx High

School of Science, one of the city's elite public schools that require a rigorous entrance exam. But once accepted, he transferred almost immediately to Forest Hills High in September of his freshman year. He would complain years later about the long commute from Queens to the prestigious Bronx school, which left little time for him to work in the family businesses. Once he switched to his local school, he was again able to spell his father each day at the Spa Luncheonette. But the job limited his social life. The only extracurricular activities he could fit in involved playing saxophone for the high school band and checking hall passes as a member of the Marshall Club. Both were viewed by most students who bothered to notice as the diversions of a geek, at a time before geeks were popular.

Blazer played no sports, including soccer, even though Forest Hills was one of the first high schools in the country to field a team. He considered himself an excellent bowler, however, and once boasted that he won a trophy at Hollywood Lanes on Queens Boulevard. Yet no one on the Forest Hills High bowling team, which practiced and competed there, remembered ever seeing him.

Blazer wasn't so much awkward at school as he was simply out of sync with his peers. He was younger than his classmates, having skipped at least a grade because he was in a "Special Progress" program to advance especially bright students. He graduated at fifteen, two years ahead of most of his classmates. He was a handsome, strapping kid with a thick head of curly hair, but he was still the baby of his class; the girls paid no attention to him. "I really had nothing to do with guys my age," recalled classmate Rhoda Berke. "I always went out with the older ones." Younger boys in her class didn't have a prayer.

But in many ways, Blazer was more mature than his older classmates. He had worked independently for years before many of them had their first job. And he was a young man in a hurry. He didn't wait around for the others to catch up to him; he graduated in January of his senior year, eager to move on to the next phase of his life.

The invisible student would win sweet revenge decades later when he hosted a cocktail party at Trump Tower for his graduating class. When he learned of the planned fiftieth reunion festivities in 2011, Blazer contacted former classmate Murray Vale, a New York sales executive who was one of the event organizers, saying that he wanted to "give something back" to his class. He offered an all-expenses-paid fete on a lower level of the Trump lobby the night before the official reunion party at the Edison Ballroom ten blocks away in Midtown. By then, Blazer had already served on the FIFA executive committee for twelve years, and had been general secretary of CONCACAF for twenty.

Instead of showboating his success, though, Blazer was gracious and impressively humble as the evening's host. His former classmates enjoyed an open bar and copious hors d'oeuvres while being entertained by Lonnie Youngblood. The Harlem blues saxophone player and his fellow musicians were Blazer's go-to band for CONCACAF events. Chuck and Lonnie had first met at the fabled Manhattan restaurant hangout Elaine's, and Chuck subsequently flew Youngblood and his wife and band to the tony Atlantis Paradise Island Resort in the Bahamas to perform at a FIFA gala. "Chuck knew how to throw a hell of a party," said Youngblood. "He was second to none when it came to that."

Throughout the cocktail party, Chuck sat in the back of the room with Blanks and his own coterie of friends, including sex therapist and media personality Dr. Ruth Westheimer and Shep Messing, a well-known soccer broadcaster and former goalkeeper for the old New York Cosmos. He "looked like Santa with his elves," recalled Berke. Former Forest Hill students came to his table to pay court and to thank Blazer for the party. Almost no one remembered him from high school, and he didn't know most of his guests. But many were impressed with him. He had a "quiet power," remembered Vale. "And he wasn't a bragger. If I had made one-tenth of his money, you couldn't even talk to me."

Vale was also surprised that Blazer didn't work the crowd at the party, which would have given him an opportunity to underscore and maybe capitalize on his generosity. What Vale didn't realize was that Blazer was often reluctant to abandon his mobility cart to navigate his way through throngs of people. He couldn't see his feet when he walked, and he risked treading on toes or tripping on some unseen obstacle.

Blazer marked the event on his blog, *Travels with Chuck Blazer and His Friends*, by quietly underlining both his alienation from his class-mates and his own success. "While I have had very little contact with my fellow high school graduates, it was a refreshing opportunity to hear the stories of the roads people have taken to the present," he noted, calling the reunion a "celebration of a half century of memories and accomplishment."

After high school, Blazer earned a degree in accounting at New York University, graduating in 1965. His studies would serve him well in his CONCACAF work as he set up budgets and massaged the books. Soon after he graduated, he married the woman he considered the "prettiest girl at Forest Hills High," Susan Aufox. They had a daughter, Marci, in 1968, and a son, Jason, two years later.

Blazer had dreamed of becoming a psychiatrist, but was steered into accounting by his pragmatic mom. Morbidly obese at a relatively young age, Edna Blazer was largely homebound, but nevertheless a take-charge parent. She urged both of her boys to focus on a field of study that was guaranteed to bring home a paycheck. Blazer's brother, Barry, was interested in becoming a geologist or metallurgist, but his mother insisted he become an actuary, which he did.

Chuck took a different approach to probability than Barry. He often boasted that he paid his NYU tuition with money won playing gin rummy against fellow students. Gambling would become a theme in his life. After he split with his wife in the 1990s, Blazer hosted Thanksgiving for friends and extended family at Aqueduct Racetrack in Jamaica, Queens, giving each person $100 to place wagers. In a story he liked to tell, his daughter, Marci, asked for tuition money for law school at the festivities. He promised to give it to her only if she won her bet. If she lost, her mom had to pay. He never revealed who ended up footing the bill. He prided himself on being a "systems" player, whether it was gambling or trading shares on the stock market. He relied on Oswald Jacoby's book *How to Win at Gin Rummy* for playing cards, and used graphs to time the market when he traded stocks using commissions and kickback money from the various CONCACAF contracts he negotiated. Chuck rarely made the stock profits he claimed he did, according to his Merrill Lynch records. Most people who knew him assumed he was independently wealthy because of the trades that he boasted made him as much as $1 million in a single day.

From the beginning, Blazer eschewed a conventional work route. The hustler from Queens concocted several marketing companies— at least on paper—usually registering them in Delaware to capitalize on the state's liberal corporate tax laws. He devised a new entity for every idea, starting a pattern that would shape Blazer's reputation as a sharp-eyed opportunist who was never at a loss for a moneymaking venture.

When Blanks told Blazer that she worked for an exhibition booker who kept close to two-thirds of the fees that companies paid for Coliseum work, Blazer created Narrators & Models Inc. He was convinced that he could organize a solid stable of talent and pay models more but still make plenty for himself. Blazer later told Blanks that the operation was also a way to keep him in her life—and to check out other available "talent." (He also told Blanks that he was selling mail-order sex toys in the 1970s through one of his ventures with a guy named Pinky, who Blazer claimed ended up in prison.)

Blazer's luck with women changed radically after his high school days—to hear him tell it. As a young marketing consultant, he passed out joke business cards touting himself as a "sex education expert" available morning, "nooner," and night. He would later brag to Blanks that he was having sex with various partners several times a day while he was courting her. He was big and handsome, and his dark ringlets were now fully unfurled. He once thanked singer Tom Jones backstage for inspiring his new hairdo after he'd witnessed women throwing their underwear onstage while the ringlet-maned crooner performed.

During this unorthodox wooing period, Blanks was introduced to what she would later discover was the Blazer "lore": a backstory, advanced relentlessly, that accentuated Blazer's intelligence and creativity. His often-repeated personal success stories were either exaggerations or outright lies. Bizarrely, he told Blanks that he was part of a high school student brain trust that was trying to predict Fidel Castro's plans to wreak havoc on America as well as determine, once and for all, who murdered John F. Kennedy. He also dropped hints that he had graduated from NYU Law School. He hadn't. If people began to question him about his law school experiences, he suddenly became a master of distraction.

Remember the Smiley Face button? That was my invention, Blazer boasted while seeking marketing contracts. According to Blazer, he first spotted the cartoon Smiley Face on an insurance company's mailing envelope. In fact, the image was created in 1963 by graphic artist Harvey Ball for the State Mutual Life Assurance Company of Massachusetts to raise employee morale. In Blazer's version of reality, he came up with the idea to turn the face into a button and manufacture it at five US factories he purchased expressly for that purpose. But when sales turned out to be lackluster, he created a smaller version that caught fire and made him a millionaire. Blazer retired on his profits, but returned to business, he told Blanks, because he was bored. Why then, Blanks always wondered, did her rich boyfriend stay in bargain-priced Holiday Inns?

It's true that Blazer played a role in the Smiley Face fad, but not the pivotal one he conjured up. The button was actually created by entrepreneurial brothers Bernard and Murray Spain, who went on to found—and sell for multimillions—the Dollar Store. The Spains owned a group of Hallmark stores in the Philadelphia area, where they invented and sold various popular tchotchkes aimed at young people. During the Vietnam War, they sold buttons sported by Americans on both sides of the argument about continuing the conflict: US flag and "Support Our Troops" buttons, as well as peace-sign pins. The Spains aimed for a neutral button they hoped could be worn by everyone, regardless of a customer's position on the war. So around 1970, Bernie slightly modified the Smiley Face icon created by Ball, added the phrase "Have a nice day!" and stamped it on a dime-sized yellow button that sold for a quarter. "The buttons were a runaway success," he said. "We were shocked. I think America was in the mood for something happy."

Demand for the buttons quickly outstripped the capabilities of local Philly manufacturers, so the Spains turned to Blazer, who at the time was running a button factory in Queens owned by his wife's uncle. "Chuck was surprised the button was doing so well, though he was happy to start filling our orders," said Spain. "But he turned out to be a greedy son of a gun. We discovered he was selling our buttons to rivals out the back door for cash." The scam was exposed when the Spains' brother-in-law drove to Queens to pick up an order of buttons from Blazer and watched the Smiley Faces being loaded into trucks from other companies. "When you go into business, you assume people are going to be honorable," remarked Spain, who said he "wasn't surprised at all" when Blazer pled guilty to tax dodging and taking bribes in the FIFA scandal.

Hoodwinking the Spain brothers foreshadowed what would become Blazer's lifetime pattern of cutting corners. In 1982, after he was hired by Direct Marketing founder and Westchester County neighbor Fred Singer to do computer work, Blazer asked Singer for a ninety-day interest-free loan of $27,000 for "bridge funding" until receivables came in for his own marketing company, this one called Windmill Promotions. Or was it Sand Castle Distributors? Blazer named both companies as loan recipients when he responded to a lawsuit by Singer in 1984 after he'd blown off repaying most of the debt. Singer's attorney spent much of one afternoon quizzing Blazer about his income. Asked why the loan had not been repaid, Blazer responded simply: "Unavailability of funds."

Singer claimed that the money was being used to prop up the Blazers' lifestyle (the family had moved from New Rochelle to more upscale Scarsdale by the time the lawsuit was filed) and not to keep Windmill running, as Blazer had claimed. According to Blazer's testimony, his wife paid most of their living expenses, including tuition for the children, life insurance on him, lease payments on three cars, including a Mercedes and a Lexus sedan, and the Westchester mortgage.

He was also dodging his taxes, another lifetime habit. In pursuit of a document revealing his income, Singer's attorney asked if Blazer had filed a tax return in the previous three years. He answered: "Extensions; they are out on extensions," adding that "some" had expired. The IRS was coming after Blazer as early as 1983. The tax man attached several liens against Blazer's property from that year to 1987, according to Westchester County Court records. Social Security records show that Blazer had no taxed Social Security income from 1977 to 1986.

Singer also charged that Blazer shifted assets to his wife to keep him "judgment safe." Susan, meanwhile, resigned as vice president of the two-person Windmill operation to sidestep liability, argued Singer's attorney. Singer would eventually get most of his money, but not until years later.

While Blazer was cooking up schemes and dodging Singer, what would become his unimaginably lucrative future was taking baby steps at a most unlikely place: on the green soccer fields of New Rochelle. The amiable Blazer volunteered to coach his children's teams, beginning in the mid-1970s. He loved to boast of Marci's booming kicks when she played with the boys. Because of the sporadic nature of his work, Blazer's schedule was more flexible than many of the nine-to-five commuter dads. He had more time for practices, games, and organizing the local league.

Though nothing special as a coach, Blazer discovered that he had a knack for what he called "sports politics," soothing complaining parents and building a stronger league with more dues-paying members. He also found that the field belonged to the bold. As one of the few in his community to own a computer, he had the facility to organize tournaments, devise schedules, orchestrate fund-raising events, compile player and team data, and write newsletters—the kind of grunt work that the other parents were grateful not to do. Blazer created special soccer patches for events and teams much as he designed branded gifts for the high-performing salespeople of his client companies. He also boasted of arranging one of the first sponsors of a youth soccer team in the nation: Nike agreed to pay for uniforms on Jason's team.

After the Nike deal, Blazer began wondering if soccer could yield an even bigger payoff. Where other parents saw endless practices, tournaments, and half-time snacks each season, Blazer spotted a growing market among the generation of children tearing across the suburban fields—and one more possible way to make money. The kids were the key; that's how sports flourish. "Get the little ones playing, and soon you'll have soccer in everyone's backyard," said Clive Toye, a former top London soccer reporter who famously brought Pelé to America when he was the general manager of the fabled New York Cosmos and later, in 1988, launched the American Soccer League (ASL) with Blazer. Then "start a league and grow it gradually."

The energy that Blazer poured into the youth teams earned him a spot as vice president of the New Rochelle Soccer Club, which organized competitions for local kids. He was then quickly elected to the board and became a vice president of the regional Westchester Youth Soccer League, for which he ran the Select Team program for top players. He was named president of the Eastern New York Youth Soccer Association (ENYYSA), which would induct him into the organization's Hall of Fame in 1998, dubbing him the "most powerful American in the world of soccer, both home and abroad." At ENYYSA Blazer met Sunil Gulati. The Columbia University economics professor would later head US Soccer and serve with Blazer on the CONCACAF board. After Chuck was nabbed by the feds, Gulati would replace him on the FIFA Ex-Co.

His Westchester soccer experience would eventually become part of the Blazer myth. When asked, in FIFA circles, about his beginnings in the sport, Blazer would say that he "used to coach," failing to point out that most of his players had been in elementary school.

As he was working his way up the soccer food chain, Blazer was also quietly but persistently courting Blanks within the confines of their trade show work for more than three years. In 1976, when Blanks returned to New York after eleven months caring for her dying mother in her hometown of Miami, Blazer arranged for her to work at a Coliseum trade show for Sony, one of his clients. They met to catch up at the bar in the Essex House on Central Park South. After a quick hello, Blazer blurted out that he had loved Blanks since the day he met her. He said his marriage was over and that he was only holding it together, barely, for the children. "He did the full-court press," Blanks said. "I had never been wooed like that by anyone. A few cocktails later, we were upstairs."

Blazer, who already had an office a few blocks north of the United Nations building in the East Forties in Manhattan, rented a one-bedroom condo for him and his new lover in the same building. His office phone was moved to the apartment, and Blanks was ordered never to answer it, so that Blazer could field calls from his wife. That arrangement blew up six months later in the blood-spattered confrontation in the couple's bedroom.

When Blazer reached out to Blanks again after her fiftieth birthday in 2002, she was in a desperate situation. Her husband, Bobby, had opted out of their twenty-three-year marriage and was seeing another woman. Mary Lynn was consumed with anxiety about supporting their two sons, Christopher, thirteen, and Nicky, nine. Checks were bouncing, bills were unpaid, they were in danger of losing their apartment. In retrospect, Blanks has often wondered if Blazer had somehow discovered her precarious financial situation—the eviction notices for the family home were public record, which Blazer could have found easily through a computer search. "Nothing's a coincidence with Chuck," said Blanks, who later learned that he kept tabs on most of his old girlfriends online.

Blazer also needed an acceptable escort for FIFA events. He was the only single man on FIFA's twenty-four-member Ex-Co at the time. While some members of the Ex-Co had mistresses, they weren't warmly welcomed at the tony dinners and official events that members were required to attend. Blanks was the perfect candidate for FIFA fetes: she was attractive, smart, and personable. She had grown up traveling the world for free because her dad was a Pan American Airways mechanic. She was even a licensed pilot should Blazer ever acquire a private plane. (He did later dream of his blonde companion, dressed as a chauffeur, driving him around New York in his newly purchased Hummer, paid for by CONCACAF.)

Blanks remembered the good times with Chuck, and she welcomed the thoughtfulness of Chuck's birthday greeting at a low point in her life. She contacted Blazer after reading his letter, using the e-mail address he had included. Maybe he would finally apologize for striking her, she thought. Perhaps he felt so badly about it that he would help her out now, so long afterward, possibly with a job. They caught up on the phone and in a stream of messages. Blanks recalled incorrectly pronouncing FIFA as "fie-fah," and feeling badly for him because he was only a secretary after all those years. No, he corrected her, he wasn't a secretary of CONCACAF, he was the *general secretary*, "like in the United Nations," Blazer explained. He was tender and funny—the man she had fallen in love with.

They exchanged photos, but Blazer's weight had ballooned so grotesquely that Blanks was unable to pick him out in the group shot he sent. He blamed the weight gain on various health problems. Within weeks, he persuaded her to visit him at Trump Tower. "He love-bombed me," said Blanks. "He seemed so infatuated with me and wanted to move so fast. It was flattering."

Welcomed into his apartment at 49J by a CONCACAF assistant, Blanks was escorted down a long hall to the living room, which fronted Central Park. The curtains were drawn, and the room was dark; for a moment, she didn't see Blazer. As her eyes adjusted to the gloom, she beheld the mound of a man sitting in the shadows in the corner of a sectional sofa, wrapped in an enormous brown-and-blue-striped velour bathrobe. He didn't rise to greet her. He was embarrassed about his weight, he said, and didn't know what to wear or how best to present himself to her. He couldn't adequately express his feelings to her, Blazer explained, so instead he played a CD he had made of songs that he believed spoke to the relationship they once had. One of them was "A Heart Full of Love" from the Broadway show *Les Misérables*; another, "All I Ask of You" from Andrew Lloyd Webber's *The Phantom of the Opera*, with the lyrics "Then say you'll share with me one love, one lifetime, let me lead you from your solitude. Say you need me with you here, beside you."

He told her, again, that she was the love of his life and that he wanted to make a home for her and her sons. He would treat the boys like his own, he vowed. By the end of the evening, they were embracing.

Less than three months later, Blanks and her sons moved in with him. The lovers first traveled as a couple to Charleston, South Carolina. Then Blazer insisted that Blanks and the boys accompany him to the Bahamas (to an apartment paid for by CONCACAF) on Christmas Day. He always took his two crazy cats on trips to the Bahamas, but on that day, the airline wouldn't allow him to take both of them in first class, so the entire traveling party left, returning to fly the following day. "It was nuts, dragging my kids back home on Christmas Day," Blanks recalled. "There were warning signs about a life with Chuck that I ignored. Then we moved in with him. Dumb. Dumb."

Their relationship became part of the Chuck Blazer myth. The couple had a once-in-a-lifetime love, he told friends and associates. They had split up when they were young only because Blanks demanded too much of his time—like all mistresses do, he explained—and he had a family to attend to. They finally got together again years later, he said, when he was divorced from his wife. At fifty, Blanks was the "oldest woman" he had ever dated, he made a point of saying. Blanks always joked that she had to wait until he grew up.

Neither one of them mentioned the bloody altercation in the bedroom.

THREE

BIRTH OF A SOCCER FIEFDOM

CHUCK BLAZER NO DOUBT MISSED THE SHABBY BUT BUSTLING NEW YORK COLISEUM AS he plotted his next moves during a brief visit to a rickety office in Guatemala City in 1984. The cramped space in a small building at the edge of town was the unimpressive headquarters of CONCACAF. Blazer had managed to parlay his youth soccer activities in Westchester County up the organizational ladder to a berth on the CONCACAF board. Like the office, the appointment was hardly formidable, and Blazer still clung to his day job hustling promotional products in New York. He tried to breathe life into the federation's then-lackluster business, mostly by working the phones from his Westchester home office.

CONCACAF, the confederation representing the Western Hemisphere—from the Caribbean and Latin America north to the United States and Canada—hadn't made much headway in the twenty-three years since its birth in Mexico in 1961. Timid, underfunded, and

25

disorganized, the association had managed to put together only a handful of international matches the year Blazer joined, and was close to dead broke. Typical of its early fumbling was a proposed showdown between the ambitious Rochester Lancers of the North American Soccer League (NASL) and a Mexican team as part of CONCACAF's 1971 international Champions Cup. The match was scheduled for February—in frigid upstate New York. That setting favored the Lancers but even the cold-proof citizens of Rochester would be disinclined to attend, and players couldn't function in snowdrifts. "It was a complete fiasco," remembered Clive Toye.

American soccer officials were so dismissive of CONCACAF that they preferred to bypass the association to seek competition with more glamorous Continental teams such as Italy and Germany from the high-profile Union of European Football Association (UEFA), another one of FIFA's regional associations. "Setting up games with tiny Caribbean countries through CONCACAF didn't seem to be the best way to grow the US league," said Toye.

Nothing about the association then hinted at the organizational powerhouse it would become, nor the millions it would generate for its opportunistic new leaders. "Chuck and Jack pretty much started CONCACAF, even though it had already existed for years," said Toye. "Obviously, as it grew, they clearly enjoyed luxurious lives. But in the beginning, any commission they might have collected on soccer contracts wouldn't have paid for a bus ticket to Atlantic City."

Nearly three decades later, after CONCACAF jettisoned Blazer cohort Jack Warner amid accusations of corruption, the organization's annual revenue had soared to tens of millions of dollars. An investigative report commissioned by CONCACAF in 2013 linked Blazer and Warner to millions of dollars in graft—but also praised their acumen in transforming the humble association into a wealthy force in global soccer.

Blazer and Warner were—and still are—respected as formidable rainmakers. And most were happy to be riding their gravy train. If anyone had suspicions about kickbacks and bribes, no one was airing them publicly. "Imagine you're a soccer official in a small Caribbean nation, and it's tough to get your expenses paid to travel to the other side of an island to watch a game," noted Toye. "Suddenly, in the era of Chuck and Jack, you're flying first-class to New York City. No one's asking questions."

Toye was filling seventy-thousand-seat stadiums with excited Cosmos fans in the mid-1970s, when Blazer was still passing out oranges to his son's team in Westchester. For years, the two men occupied parallel sports universes. But decades after the demise of his beloved Cosmos, Toye was working for Blazer. Toye was in on the pulse-quickening first wave of US soccer, which sputtered and died in the mid-1980s; ten years later, Blazer caught the far bigger second wave, one stoked by a massive new infusion of media and sponsorship money.

Toye, a longtime sports reporter for London's *Daily Express*, moved to America in 1967—while Blazer was plugging products at the Coliseum—to become the general manager of the Baltimore Bays, one of ten charter members of the fledgling US National Professional Soccer League (NPSL). The league was launched that year by a group of British and American soccer entrepreneurs, with support from several baseball and football team owners who had stadiums sitting empty much of the year. The principals were convinced that they would be the first to bring real football to the large and wealthy (if soccer-clueless) US market. Hopes were fueled by the surprising popularity among American viewers of the first World Cup game televised in the United States—the 1966 final that England won 4–2 against Germany in extra time after breaking a 2–2 tie with a controversial goal that soccer fans still argue about today.

Although soccer had been played in America for a century, especially in immigrant communities, it continued to be viewed as a "foreign" sport in the hidebound US television market. NPSL did manage to win a contract with CBS to televise a game of the week—promoted with the slogan "just for kicks." But in one of the first signs of soccer's disconnect with its new nation, network officials were stumped by a game that didn't have built-in breaks for commercials. In his book about the genesis of the NPSL, *Kick in the Grass*, Toye writes that when Bill McPhail, the head of CBS Sports at the time, asked league executives how they would stop the game for commercials, he was told: "You don't. Television will have to change for soccer." Toye knew from the "pitying looks" on the faces of the CBS guys what was coming next. "That will never happen," said one of McPhail's assistants.

In fact, the game would bend for CBS. Referees wore an earpiece to hear producers' requests to slow the action during penalty, corner, and goal kicks to give the network time to squeeze in commercials. Throw-ins became "studies in still life," quipped Toye, and injured players were encouraged to writhe on the ground a bit longer. In the Pitts-burgh Phantoms' 2–1 victory over the Toronto Falcons only a month into the 1967 debut season, referee Peter Rhodes admitted after the game that he had pressured players to milk—or even fake—injuries to give CBS time to cut away. It was an early indication of the powerful role media would play in the game.

Few elite American athletes played soccer, so almost all the early players were foreigners. In 1967 the combined rosters of the ten NPSL teams included just eight US citizens. The Baltimore Bays had a single American, who was asked to wave the Stars and Stripes before the team's home opener against the Atlanta Chiefs, which drew a crowd of 8,434 and was televised nationally by CBS. Curious fans turned out in respectable numbers early in the season, but attendance waned as the year wore on. The league would average a paltry 4,800 fans a game for the season.

The NPSL also had to battle for fans with its competitor: the new United Soccer Association (USA), which, unlike the NPSL, was officially sanctioned by FIFA. There wasn't anything American about that league either, except that the games were played on US soil. The USA consisted of twelve renamed European and South American teams imported wholesale: Ireland's Shamrock Rovers became the Boston

Rovers, England's Wolverhampton Wanderers masqueraded as the Los Angeles Wolves, and Scotland's Dundee United morphed into the Dallas Tornado. Each USA franchisee paid about $250,000 to import a team.

Both newbie leagues struggled through the 1967 season, and in December they came together to form the now-defunct North American Soccer League (NASL). The merger combined resources and eliminated redundant teams, but the reconstituted, streamlined league didn't fare any better. The Bays were owned by baseball's Baltimore Orioles, but when the soccer players took the field, "with very few exceptions, the hostility of the baseball people at Memorial Stadium could be felt from start to finish," Toye wrote in another of his books, *Anywhere in the World*. "We were plainly not wanted, and our game was not wanted." Years later, the flag-waving New York *Daily News* columnist and sports editor Dick Young, one of the writers most hostile to the sport, would famously advise the paper's young beat reporter David Hirshey: "Don't waste your time on soccer, kid. It's a game for commie pansies."

NASL television audiences continued to shrink, and CBS canceled its contract after the 1968 season, citing low ratings. Most of the teams folded by the end of the year. League commissioner Phil Woosnam, a former professional player from Wales who had coached the Atlanta Chiefs, scrambled to eke out another season—and then another—by providing a mix of competitions between foreign and domestic teams.

Despite the troubles at the pro level, the number of Americans who played the game kept growing, as did the talent level. In Saint Louis, a city with a long soccer heritage, the Stars placed fourteen Yanks on its eighteen-man roster, and could hold their own against other NASL teams packed with foreign players. (US players derided the NASL as the Non-American Soccer League for its bias against native talent.)

The professional game would make its great leap forward with an infusion of money and celebrity that could happen only in New York City. Ahmet and Nesuhi Ertegun, soccer-obsessed Turkish American brothers and the founders of Atlantic Records, convinced Steve Ross, the CEO of Warner Communications (which bought the powerhouse rock and rhythm-and-blues music label from them), to bankroll a dream team for Toye to run. They believed the league needed a marquee flagship in New York, a natural soccer market that teemed with passionate, ethnic fans desperate for a team in their adopted country to call their own. Inspired by the New York Metropolitans, aka, baseball's beloved Mets, Toye christened the players the Cosmos—short for the Cosmopolitans.

In 1975 Toye pulled off the soccer coup of the century by luring Brazilian superstar Pelé a year after his retirement at the age of thirty-five to play for the Cosmos. The enticement was a then-astounding $2.8 million for three years. The astonishingly balletic player who began playing professionally at the age of fifteen and would score 541 league goals in his career was probably the only soccer player most Americans knew by name. "Clive Toye kept after me for years, obsessively, like some kind of crazy hunter—I was Moby Dick to his Captain Ahab," Pelé wrote in his book *Why Soccer Matters*.

Toye still boasts today that he landed Pelé because he convinced the superstar he could win over a nation, not just the fans of a team. At first, Pelé was skeptical. The league was "semiprofessional," he wrote, "one that was living on a hand-to-mouth basis, its future totally uncertain." He was also reluctant to leave Brazil, and the nation didn't want to lose its national treasure. Henry Kissinger, former US secretary of state and a soccer nut, huddled with Brazilian officials to persuade them that it would be an inspired diplomatic move to share Pelé with the American public. Pelé said he finally accepted Toye's offer for one simple reason: he was broke.

Pelé had a blast in New York and helped change the course of US soccer. With a media-mobbed announcement at the posh 21 Club in Manhattan on June 10, 1975, the soccer god and gracious off-field ambassador was presented to his adoring public. His Cosmos debut against the Dallas Tornado was broadcast by CBS to twenty-two countries. Pelé was a rock star even among teammates, who couldn't take their eyes off him. "It was hard not to be in awe—every day," said Cosmos defender Bobby Smith in the documentary *Once in a Lifetime*. Team Captain Werner Roth added, "The biggest challenge for us on the field was not stopping and watching him play, because he still had these incredible moves."

Thanks to Pelé, seventy thousand wild, screaming fans in 1977 packed the Cosmos' new home across the Hudson River in New Jersey's Giants Stadium, built the previous year for New York's professional football team. The Cosmos had left the creaky, twenty-two-thousand-seat Downing Stadium on Randall's Island, under the Triborough Bridge, where the dirt had to be spray painted green for TV cameras. Though the skill level of the game had light-years to go, the Cosmos infused the sport with uniquely American razzmatazz. A Bugs Bunny mascot patrolled the sidelines, and celebrities such as Mick Jagger, Robert Redford, and Barbra Streisand were frequent visitors to the team's locker room.

Pelé became the first soccer "brand" in the United States and hinted at the massive commercialization and money that were to come. When Ross trotted out his team and trophy player for exhibition games around the world, the Warner corporate logo was displayed prominently on their uniforms. Pelé also attracted Pepsi, Honda, and the Pony International shoe company as sponsors. FIFA president João Havelange was so intrigued by the sponsorship concept that he contacted Toye to discuss "commercial matters." Toye passed Havelange's inquiry along to Warner, but the company's Licensing Corporation of America subsidiary dropped the ball and opted not to do business with FIFA.

The Pelé Cosmos were fun while they lasted. After the superstar left in 1977, following a rapturous farewell game, the team's success proved to be ephemeral. The NASL took a precipitous dive. The "league died of fame," said Toye, who was stunned by how quickly interest imploded. The Cosmos model might have worked in New York—for a time—but it wasn't sustainable in smaller markets. Toye blamed mismanagement of a staggering injection of money controlled by "egomaniac" meddling owners lured by the relatively cheap cost of a franchise in a new sport. "They didn't understand the steady, constant, thoughtful work required in developing and maintaining a league," he said.

The Cosmos were plagued by infighting, according to Toye. He brought in the great German sweeper Franz Beckenbauer, and Ross snared star Italian striker Giorgio Chinaglia, but ownership continued to push for more expensive foreign superstars against Toye's advice. He had hoped to stick to a handful of overseas stars to help groom US players. "My idea was to anchor the middle of the field with Beckenbauer and bring in young American talent who could be mentored by an experienced, talented player," said Toye. "I thought developing American players was the whole bloody idea." The team incurred astronomical travel costs and a payroll padded with friends, relatives, and mistresses, according to Toye, who was ultimately forced out as Cosmos president. The Cosmos folded in 1985, and the NASL soon followed. It would take American soccer years to recover the fan enthusiasm lost in the seventies.

In a weird confluence during the Cosmos phenomenon, Toye and Chuck Blazer—who was still on the periphery of the sport—would meet on the fields of youth soccer in Westchester County, where both men lived and coached their children's teams. Toye's Scarsdale Hornets trounced Blazer's New Rochelle team in the competition for the 1978 Westchester Cup. "He did the best he could," Toye said dismissively of Blazer's coaching skills. "I don't know what he thought he was doing there; he didn't really know the game."

Whatever Blazer's shortcomings as a coach, he became a crack "sports politician," which is how he often described himself. He had a "shrewd business sense that ultimately grew soccer tremendously," said Toye. "He had great, creative ideas, and he had the ability to recognize the good ideas of others and put them into effect."

While Toye was helping to develop the professional game in the

United States, Blazer was taking a far different path to the pinnacle of international soccer administration—one that included the very odd detour to Guatemala City. After his stint in Westchester County youth soccer, Blazer eventually reached the board of the Eastern New York Youth Soccer Association (ENYYSA). He then cleverly leveraged that platform for the next stage of his soccer evolution. In 1984 he arranged for ENYYSA to host the annual meeting of the United States Soccer Federation (USSF) in Midtown Manhattan. He wrangled an endorsement from Pelé, and a quickie, on-the-spot campaign with the star won him a seat on the USSF board. He served as the federation's executive vice president of international competition, which automatically gave Blazer a berth on the CONCACAF board.

The suburban soccer dad had now ascended to a power perch in soccer. Just as he did in youth soccer, and would at CONCACAF, Blazer pushed for more matches to raise American soccer's profile and generate more income. In an interview in a local Westchester paper, Blazer vowed to help wipe out the soccer federation's $600,000 debt. "There's no magic," he told a local reporter. "To erase the debt, we have to have a viable, saleable product that attracts sponsors."

During the two years that Blazer was on the USSF board, he worked "incredibly hard," said a colleague. To showcase American soccer, Blazer increased the number of US national team matches to nineteen compared with just two in the same period before his election. Despite that record, Blazer failed to win reelection to the USSF board in 1986. "Chuck always thought he was the smartest guy in the room, and he wanted everyone to know that. That didn't sit so well with some of the USSF brain trust," said one official. Though he lost the USSF board spot, Blazer still held on to his leadership role in CONCACAF, and the pragmatist turned his focus to raising that association's profile.

He would find a confederate in Jack Warner, who had been automatically elevated to the CONCACAF board—and to the powerful FIFA Ex-Co—in 1983, when he became president of his home regional soccer association, the Caribbean Football Union. Like Chuck,

Jack recognized opportunity. Early on, Warner became aware of CFU's "major revenue-earning opportunities," Warner's official biographer, *Trinidad & Tobago Express* sports editor Valentino Singh, wrote in his book *Upwards Through the Night: The Biography of Austin Jack Warner*. Warner also recognized that he could be a kingmaker in FIFA, a position he would milk tirelessly for personal profit. The CFU represents 25 of the 35 nation-votes in CONCACAF, a surprisingly significant chunk of the 209 total votes at FIFA—critical to any candidate who wants to be president of FIFA. Warner once boasted that he wielded those votes to mold the CFU into a "frightening" political force. Warner was also the general secretary of the Trinidad and Tobago Football Federation (TTFF), a member association of CFU. He officially gave up that role when he rose to the CONCACAF leadership, as required by the board, but remained a "special consultant" and de facto head and power broker of TTFF, which would extend his influence throughout his CONCACAF career.

In 1987 Blazer joined forces with his neighbor and youth-coach nemesis Toye to launch the American Soccer League (ASL) in the wake of the NASL's demise—"to keep things going"—said Toye, and ran it out of Blazer's Westchester basement. The new league focused on East Coast and Florida teams with American players and stripped-down budgets with no imported superstars. At least, that was Toye's vision. Toye was the president, an unpaid position, while Blazer, the self-appointed commissioner, paid himself $48,000 a year—even though he had capped *total* team salaries at $50,000. The league began with five teams, grew quickly to ten, and drew a respectable 250,000 fans to 250 games in 1988.

It would be an exceptional year for American soccer. The United States was selected to host the 1994 World Cup, a watershed event for soccer's largest underdeveloped Western market. The USSF, rebranded as US Soccer, promised to use most of its World Cup profits, close to $100 million, to establish a top-tier national professional soccer league. Major League Soccer (MLS) began play in 1996 with ten teams and expanded rapidly to twenty.

The ASL died quietly a year later. Toye and Blazer had butted heads over strategy and organization, profits were marginal, and some of the team owners wanted more transparency. As the ASL was sputtering, Blazer became president of one of the teams, the Miami Sharks, but was let go after only five months when owners accused him of draining the franchise's dwindling income for pricey dinners, five-star hotel rooms, and first-class travel. It was a pattern he would soon repeat on the CONCACAF board.

Through it all, Blazer and Warner continued to plot strategy at a string of CONCACAF-related events. The men particularly bonded during the 1986 World Cup in Mexico. Blazer took his teenage son and daughter to the matches and was touched that Warner helped arrange sightseeing and other activities for the kids, despite his hectic Cup schedule as an Ex-Co member. "I was able to see past the officialdom of a person in high office and find out something about the man himself," Blazer told Singh. "His attention to my kids was unparalleled. This was the basis for the friendship which was cemented during that period and has lasted ever since."

In appearance, Blazer and Warner seemed an improbable pair. Warner was a trim, black, balding, devout Caribbean Catholic, nearly always attired, like his countrymen, in a guayabera, the loose-fitting, light-colored shirt designed for the heat of the Caribbean. Blazer was Jewish, a literally larger-than-life Yank with a Falstaffian laugh and a cloud of curls encircling an enormous head. Blazer almost always wore a suit and tie to events and matches, no matter the temperature. While Blazer was solidly upper-middle class and resided in one of the largest, most powerful cities in the world, Warner had a tough upbringing in a tiny village in southern Trinidad, where he and his five siblings were raised by their mother. Warner's hard-drinking dad was largely missing from his life. He attended school with the help of scholarships and eventually became a history lecturer at Trinidad's top Polytechnic Institute.

But the men were far more alike in other ways. Both were affable, seductive sports politicians, and cunning, indefatigable strategists. Both publicly attributed their success to God. Their quiet beginnings belied their soon-to-be burgeoning wealth—and their plunge into worldwide ignominy.

After Mexico, Blazer and Warner were together again in the VIP seats for the electrifying 1989 World Cup qualifying match between Trinidad and Tobago and the United States at the National Stadium (now the Hasely Crawford Stadium) in Port of Spain. America needed a win to qualify for the Cup; a draw would punch T&T's ticket. Blazer was torn about the contest and was worried for Warner. "One cannot imagine how I felt seated in that box with my best friend standing in the back with the whole world on his shoulders," Blazer told Warner's biographer. "Yes, I wanted my country to win . . . but no, I didn't want Trinidad and Tobago to lose. It was not a nice feeling."

The Strike Squad, as the team was known, lost to the Yanks, 1–0, thanks to the "shot heard round the world": a goal by US midfielder Paul Caligiuri that sent the American team to the 1990 World Cup in Italy. Caligiuri's thunderbolt reignited US Soccer—the men's national team has participated in every World Cup since—but the qualifier plunged Warner into his first dark scandal. Warner was accused of printing and selling tens of thousands of dollars' worth of counterfeit tickets and boosting the number of spectators dangerously beyond the stadium's safety threshold. FIFA officials had warned that the emotional match could trigger turmoil in the stands, and recommended that the number of tickets be reduced 5 percent from the 28,500 capacity, to create some breathing room and make effective crowd control possible. Instead, Warner was accused of arranging to sell up to 45,000 tickets, as fans squeezed into every available inch of space in the stadium. "The place was packed like sardines; if we had had an emergency, a lot of people would have died," Strike Force coach Everald

"Gally" Cummings said after the match. Warner also lifted restrictions on the sale of alcohol, against FIFA orders.

The situation was even more dangerous outside the stadium, where many fans with bona fide tickets were shut out by those who had entered with counterfeit paper, triggering a near riot. A minibus carrying the Trinidad and Tobago team was unable to get through the angry mob, which pounded on the windows and rocked the vehicle. Soldiers had to hoist players over the heads of the furious fans and into the stadium. The event was so chaotic that journalists speculated that Warner had deliberately undermined his own team because FIFA's leaders were hungry to bring the United States—and its potentially lucrative market—solidly into the soccer fold with a berth in the World Cup.

Coach Cummings later refused to go on national TV and read from a script provided by Warner saying that the stadium had not been oversold. Cummings claimed that in retaliation for refusing to lie about the tickets, Warner had him fired and prevented him from getting professional coaching jobs anywhere in the Caribbean.

Warner flatly denied selling extra tickets and vowed to launch an investigation into the counterfeits, a diversionary tactic that CONCACAF would use again in future scandals. Four months later, Warner admitted that, yes, he had arranged to sell forty-three thousand tickets because he feared organizers were failing to meet demand and Trinidad's soccer federation needed the extra ticket fees to cover its costs. He had lied earlier, Warner said, because FIFA ordered him to do so. He also said he lifted restrictions on the sale of alcohol because the team's major patrons included the Caribbean Development Company, which sold beer during the match, and rum maker Angostura.

When the government of Trinidad and Tobago launched an independent investigation into the fiasco, the head of the commission asked, "Did Warner believe he was God or merely think he was running the country?" Soon after the match, Warner's number one mentor on the FIFA Ex-Co, President Havelange—who owed his presidency to CONCACAF votes—awarded Trinidad and Tobago the FIFA Fair Play

Award for fan behavior at the do-or-die qualifier. The government's inquiry into the ticket scam fizzled. Warner pointed to the FIFA award whenever he was challenged on the phony tickets.

By the time the fans were mobbing the National Stadium, Blazer had already identified Warner as someone he could work with. He approached the Trinidadian with an idea the day after the big game: Warner should run against aging CONCACAF leader Joaquín Soria Terrazas and become president of the organization. Blazer, who could have been a contender himself, never considered the presidency seriously because he was convinced that a "white man" couldn't head an association of largely Caribbean and Latin American organizations, he told a confidant. Besides, Blazer said, he'd rather be the "man behind the man"—a man Blazer hoped to control—in CONCACAF.

Once Warner agreed to run, Blazer used his considerable politicking skills to extol his pal and quietly denigrate Terrazas, who had held the job for twenty years—although, in truth, he had hardly been dynamic. Blazer's participation turned a "long-shot candidacy into a sure thing," said the 2013 CONCACAF investigative report that would lambaste the men. Warner also received another of many repayments from Havelange for delivering those presidential votes. The FIFA boss traveled to Costa Rica, where the ballot took place, to campaign for Warner personally. Terrazas was trounced, getting only 30 percent of the vote.

Warner took office in 1990 and immediately named Blazer his general secretary, hailing his new friend as one of the "top international businessmen" in the US. Blazer quickly moved CONCACAF's headquarters from Guatemala City to New York City: first to a small office opposite Trump Tower and then to the entire seventeenth floor of the building. By the summer of 1990, Blazer had signed a CONCACAF work contract, devised by him, that provided fees and a 10 percent commission on every CONCACAF deal he negotiated. The money would be diverted to one of his many companies, this time to Sportvertising, which was eventually registered in the tax haven of the Cayman Islands in an account established with the help of banker and Cayman

Islands Football Association president Jeffrey Webb—who would later become president of CONCACAF.

The 1991 Gold Cup, an eight-team tournament played in Los Angeles for the federation championship, became the first significant project launched by Blazer and Warner. The biennial tournaments would become the major financial engine of CONCACAF—and the key source of wealth for the men. After 1991, the two were off to the races: Blazer would admit to taking bribes for the rest of the Gold Cups during his CONCACAF reign.

The way was clear and green for Blazer and Warner. They had closed a loop at the top of CONCACAF. They could run their schemes with impunity, and Blazer would hide the evidence in his budgets and accounts. "Warner had the votes, and Blazer had the brains," said an investigator. For the next twenty-one years, the field belonged to them.

FOUR

PLAYBOY OF WESTERN CONCACAF

IN THE SUMMER OF 2001, CHUCK BLAZER WAS RIGHT WHERE HE WANTED TO BE: POOL-side, at a mansion in the Hamptons that he had rented, he boasted, for $100,000 for three months. The place was opened up to close pals and a rotating cast of alluring women who were encouraged to go topless or play nude water polo as often as possible. Chuck, who was fifty-six at the time, didn't frolic in the pool. His weight hovered around 360 pounds and hindered his mobility. But he liked to watch.

What a decade it had been. He and Jack Warner had already made CONCACAF millions of dollars and had helped themselves to millions more. Chuck was living the dream. He had eased into his work and the opulent lifestyle as if he were born to it.

The rental that summer was within sight of the Atlantic and, Blazer bragged, close to a compound occupied by hip-hop impresario P. Diddy. The place bordered an open savannah of tall, golden beach grasses, where Blazer enjoyed photographing women willing to pose au naturel—two by two. The storied beach communities on Long Island's East End had once been the exclusive province of New York society—back when New York society meant old money, old-school propriety, and old-fashioned discretion. It was no place for glitzy show-biz types, nouveau riche media and corporate honchos, or their publicity-seeking handlers. But that was changing in the 1990s, when over-the-top arriviste parties and high-level scandals were not only commonplace but almost de rigueur.

None of it meant much to Blazer; his usual getaway was in the Bahamas, where he could entertain friends, family, and associates in the sun while also cultivating a power base in Jack Warner territory. That summer expenditure was primarily an attempt to impress C.T., a longtime girlfriend. When he had been introduced to her on the CONCACAF circuit in 1994, she was twenty-four, an exotic beauty from California with jet-black ringlets and a spray of freckles across her nose. The confederation's schedule of dinners and galas attracted a coterie of single women who chatted up the soccer players and the men with the money behind them. Blazer's young lover had been seeking an advantageous marriage, but by now, she was growing bored and frustrated with him. His physique was heading south, though she repeatedly admonished him to lose weight. C.T. also wanted children; Chuck did not. But he was desperate to keep C.T. interested, and so, the manse on the South Fork. He had even turned over a CONCACAF office to C.T., ostensibly for her to work on association events. In reality, she spent much of her time at her desk "doing her nails," Blazer conceded.

C.T. moved in with Blazer in 1994 in his first Trump Tower residence—a condo next door to Donald Trump himself on the sixty-sixth penthouse floor; it was actually the fifty-sixth floor, but Trump inflated the number of stories in his building as a marketing ploy. (Trump once boasted to the New York Times that he was the first high-rise developer to start the floor-inflating practice. Buyers "like to have apartments that have height, the psychology of it," he said.) The main bathroom, overlooking Central Park, had a large Jacuzzi where C.T. sometimes posed for photos. Chuck kept images of C.T.—and a group of his other favorite women who would remain in his life—on his computer desktop. In addition to the pictures, Blazer maintained files on women he knew, with information on their personalities and sexual proclivities. It was one of the few organized records he kept; he had a difficult time letting go of any dalliance.

C.T. came to a big decision during those leisurely summer months. She had another paramour on the line: a wealthy financier who had offered to marry her. Chuck's lush Hamptons digs weren't enough to convince her to stick. Their affair was at an end. The only things that remained of C.T. in Blazer's apartment were her two oddball cats and an expensive fur coat. Blazer wouldn't see her again for several years, until they spotted each other near the Plaza hotel, just off Fifty-Ninth Street. She was pushing a baby stroller. By that time, Blazer had grown so huge that he was reduced to perambulating on a mobility cart. "Hello, Chuck," she said with a small, rueful smile as they moved off in opposite directions, each commandeering a different vehicle.

Despite his heartache that summer, Blazer still enjoyed himself in the Hamptons: flirting with female guests, sharing his bed with at least one of them, telling his stories, laughing, drinking. Those three months were a relaxed if relentlessly hedonistic vacation from Manhattan. One photo that epitomized those days featured a voluptuous woman curled up nude on the grill of a barbecue near the pool, looking like a large, pink-fleshed salmon ready for the coals.

That was the name of the game for Blazer: conspicuous consumption in everything. As CONCACAF's general secretary, he had become a star in soccer circles, and was growing ever wealthier by helping himself to every perk his position afforded. He had hefty offshore bank accounts, enjoyed a luxurious lifestyle, and was reveling in thoughts of what even more money could bring. He had shifted all of his living expenses—his apartment, meals at Manhattan's priciest restaurants, travel, hotels, maids, and a chauffeured limo—to CONCACAF.

Chuck's golden ticket was the Gold Cup, a mini-iteration of the World Cup launched by Blazer that would remain the association's cash cow throughout his tenure as general secretary. At the start, Blazer expended long hours to make sure it would succeed. "There were always a million details to work out, and if I called late, Chuck would stay on the phone until every question was answered," recalled Jill Fracisco, who ended up working for Blazer for almost twenty years. She was employed by a Los Angeles promoter for Mexican media giant Televisa when she was asked by her bosses to help CONCACAF orchestrate the first Gold Cup in 1991. "What in the world is CONCACAF?" she remembered wondering. Fracisco took on the job, and worked closely with Blazer in the months leading up to the inaugural event in Los Angeles, where tournament games were split between the Rose Bowl and the Los Angeles Memorial Coliseum. She described Blazer as already being "hefty" at that time, but also gregarious, intelligent, engaging, and willing to pitch in. "I would work all day in the office, and about nine o'clock I would head to the headquarters hotel and review with Chuck all the team changes and needs. We would finish up at midnight and be back for an eight o'clock meeting with the staff," she recalled.

Eight teams played in that first Gold Cup. The United States was the surprise winner of the tournament, upsetting Mexico in the semis before forty-one thousand fans at the LA Coliseum. The intensifying rivalry between Mexico and the increasingly popular American team would help drive the business. The event marked the start of CONCACAF's long, lucrative relationship with Televisa and the sports marketing firm Inter Forever Sports, which later became part of Traffic Sports International of South America and its American affiliate, Traffic Sports USA, both major targets in the federal indictments. The first tournament, which was broadcast on closed-circuit pay TV in the

United States and Mexico, brought in $1 million, the most money earned at a single event in CONCACAF's thirty-year history.

By 2009, the Gold Cup had helped boost CONCACAF revenues to $35 million. CONCACAF had long been responsible for arranging World Cup qualifying matches, but "Chuck understood other tournaments could be major moneymakers for the association at a time when it was surviving paycheck to paycheck," noted Ted Howard, who would become Blazer's deputy general secretary in 1998. "He had a head for marketing, and he never lacked confidence that he could make money for CONCACAF."

CONCACAF soon tacked on an under-twenty-three and an under-seventeen tournament series to provide qualifiers for the World Cup, and by 2008, Blazer had added the Champions League, modeled on the European competition of the same name, which pits top-ranked club teams against one another. The soccer dad who had coached his daughter was also one of the first to expand women's events beyond an initial senior national team tournament. American women would become a formidable force in the wake of the federal Title IX law passed in 1972, requiring equal access to sports activities in American schools.

But with that first Gold Cup, Blazer realized quickly, noted an investigator, that he had a tournament valuable enough to attract bribes. Not only did Blazer take a 10 percent commission on every Gold Cup contract, but he also padded his take with bribes and kickbacks in handing them out. Traffic president Jose Hawilla, fresh from bribing his company's way into commercial rights for South America's lucrative Copa Cup, came to the United States in 1993 seeking greener shores—and Blazer and Warner. With an initial "six-figure" bribe to the men, he forged a $9.75 million deal for media and marketing Gold Cup rights for Traffic USA through 2003, according to the Eastern District indictments. The deal was "amended and renewed in negotiations" that took place by phone or in quiet face-to-face meetings in Manhattan, Miami, and Los Angeles. For each event, hundreds of thousands of dollars in bribes and kickbacks—the amounts soaring with tournament revenue—were wired to offshore accounts controlled by Blazer. When banks requested documentation for the source of the funds, the general secretary concocted fake, backdated consultant bills to make it appear that CONCACAF had paid for services rendered to an offshore sports marketing firm—owned by Blazer. In a sign of the exploding value of the CONCACAF events, Traffic would later offer $15.5 million for worldwide exclusive rights for the single 2013 Gold Cup and the 2013–14 Champions League series, and agree to pay a $1.1 million bribe to new CONCACAF president Jeffrey Webb, which was funneled through New York banks, according to the first round of the federal indictments.

Swelling revenues did not prevent CONCACAF from being the beneficiary of millions of dollars in "soccer aid" and pork-barrel projects delivered by FIFA presidents João Havelange of Brazil and his Swiss successor, Sepp Blatter, to ensure the critical votes they needed to stay in power. In the FIFA system, each member nation, no matter how small, has one vote in the organization's elections. Montserrat, with a population of just five thousand, wielded the same electoral clout as the three hundred million people of the US sports market and the two hundred million of soccer behemoth Brazil. The Caribbean has more votes than all of South America. So CONCACAF, with its thirty-five votes, controlled an astonishing one-sixth of all FIFA votes, which were always delivered in a single bloc by Warner to the FIFA presidential candidate of his choice.

CONCACAF's US headquarters opened for business in 1990 across the street from Trump Tower, but by 1994, Blazer had worked out a deal to move into the luxury high-rise that he cherished above all other addresses: the first year was free, and the remaining eleven-year lease was discounted. Most of the office space remained empty after the lean CONCACAF staff took up residence, so Blazer either rented it out or used it as favors, on the federation's dime, in what one staffer branded a "barter system." The occupants included a rotating crew of escorts, a pair of hedge fund advisers, and others whom Chuck might find useful. One of the offices was occupied by two shoe manufacturers who were working with Blazer for years on a scheme to make inexpensive Disney-themed shoes in China. It was run by yet another Blazer operation, this one called Asia Pacific Initiatives Limited, located in the CONCACAF offices. In 2008 Blazer was seeking $6.5 million from investors, according to a proposal he shopped around. But that was one Blazer brainstorm that went bust, though he likely risked very little of his own money in the scheme. By 2010, CONCACAF had twenty-five employees in New York, with another ten in Miami.

CONCACAF's dramatic growth caught the attention of FIFA's executive committee. The board was eager to tap into the shrewd mind of Blazer, who to many Ex-Co members personified the uniquely American Midas touch of a New York businessman with marketing moxie. FIFA also wanted to bring the massive US market more deeply into the fold following the wildly successful 1994 World Cup. In 1996 Warner helped Blazer get elected to the FIFA Ex-Co to fill a vacancy. Chuck beat out high-profile Los Angeles lawyer Alan Rothenberg, who had been president of the USSF and the director of the 1994 Cup.

Rothenberg represented the pedigree, but Blazer embodied the prospect of future income. He vowed to help fill FIFA's coffers. Blazer's greatest contribution to FIFA was in boosting income from the sale of American television rights for future World Cups (which in turn increased commissions and bribes) and stimulating the US hunger for still more televised soccer games. Blazer persuaded FIFA to retain control of World Cup rights in-house rather than farm them out at a flat rate to a third-party marketing company. But the sports marketing companies were never really jettisoned from the business. Instead, FIFA—and CONCACAF—essentially became partners with the corporations, sharing a percentage of the sales of TV and sponsorship rights as they dickered over income and, in many cases, bribes.

A key Blazer coup was convincing the FIFA Ex-Co to terminate a 2007 deal to sell NBC the US rights to the 2010 and 2014 World Cups for $350 million. Instead, Blazer dodged a bidding process and forged a combined agreement with Univision and ESPN for $425 million, dwarfing earlier deals. ESPN also agreed to pay to carry Major League Soccer games, which satisfied Blazer's strategy to grow American demand for soccer by feeding audiences a steady diet of the sport. FIFA reaped a record $631 million profit between 2007 and 2010 thanks to various TV deals.

In 2010 a grateful Blatter rewarded Blazer by naming him chairman of FIFA's marketing and television committee. He was also put in charge of FIFA video game licensing operations and appointed to other committees. Still, the two were never easy friends and clashed often. Blazer sometimes referred to the Swiss leader as an "old Nazi" and often "Septic Bladder," a moniker coined by Blazer's friend Clive Toye. But Blatter clearly valued Blazer's business acumen—and was willing to pay for it. Each committee appointment came with an extra dollop of salary on top of FIFA's annual Ex-Co pay, estimated to be at least $250,000, with a minimum $100,000 yearly bonus, according to Blazer. Payments were made in Zurich—in cash if preferred. Or it could be wired directly to an offshore account, some set up for Ex-Co members by Cayman Islands banker Jeffrey Webb.

Blazer's burgeoning bank accounts and expense money translated into an ever-more splendiferous life in New York, while in the soccer-obsessed lands beyond the United States, he was becoming something of a celebrity. "You watch, Mary Lynn," he told Blanks after she moved in with him in 2002. "We will be treated like royalty by kings, queens, and statesmen all over the globe." As testament to that, Blanks and son Nicky once enjoyed a private tour of King Tut's tomb in Luxor, Egypt. Blazer couldn't negotiate the narrow mud corridors to the inner sanctum of the boy-king's final resting place, so he sat waiting outside on a low stone wall. When Blanks and Nicky emerged into the hot sun, they found Blazer surrounded by a gaggle of excited young men who had recognized the FIFA bigwig and were questioning him eagerly about the World Cup. "That's how it was in many places," Blanks said.

"People recognized him on the spot because he stood out, and they knew he was a big deal in the game."

Blazer's profile was much lower back home in a nation increasingly fond of soccer but largely oblivious to the inner workings of FIFA and CONCACAF. He still managed to live like a sultan, though. His calendar was packed with parties, dinners, and bimonthly trips to FIFA headquarters in Zurich, as well as monthly stays in the Bahamas, where CONCACAF was incorporated. He bought an apartment in Miami, and often headed to Las Vegas for tech and electronic exhibits—gambling—and strippers. "Hey Chuck, I'm glad you're in town," e-mailed a working girl to Blazer during a 2007 Vegas visit. "If you decide to come out tonite I will be at Scores. Really nice place and they have a restaurant."

On a whim, Blazer purchased a speedboat in the Bahamas through the hastily constructed shell corporation Gondola Ltd. and hired a pilot to squire guests. He rarely rode along, as it was too difficult for him to climb aboard. He began to dream of becoming a Bahamian citizen and living beyond the clutches of the IRS. The soccer king even wondered aloud to Blanks if he might one day be featured on the Bahamian currency.

Blazer certainly spent money like he was printing it: he rang up $29 million in expenses on his black Amex card over seven years and reimbursed CONCACAF only $3 million of it as personal costs. He dined almost nightly at exclusive places such as Nobu, Lavo, and Tao nearby, sometimes Campagnola, and he always picked up the tab for the shifting entourage that accompanied him. Chuck often spent $400 on Chinese takeout. He also enjoyed dining a block away from his apartment at Rue 57 on the corner of Fifty-Seventh Street and Sixth Avenue. When weather permitted, he parked his scooter to sit at an outside table with his pet macaw, Max, perched on the chair next to him. Blazer fed Max chicken legs, looking like two characters in a twisted modern-day scene from *The Fall of the Roman Empire*.

By 1998, Blazer had ascended to what he considered restaurant heaven by taking his anointed place among the journalists, novelists, actors, athletes, detectives, politicians, and a cast of beautiful women at Elaine's. The Upper East Side establishment drew the city's stars and movers and shakers, and the people who wanted to be like them. Proprietress Elaine Kaufman awarded Blazer his own spot: sought-after table 4, near the front, where he could be found many nights—almost always Thursday but never on Friday. That was when the place was overrun by the bridge-and-tunnel crowd, he complained: people from New Jersey . . . and Queens.

One evening, "special ladies" Miss USA 2006 Crystle Stewart and Miss Universe 2008 Dayana Mendoza flanked Blazer, who never missed the Miss Universe pageants when it was owned by Donald Trump, in Vegas or Miami. "Guys, consider me lucky," Blazer wrote in his blog the next day. The meals and free-flowing $400 bottles of wine, often Ornellaia or Château-Figeac, all went on Blazer's tab—or rather, CONCACAF's. One journalist described Blazer as having a "childlike innocence" in his joy of good company and the high life.

"The room lit up when Chuck walked into Elaine's, and there's no doubt Elaine was very fond of him," recalled famed sports photographer Neil Leifer, who took the iconic 1965 shot of a snarling heavyweight champion Muhammad Ali standing over a prone Sonny Liston in the boxing ring. "He was generous, warm, fascinating." Leifer, a regular at table 3, bantered frequently with Chuck. "He always offered me a ride home with his driver, even though it was out of his way." Reminded that Blazer's generosity was funded by CONCACAF, Leifer responded, "Who knew? He seemed like a fabulously wealthy American who was having a ball. He wore his wealth well. When I read the news about him, I was one hundred percent stunned. I'm sure I felt the same way people who thought Bernie Madoff walked on water did when they discovered he was a crook."

Leifer said he was particularly impressed that Blazer had made it to the top of FIFA as an American. The photographer covered four World Cups for *Sports Illustrated* and ran smack into the European disdain for Yanks' understanding of soccer. (FIFA's new reform committee boss, Michel Carrard, noted after he was appointed in 2015 that soccer wasn't a "true American sport. There, it's just an ethnic sport for girls in schools.")

Blazer and the scratchy-voiced Elaine, who usually sat with him at table 4, treated each other like a brother and sister from another mother, with Elaine loudly and sarcastically passing judgment on Blazer's friends and girlfriends. Blazer often boasted that he was so close to Elaine that he hauled himself out of bed in the middle of the night to bail Kaufman out of jail after her notorious 1998 arrest on an assault charge for allegedly slapping an unruly patron. That tale was likely another invention of Blazer's. Kaufman was released from the Nineteenth Precinct station house an hour after her arrest when Police Commissioner Ben Ward reportedly made a call on her behalf. (The charges, and a subsequent lawsuit filed by the bruised customer, were dropped.)

Like Blazer, Elaine was a surprisingly effective, engaging, over-weight know-it-all with a sharp wit and sharper tongue. She once called herself a "fucking icon," adding, "You get points for surviving." Kaufman was born in Manhattan but raised, like Blazer, in the bor-oughs: Queens and the Bronx, in her case. They were both crafty su-perachievers from inauspicious beginnings who beguiled the best and the brightest of Manhattan, people who never saw them coming and were completely in their thrall. Kaufman considered herself "at the top of the hill" during her restaurant heyday, sounding very much like a preening Chuck Blazer.

"We have been friends for years," Blazer wrote about Elaine in his blog. It was clear that his effusive welcome at her restaurant was a coveted prize for Blazer. Elaine's embrace represented to him the im-primatur of social success, similar to the way he viewed his residence high in Trump Tower. They were both incontrovertible proof of his as-cendency from his humble beginnings in Queens. And Elaine's wasn't a place for the stuffed-shirt wealthy. The restaurant often celebrated the creative mavericks—and their sycophants. Now he was part of that inner circle. When Kaufman died in 2010, Blazer lamented, "There was hardly a night that she didn't anchor my safe harbor; there will hardly be a day when I don't think of her."

Blazer celebrated his sixtieth birthday at the packed restaurant with friends from a glittering eighty-person guest list that included cops, journalists, public relations execs, and close pals Shep Messing and Ruth Westheimer. Henry Kissinger was invited but couldn't make it. FBI special agent Anne Beagan had a wardrobe malfunction that night as she flirted with the birthday boy—and weeks later stayed with her sister-in-law and two girlfriends in Blazer's Bahamas apartment. He flew out, alone, to "entertain" them, he would tell Blanks, ordering her to stay home. Blazer also later escorted Beagan to Zurich to meet Sepp Blatter. According to Beagan's brother-in-law, David Bookstaver, Blatter was recruiting federal agents at the time to help with tournament security procedures. "It was not an official trip," said Bookstaver, who is the communications director for New York State Courts and spoke for Beagan. "She was not speaking on behalf of the FBI. It's important to remember that in 2005 Blazer was not a pariah, not a bad guy, and had a variety of friends from all areas of the world. Agents are allowed to have friends." A spokeswoman for the New York office of the FBI declined comment on Beagan's relationship with Blazer, saying only that the agency doesn't discuss agents' personal lives.

For the party, Blanks had tracked down several of Blazer's childhood addresses to surprise him with copies of the deeds she obtained through the Adopt-a-Building program. But when Blazer opened the gift and examined the documents of the homes of his past, his face darkened in rage. "What is this?" he demanded angrily before hurling them back at her across the table in front of shocked guests. "I spent my whole life trying to get out of Queens! Why would I want this?"

Blazer's whirlwind social life extended beyond Elaine's to less rarefied joints: he made regular trips with friends to posh Manhattan strip clubs. He never went alone to watch the lap dancers, who swarmed the frequent, generous customer whenever he entered with his entourage of friends and CONCACAF workers. He loved paying for two women at a time to perform dances for his pals. The clubs were an integral part of the culture of virility that infused the lives of the all-male FIFA Ex-Co members, some of whom alternated between squiring their educated, sophisticated wives at official FIFA functions and stepping out with their much younger, less accomplished, not-quite-ready-for-prime-time mistresses and dates.

But in Blazer's case, women were also a compulsion. He needed frequent attention from sexy, exhibitionistic women, even though his weight made any bedroom gymnastics moot. In addition to strip clubs, he also frequently sexted or Skyped with women on his computer. In one conversation, he boasted to an apparently young "Oh Kissa" that he was about to participate in a press conference for an upcoming World Cup. "Oh," responded Oh Kissa, "I wish my dad could go to the World Cup."

Blazer's strip clubs of choice were Scores and the now-defunct Stringfellows. Sometimes he switched to the Penthouse Executive Club because Scores' managers, classy as ever, decided to separate the dining area from the dancers. Blazer preferred to eat while gawking, something he could do at the Penthouse. He got a kick out of adding "SONY" to the bills that he expensed to CONCACAF. It stood for Stringfellows of New York, not the electronics giant. "When I first went out to the clubs with Chuck, I thought, 'What a generous guy,'" said former CONCACAF staffer Mel Brennan. "But over time, I noticed everything went on that CONCACAF charge card, and I saw the costs paid by the office. That's not what the money was supposed to be used for. Man, the guy had a lot of energy for what he was interested in—not so much for helping people through sport." Brennan became disturbed by the nocturnal outings and left the organization a short time later.

Not everyone saw that warm, magnanimous, public side of Blazer that garnered so much loyalty—to this day—from friends and associates. Man-about-town Chuck could morph into mean-around-the-office

Chuck, a boss known at times to reduce staffers to tears with his angry tirades. Though he had difficulty moving around, Blazer was big and imposing and could be physically intimidating. He once threatened to throw CONCACAF tech expert Tim Longo out the window, vowing to "show you the quickest way to the first floor," Longo recalled. Blazer could turn from friendly and gregarious to frightening and angry in a heartbeat.

Few experienced this more dramatically than his live-in lover. Shortly after Blanks moved in with Blazer, she was startled when he suddenly pounded on the door of the locked bathroom while she was taking a bath. Her two sons were playing in the living room as Blazer shouted at her to "Get out!" and "Balance your checkbook!" Blazer had looked at Blanks's open laptop and seen that she had bounced checks. Blanks had just discovered that her estranged husband had stopped depositing money in their joint account. She told Blazer she would handle it when she got out, but he continued to pound at the door and then used a claw hammer and screwdriver to try to break in. He ended up punching out the doorknob, but still couldn't force his way through the door. "Goddamn it, Mary Lynn, now I have to call a repairman!" he yelled. When the handyman arrived, he put his arm protectively around Blanks, by then wrapped in a towel and shaking.

Blanks told her sons to pack up, but the older boy refused, saying that Blazer had offered to buy him an expensive computer if he stayed. She moved out with her younger son, but Blazer wooed her back by promising to see a therapist for anger management. Dr. Ruth recommended psychiatrist Steven Herschkopf, who wrote the book *Hello Darkness My Old Friend: Embracing Anger to Heal Your Life*. He saw Chuck and Mary Lynn together for a time, though Blazer soon begged off, citing business obligations. Herschkopf declined to discuss the therapy sessions because of doctor-patient confidentiality, but Blanks said he advised her that if she didn't have an "alternative" to living with Blazer, "keep your head down." The next time Blanks walked, Blazer offered her a lump sum payment to stay with him. Months after the bathroom incident, Blanks ordered a replacement door, but Blazer commanded an assistant to remove it. The battered door with the gaping hole where the doorknob was supposed to be served as a jarring reminder of the confrontation for the entire ten years they lived together.

Blazer's obesity complicated daily living for him—and for Mary Lynn. Because of the weight pressing on his lungs and years of heavy smoking (he finally gave it up for a worried Blanks), Blazer had to sleep propped up on pillows in his king-sized bed so that he could breathe. Each night, he was hooked up to a BiPAP (Bi-level Positive Airway Pressure) machine. The BiPAP forced ambient air into his lungs through a hose connected to a mask, which covered his mouth and nose and was strapped onto his head. The sound of the Darth Vader–like rhythmic pumping of air filled the apartment long after everyone was asleep.

The CONCACAF general secretary spent almost every morning working from his apartment, often trading stocks, clad in the black boxers and one of his 6-X Ralph Lauren polo shirts (he had at least a hundred of them) that he typically wore to bed the night before. When he was overheated, as he often was, he would strip off his shirt and blithely sit there half naked as staffers shuttled back and forth from CONCACAF offices for his signature or their marching orders. For a short time, he worked in an adjacent one-bedroom apartment that he converted to a home office at an additional monthly cost of $6,000, paid by CONCACAF. But Blazer ended up turning over the apartment to C.T.'s old cats, Bear and Cosmos, who suffered from serious bladder control issues. The white rugs in the main section of his home were already spotted with yellow stains from the cats. When the felines soaked business documents in Chuck's new office, he ceded the space to them and returned to working in his living room or on the edge of his bed. The cat apartment, its parquet tiles curling up from urine (branded "disgusting" by one of Blazer's employees), was only part of the increasing rot beneath the elegance of Chuck's home. He was negligent about home maintenance and sometimes ignored bills from his handymen, making good workers more difficult to find to keep up appearances. As a result, the kitchen and bathroom cupboards were streaked with rust, strange molds bloomed on ceilings and walls, and fabric-covered walls were soiled and heavy with dust.

Blazer was unable to bathe or dress himself, so Mary Lynn was expected to wait in the apartment so she could shower with him to help him get ready for the office. She needed several large bath towels and a blow dryer to completely dry him. He almost always wore a suit to work; he had five favorite tailor-made suits from Rochester Big & Tall along with dozens of pastel-colored dress shirts. Ties were the pride of his closet. Hundreds of $300 silk models handmade in Italy for the Leonard Paris fashion company featured his favorite vivid floral and sea themes.

His lengthy dressing ritual included matching one of his fancy ties with the right shirt and suspenders. Blanks emerged each day from his closet with several ties draped over her outstretched arms. Blazer would point, and she would try to guess which one he wanted. "No, *dear*," he would say, growing more irritated, "not that one," or "No, *darling*, that's not the one I mean." When Blazer traveled, he added his FIFA pin encrusted with four diamonds to his jacket lapel. The pin was stolen twice while his suit jacket hung in a closet in the first-class section of his flight.

As a boss, Blazer wasn't known for his human resource skills and sometimes put people on the payroll after meeting a likeable person at a bar and talking soccer. Blazer also added his son, Jason, a physical therapist, to the payroll as CONCACAF's "medical director" at $7,000 a month, and used association funds to produce a series of videos on soccer and health that were distributed free to teams and any organization with an interest. Chuck's attorney daughter, Marci, was later handed a post on FIFA's legal committee for an undisclosed sum.

As CONCACAF began to percolate, and the New York staff grew, Blazer handled fewer and fewer of the details. He was too busy trading stocks. Staffers, most of whom believed their boss was independently wealthy, were under orders not to bother him until the closing bell sounded; Warner would later accuse him of being "addicted" to trading. Blazer bought and sold stocks through a Merrill Lynch account registered offshore, according to CONCACAF investigators—though clearly, he was trading from New York. His broker, Steve Teixeira, worked just across the street in Merrill's midtown office. Teixeira often showed up at Blazer's apartment to apologetically collect checks, apparently to cover margin calls on trades that Blazer had misjudged. According to Merrill records, a Blazer account registered to MultiSport Games Development Inc. held $4.5 million the end of 2011 after peaking at $5.5 million that year. Blazer traded in a variety of companies, including Adobe, Cisco Systems, Yahoo!, Disney, Intel, and the Sands Corporation of Las Vegas.

Merrill dumped Blazer as a client in 2011 as information about the CONCACAF scandals emerged. Teixeira delivered the bad news personally, showing up at Blazer's door with tears in his eyes. When he left, Blazer told Blanks: "He should be crying. I put his kids through college."

While Blazer assiduously guarded access to most of CONCACAF's accounts to protect his crooked books, a small, dedicated crew labored long hours to accomplish much of the key work of the increasingly powerful association. Each tournament sponsored by the federation involved an enormous number of tasks. Years before the Gold Cup was launched, venues had to be selected, insurance obtained, schedules organized. Merchandise—apparel, banners, mugs, and myriad other items, all branded with logos and slogans—had to be designed and ordered, vendors found. Agreements with teams were crafted, hotel rooms and transportation—including frequent team bus trips to practice fields—arranged.

Some of Blazer's most effective employees, like Fracisco, were women. Jill was head of competitive tournaments and events, the guts of the organization. She often worked seven days a week, sometimes past midnight. Despite Blazer's philandering, she considered him largely blind to gender in the workplace and was grateful for the trust and responsibility he gave her, particularly in an association where she was often exasperated by the machismo she encountered. But Fracisco became vexed over the years to see men join the staff much later and get paid far more for what seemed to be mystery work.

She also found Blazer annoyingly stingy. When Chuck was working late, he typically ordered food for himself but not for the staff. He often insisted on lavish hotel suites for himself, but demanded that his staff stay in inexpensive rooms. "I'm on a champagne budget, you're on a beer budget," he once told Fracisco. Jill knew that employees in other sports organizations were often rewarded with bonuses after successfully pulling off big events, but that was not the case with Chuck. When she asked to earn commissions on some of the sponsorships she'd arranged for Gold Cup tournaments, Mr. Ten Percent told her: "I don't believe in commissions."

Fracisco much preferred traveling with Warner, who stayed in the same hotels as the tournament staffers, ate at the same restaurants, and took the same flights. He also sent handwritten thank-you notes after a big event. "I feel like such a fool now," said Fracisco. "We were so proud of ourselves when we managed to save three hundred dollars on an airline ticket or negotiated a string of hotel rooms at a discount. All those savings probably ended up in one of Chuck's offshore accounts." Added Toye, Blazer's longtime associate, "The real shame of it is that the mountain of work was done by very few people, none of whom, along with the rest of the staff, ever saw a single penny from the corrupt deals going on around them."

Not all Blazer's employees were hard workers. Some were useless, and in a few cases, that was apparently part of the plan. The controller was a heavy drinker who, he confided to his colleagues, downed a bottle of vodka a day, topped off by a couple of painkillers. He sometimes offered the pills to coworkers, calling them "Gummy Bears." One visitor to the office told Blazer that his controller appeared to be inebriated. "That's just the way we like him," Blazer responded.

Office tech expert Longo tracked down a series of viruses infecting office computers linked to the controller's machine and discovered that he spent hours each day on porn and gambling sites. After he reported the controller, Blazer called the man into his office and angrily scolded him loud enough for the office to hear. But he later told Longo to get the offending employee his own laptop and a dedicated phone line. "I was stunned," said Longo.

CONCACAF had no accurate, functional accounting system. When it came time to compile the annual financial report, Warner's pal and accountant Kenny Rampersad, of Kenny Rampersad & Co., was flown in from Trinidad to assemble the financial statements, according to staff members. Then he would apparently audit his own figures. Over the Warner and Blazer years, Rampersad's financial creations were always approved by the seven members of CONCACAF executive committee, who were elected by the association congress after getting the stamp of approval from the two leaders. Most board members turned quickly to the bottom line to make sure expenses weren't far off the previous year's and, hopefully, revenue had increased. If anyone hesitated or challenged Blazer, he projected an imposing, bullying impatience that brought most to heel. The financial statements were challenged only a handful of times, according to meeting minutes that the integrity committee examined. Occasionally, FIFA conducted an "audit" of CONCACAF expenditures, consisting of a request for certain invoices, which suddenly materialized where none had been before, according to staffers.

For Blanks, the clock on her Cinderella story was starting to tick toward midnight. She had enjoyed the fairy-tale trips to Europe, tea with the Queen of England, photo ops with Mick Jagger, Prince William, actor Morgan Freeman (one of the pitchmen for the US bid to host the World Cup), and the opportunity to chat with Nelson Mandela aboard a private jet. But her charmed life was becoming infected by suspicion and Blazer's troubling control. It took less than a year after she moved in for Blanks to suspect strongly that Blazer was cheating on her. After intercepting computer conversations between Blazer and another woman, Blanks confronted him. "I thought this was supposed to be a monogamous relationship," she said. "Absolutely," he insisted.

As the years unspooled, Blanks felt as if she were in the grip of a fearsome Svengali. She served as Blazer's fill-in wife, womanservant, travel companion, aide, and hostess, yet she could never quite satisfy him. He would call her to his bedside every morning and upbraid her for the things he decided she had bungled the day before: from asking a misguided question at a FIFA dinner, to wearing the wrong dress, to stepping in front of him at a red carpet event.

Blazer slowly choked off Blanks's relationships with her circle of friends, and she came to rely more and more on the FIFA wives as companions. She looked forward to seeing them during the six to eight trips she and Blazer made to Zurich each year. Early in the relationship, Blanks invited one of her closest New York pals to her apartment to enjoy the view. The friend lit up a joint at almost the same moment that Blazer opened the front door, returning unexpectedly from a CONCACAF trip. The instant he spotted the stranger and smelled marijuana he morphed into a furious Zeus. The man who would later plead guilty to dodging taxes and taking bribes banished the friend forever, telling Blanks angrily that he had an important post at the very pinnacle of world soccer and could brook no lawbreaking in his home. In fact, some people who know Blazer, including one investigator, believe he was convinced he wasn't doing anything wrong. He shrugged off dodging the IRS and regarded his bribes as his just desserts for the CONCACAF business he generated.

Blanks became increasingly mystified by—and suspicious of— their living expenses. Why, she repeatedly asked Blazer, was he paying $24,000 a month in rent when he could easily invest some of his millions and own a home in a Manhattan? He would tell her there were tax reasons that she wouldn't understand. Still, he indulged her interest in home ownership by sending her on real estate shopping trips, during which she searched for appropriate brownstones. Blazer even sent decorators with her to discuss possible renovation plans, but he apparently had no intention of ever buying a house.

Nor would he allow Blanks to work. The onetime model and actress who appeared in *All My Children, As the World Turns,* and *Loving* was offered audition opportunities while living with Blazer, but he told her, "Your job is me."

Finally, out of desperation, Blanks pleaded with Blazer to allow her to work in some capacity for CONCACAF or for one of his many corporations. He was becoming more distant, often traveling without her, and she feared for her financial future. She revealed her concerns in an e-mail to him the summer of 2009 while he was out of town for a soccer event:

> I am very grateful for all the bills you have paid over the past seven years. You have been most generous with me and my children, as you said you would be if I left my home and husband and came to live with you. I have done everything you asked . . . I bathe you, I dress you, I am your escort, your aide, your confidant, and when you allow it, your lover.

> You have done a wonderful job providing for us so far, but I am concerned for our future. I have no family, no savings. You have not let me work. I need to have a job history, or I won't even be able to get unemployment, much less a job. I do not know your intentions to me or my children anymore . . . you seem so different and distant, and your health does not look good . . . I am asking that you honor your promise to me, and do the right thing.

Blazer promised, in an uncharacteristically tender e-mail response, to explain everything to Blanks as soon as he returned home:

> Unfortunately, you have never understood why I can't pay you from one of those companies. I've told you that I can't, but that has never satisfied you. I will

have to explain it in person. The answer is actually quite simple and cannot be compared to anything in your life experience, but it is a true and honest answer and a very good reason which I didn't want to put on your shoulders. I will do so now.

There are no issues over which you should have concern, other than my dropping dead, which I am trying not to do (believe it or not).

So sit tight and I will be home in a few days, and you will see some of my warts. Nobody likes showing their warts, but it is far better than you imagining a load of things which are just not true.

Love you,
Chuck

Blazer returned to tell Blanks the most dangerous secret of his life—the one that would ultimately ensnare him in the massive FIFA take-down. He sat in the living room, on the couch where he had wooed her, and revealed that the "tax reasons" behind his decisions not to put her on the CONCACAF payroll—or to buy property—were that he wasn't paying any taxes, and hadn't for decades, and that he couldn't afford to draw the attention of the IRS. He said he'd stopped filing taxes after C.T. moved in with him nearly two decades earlier. "She was an expensive girl," he explained, and he needed the extra funds.

"What were you thinking?" asked an incredulous Blanks. "You're going to end your life in a federal penitentiary."

The former chain-smoking borderline diabetic looked down at his massive lap for several seconds and then raised his face to hers:

"I thought I'd be dead before anyone caught up to me."

FIVE

MAD PARROTS AND CRAZY IDEAS

HE WAS HATED BY MANY, FEARED BY MORE. "NOBODY LIKED MAX," SAID JILL FRACISCO. With his piercing squawk and vicious beak, Chuck Blazer's macaw parrot Max was a constant, irritating presence at CONCACAF. Until Max was forced out of the federation workplace along with his beleaguered master, the bird lived in Chuck's seventeenth-floor office and terrorized staffers. He was one more odd facet of Blazer's quirky menagerie and another testament to his weirdly off-kilter affair with his pets during his soccer career. It began with his pre-CONCACAF dog Tango, a shih tzu mix who traveled with Chuck when Blazer was general manager of the Miami Sharks. After he became a CONCACAF honcho, Blazer always took his two cats on monthly trips to the Bahamas—first class.

Max was a gift to Chuck from his wife, Susan, and daughter, Marci, in the early 1990s. The bird could say "Hello" in such an eerie mimic of Susan's exact inflection that it often sounded like she was in the room. He could also squawk "CONCACAF." But most plaintively, the bird wailed a croaky "Chuuuuuuuuuck" when Blazer strode from his office and out of sight. Max loved his Chuck, and Chuck couldn't seem to get enough of Max. Whenever Blazer spoke to people in his office or talked on the phone, the jealous macaw squawked incessantly until he had Chuck's full attention again.

It wasn't a tactic appreciated by the staff, not that Blazer cared. "When I talked to people on the phone, they would ask me, 'Where are you?' because it could sound like a zoo," recalled Fracisco. "I would tell them, 'Obviously, I'm in the middle of a jungle.' But it wasn't funny."

Max had eyes only for Chuck. The macaw generally tolerated women but often tried to slash anyone else who ventured too close. Even on his outings to Central Park, where he rode on a basket attached to the front of Blazer's mobility scooter, Max eyed the fingers and faces of children taken in by his brilliant lime-green plumage. Blazer never warned anyone, and the bird sometimes lunged at kids. Chuck thought it was funny—unless Max nipped at him. A witness once saw Blazer fling the snapping bird across his office. It only seemed to make Max crankier.

Initially, Max lived in an eight-by-ten-foot octagonal iron cage in Blazer's office (he had a second cage on the office terrace), though he often emerged to sit on a perch next to Chuck's desk. He ate a rich diet of seeds, nuts, and fresh fruit daily. He attended the monthly office parties held to celebrate staffers' birthdays. That's when Max performed his lone trick: he swayed back and forth in a parrot dance when people sang "Happy Birthday to You." Blazer bragged about Max almost as if he were a son.

Max finally struck it rich, along with his master, when Blazer pitched and won funding from FIFA for a state-of-the-art CONCACAF TV broadcast studio in 2006. A first for CONCACAF, the studio was to be run by a wholly owned subsidiary created by Blazer, CONCACAF

Marketing and TV Inc. (CMTV). The new entity also took charge of selling sponsorships and television rights to association tournaments. Blazer had decided in 2003 to stop outsourcing such sales, and canceled a deal with the marketing firm Inter Forever Sports to instead directly sell the rights for the 2005 Gold Cup and Women's Gold Cup. Blazer hired Inter Forever's CEO as the director of TV and broadcasting for CMTV.

Inter Forever, struggling financially at the time, was acquired by Traffic Group of Brazil, which created its own American subsidiary in Miami, Traffic Sports USA. Even as CMTV continued to operate, Traffic would reestablish a relationship with CONCACAF and Blazer, and would continue Inter Forever's practice of providing the general secretary with hundreds of thousands of dollars in bribes for the rights to sell CONCACAF tournaments to sponsors and media companies.

CMTV hired a number of employees, including attorney Italo Zanzi, whom Blazer brought in to work as the deputy general secretary of the subsidiary. Zanzi had been a goalkeeper, not in soccer but on the US national handball team from 1997 to 2007. In 2012 after he left CMTV he became CEO of Italy's AS Roma soccer team. The handsome Zanzi, with his jet-black hair, an open, friendly face, and the ice-blue eyes of a Siberian husky, was considered Blazer's "arm candy," in the words of one coworker. Zanzi instantly drew women to his boss's side at strip clubs and restaurants; they were then weaned onto Blazer's black Amex card for drinks and lap dances.

Zanzi's actual job was a mystery to many in the CONCACAF office, though Blazer often boasted that his deputy was a crack contract negotiator and that the two worked together like "butter to bread." He was supposedly negotiating contracts for the very same Gold Cups that, according to testimony from his own boss, involved hundreds of thousands of dollars in bribes. Zanzi's LinkedIn résumé states that he worked from December 2007 until October 2011 on marketing and TV rights for CONCACAF—both at the very heart of federation corruption. Zanzi represented CONCACAF on FIFA's committee for fair play and social responsibility at the same time that Blazer was accepting bribes. Roma officials said four months after the first round of Eastern District indictments that a background check on Zanzi before he was hired came up clean, with owner James Pallotta telling the Associated Press: "We did long checks beforehand" into Zanzi. "There has been zero [allegations]. He has nothing." Zanzi was paid a $250,000 salary and a $250,000 annual bonus, according to CONCACAF records.

The year before he began working for CONCACAF, Zanzi ran as a Republican candidate against Long Island Democratic incumbent Tim Bishop for the US House of Representatives. Zanzi, from Long Island, was living mostly in Blazer's Manhattan apartment, while maintaining an address in New York's First Congressional District in eastern Suffolk County. Zanzi shared the cats' quarters, dropping his used towels on the floor and stepping carefully over the feline messes. *Newsday* touted him as a man with "tremendous potential . . . Down the road there should be a place for a bright, energetic man like him in public life." Zanzi lost the election with 38 percent of the vote, considered a decent showing by a young, newbie politician against the popular Democratic incumbent. He celebrated his thirty-first birthday that year at Elaine's, and "the owner of the estimable bar and restaurant . . . contributed a delicious nougat ice cream and strawberry whipped cream birthday cake," Blazer gushed in his blog. "Yummmy!!!!"

Zanzi and Blazer would party even more after that birthday. CONCACAF opened an office in Miami in 2008 to house the CMTV operations. Miami was chosen because of its proximity to many of CONCACAF's business partners in the Caribbean, and Latin and South America. The office started with five employees but grew steadily. Blazer and Zanzi found reason to travel there frequently and stayed together in adjoining apartments.

Though CMTV was headquartered in Miami Beach, Blazer decided to build the actual TV studio in the New York office. He wanted it close by, but the configuration of the Trump offices couldn't accommodate the facility. So the seventeenth-floor spaces were overhauled completely and the studio built at a cost of at least $3 million, though Blazer confided to some that the true cost was closer to $5 million. That's when Max got a new glass aviary with a marble floor in Chuck's office—for $150,000. The space included a perch, a view of Central Park, six food cups refilled daily at a cost of hundreds of dollars a month at CONCACAF's expense, jungle-gym netting where Max could climb and hang upside down, plus a clear sight line to Chuck's wall-mounted wide-screen TV. Blazer later gave Max his own TV inside the aviary, usually switched to the Cartoon Network, which Chuck insisted the bird preferred to the Discovery Channel or the business programs playing on Chuck's TV.

The association had to spend hundreds of thousands of additional dollars on a new cooling system to keep the broadcast equipment and computers cool when the building's air-conditioning shut down on nights and weekends in the commercial offices. Blazer had an alarm on his phone that alerted him if the temperature climbed to a dangerous level for the equipment—or for Max. When that happened, he immediately phoned an assistant to rectify the problem.

The general secretary didn't do so badly himself on the TV studio deal. Blazer collected a cut of the first $3 million installment of FIFA funds sent to CONCACAF to build the facility. Two weeks after CONCACAF received the payment, Blazer helped himself to $300,000, which he disguised on the association's books as "commissions payable" from a "Sony Equipment Sponsorship." CONCACAF's investigation found no evidence that Sony served as a CONCACAF sponsor. In fact, the confederation paid an additional $1.2 million to Sony Electronics in 2006 to purchase equipment for the broadcast studio. CONCACAF investigators were unable to track completely the money spent on the facility—or the general secretary's "commissions"— because of incomplete financial records.

CMTV also served a function other than marketing, one that CONCACAF's board didn't discover for years. The subsidiary bought

Florida real estate. CMTV funds were used to purchase two apartments at the luxury waterfront Mondrian South Beach Hotel Residences in Miami Beach in May 2010: a one-bedroom apartment and studio for a combined $810,000. The apartments, combined in a pricey renovation, were used primarily and controlled exclusively by Blazer and Zanzi, even though Zanzi had his own apartment elsewhere in Miami, according to CONCACAF investigators. Blazer bought the properties without CONCACAF authorization, in the name of CMTV and in his capacity as CMTV president. The CONCACAF investigative committee was "unable to identify a business rationale for the purchase of the apartments." The Mondrian is located less than a mile from CMTV's offices in Miami Beach, yet most CONCACAF employees had no idea the apartments existed.

Blazer had a dream for the TV studio: it would broadcast video-taped feeds of CONCACAF games with analysis by three different commentators, including Shep Messing; John Harkes, the former US national team captain; and a young soccer broadcaster, flown in from New Zealand, whom Blazer had met during a television studio appearance there. But there was no outlet for such programs other than FIFA's and CONCACAF's Web sites. Broadcast companies had their own operations and weren't interested in buying the new product. One TV network offered up to $20,000 for the broadcasts, but the money didn't even cover the travel expenses of the New Zealand commentator, according to a source who worked at the CONCACAF offices at the time.

Bizarrely, Blazer kept the studio to himself, his three "stars," and a small crew of cameramen and editors. He refused to allow Longo or any other staffer inside for almost three years until he needed help producing a series called *Inside the Gold Cup*. Despite the availability of three state-of-the-art studio cameras, eight editing bays, and a blue screen to key in backgrounds behind the commentators, the finished videos were merely downloaded to YouTube—an operation that didn't require much more than a computer and a simple video camera. "It was so disappointing to see all that work go into those films and then watch Chuck load them onto YouTube," recalled a staffer.

Licensing restrictions prohibited renting out the space for uses other than televising FIFA-endorsed soccer, although Blazer did allow Ruth Westheimer to produce a short video on her book *Musically Speaking: A Life Through Song*, according to employees. The cost of the studio was prohibitively expensive, and the operation was shut down just years after it was launched. The equipment was sold off a short time later.

As for Max, he enjoyed his CMTV-funded aviary for several years. Chuck eventually took in a pair of Eclectus parrots, Venus and Apollo, that had belonged to friends of Zanzi's parents. But they annoyed and frustrated Max because they cooed to each other all day and mated often. Max began to rip out his feathers and required hormone shots in a fruitless bid to keep him calm. Chuck stopped taking the crazed macaw to Central Park. Blazer grew fonder of his new Eclectus birds; after Venus laid two eggs, he gushed on his blog, "It looks like I am going to be a grandfather again," and promised, "Pictures of the proud parents will be posted when they finish taking turns sitting on the eggs." Unlike Blazer's schemes, the eggs never hatched.

When Blazer was eventually forced out of CONCACAF, Max and the Eclectus lovers came to live in his apartment. They were given the lone bedroom facing south, so Max lost his view of Central Park, but at least the room had its own bathroom—with Jacuzzi.

SIX

UNCLE JACK

A JUMBLE OF BLEACHED CONCRETE STRUCTURES LOOMS IN THE STICKY HEAT ACROSS
from farm fields in Trinidad's tiny township of Macoya. "CONCACAF" is
spelled out in large blue letters on a water tower. It's an hour's drive east
from Piarco International Airport along the Churchill-Roosevelt Highway, past industrial warehouses and pockets of shoulder-to-shoulder
white stucco homes. The complex includes a bathhouse that opens onto
an outdoor swimming pool, the small Marvin Lee Stadium and soccer
field, an inn, a hangar-sized meeting and banquet building with bare
slab interior walls, and a health club. The anomalous buildings are so
out of place in the tropical landscape amid palm trees near the foot of
the North Range mountains that they could have been dropped there by
aliens. But they're hardly futuristic or even state of the art. The electric-
ity sometimes flickers out at the Sportel Inn, or hot water trickles to
nothing.

This is CONCACAF's $26 million Centre of Excellence. Max's aviary and Chuck's $3 million TV studio are parrot feed by comparison. The center was created by the association to help promote the beautiful game, and develop soccer and coaching skills. Instead, it's the mother of sports boondoggles, built by the man branded by one US law enforcement investigator as FIFA's crook of crooks: former CONCACAF president Jack Warner.

Warner's greed was deeper than the Caribbean, and it would drown both the Trinidadian and his longtime American partner in crime. Blazer had staked his future on Warner when he backed him to become the association's president in 1990, an initially lucrative miscalculation that would ultimately trigger Chuck's ignominious downfall—and FIFA's. The story of Chuck Blazer's end is as tied inextricably to his tangled relationship with Jack Warner as it is to his own outlaw history. Over the years, Warner's scams became progressively brazen, his invective more and more outlandish until it exposed the Ex-Co's dirty business, which had been cloaked for decades behind impeccable manners and carefully coded conversations in low voices at elegant dinners. Though the Mohamed bin Hammam cash-for-votes scandal was the final blow that shattered Blazer and Warner's twenty-two-year relationship, the tension between the men had been growing.

FIFA and CONCACAF paid for the Centre of Excellence, which was Warner's brainchild. But the CONCACAF board didn't discover until 2012—seventeen years after the center was approved—that the complex had been built on land owned by Warner. He used soccer association funds to buy the real estate for himself and controlled all construction and operating funds. As of late 2015, he was still the owner of the center and was continuing to collect income from it. The complex is tucked away at the extreme southeastern edge of the vast CONCACAF territory that extends to northern Canada. It's surprisingly remote from any major population center within CONCACAF: 4,400 miles from Vancouver, 2,500 miles from Mexico City, and 2,200 miles from New York. "It's as if we built a ramshackle CONCACAF center for excellence for Central and North America and the Caribbean, and located it in some backwater town in Alaska," noted Clive Toye, who visited the center a number of times while working for CONCACAF. He was stunned by what he saw. "What the hell?" Toye recalled thinking when he first looked around. "Yes, there was a soccer pitch, but not a very good one, and I never saw a single person playing a game or practicing."

There seemed to be everything else, though. According to the center's Web site, it was "established to be a hub of football education, expertise, and skills training," but it "blossomed into a multipurpose facility," hosting "weddings, graduations, and parties." Over the years, the center has been the scene of concerts by popular Bollywood singers, gospel music recitals sponsored by island churches, area school graduations, banquets, and conferences that had nothing to do with any sport. The Centre of Excellence has hosted an international Islamic retreat, the Trini Ink Tattoo Convention, and the Caribbean Nail and Beauty Trade Show. It's been the site for a Barely Legal Pimp My Ride car show, and several "Drift Shows," featuring souped-up cars spinning out around traffic cones in the parking lot between the warehouse-like Sepp Blatter Hall and the soccer stadium. Weddings are the major moneymakers. The center's Web site features a gallery of photos of flowers and concrete walls disguised with gauzy curtains behind tables outfitted for receptions. Workshop blogs include helpful primers on "Designing Your Wedding Cake" and "Firing Your Wedding Planner."

As for any soccer-related activities, very occasional coaching clinics are conducted by the Joe Public Football Club, one of Warner's many family companies that also owns the FC Santa Rosa team, which plays the odd game at the stadium. The Warner family travel agency, Simpaul, arranges all transportation to the site.

The Centre of Excellence represented the epitome of Warner's skill at misdirecting FIFA funds and hiding the money behind a maze of Warner-controlled entities. He proposed the center "to help raise the quality of soccer at CONCACAF" at an association executive committee meeting on July 28, 1995, and it was quickly approved "in principle," according to the minutes. Warner estimated then that the complex would cost $7.5 million.

The following spring, delegates at the annual CONCACAF Congress were informed in a report written by Blazer that the association was constructing a "facility for coaching and player development." Then–FIFA president Havelange—who desperately depended on Jack's Caribbean votes to retain his post—praised Warner for his "vision in building the CONCACAF Centre of Excellence in Trinidad." By that time, two Warner family companies—CCAM and Company Ltd. and Renraw ("Warner" spelled backward) Investments Ltd.—had already purchased the three plots of land for the center for a total of $1.7 million. They did it using FIFA money fronted to CONCACAF, association investigators would find later. Warner's first purchase in Renraw's name was tracked directly to FIFA funds; records on the purchase details for the other parcels are missing, but CCAM and Renraw bought the land shortly after FIFA funds were deposited in—and vanished from—CONCACAF accounts.

CONCACAF spent at least $26 million on the construction and development of the Centre of Excellence from 1996 to 2006. Funds were secured by Warner through different sources of money, including a $6 million loan from the Union Bank of Switzerland guaranteed by FIFA, which later paid it off without charging CONCACAF. Other funds were interest-free loans directly from FIFA, repaid by turning back disbursements that FIFA was scheduled to allocate to CONCACAF. In some cases, CONCACAF surrendered its share of World Cup proceeds. It also turned back to FIFA $2.3 million each year from 2003 to 2006 in Financial Assistance Program (FAP) grants for CONCACAF to use on local projects (some FAP funds went to pay bills at Elaine's). "For months, every dime that came into the CONCACAF offices from FIFA went right to Jack Warner to build the center," said longtime CONCACAF official Ted Howard. Warner not only secretly purchased the center for himself using FIFA and CONCACAF funds, but also leveraged the property as collateral to obtain personal loans, according to the investigative report by CONCACAF's integrity committee. The committee was unable to determine how any of the millions spent on the center were used because all records, if any existed, were kept by Warner, who refused to turn them over.

The boldness of the scam worried Blazer. The men had colluded to collect bribe money in tournaments like the Gold Cup, Blazer confessed in court, and otherwise covered for each other on their individual schemes. But the Centre of Excellence was a monster con that devoured funds needed to run the association and its legitimate activities. "There are so many things that could have been done with the tens of millions of dollars wasted there," Blazer is quoted as saying in the integrity committee report. Blazer grew increasingly skittish about the deception, particularly each time that Toye returned from Macoya to express his suspicions about the facility.

A key part of the ruse of disguising the true nature of the center was to create annual financial statements that didn't raise any alarms with the board. Warner and Blazer flew in accountant Kenny Rampersad from Trinidad to CONCACAF's Trump Tower office to create the financial reports submitted to the federation board. In the confidential 2008 financial statement, the Centre of Excellence was listed as a CONCACAF—not a Warner—asset worth $25 million ($20 million after a twelve-month depreciation). Rampersad was also Warner's accountant for the Centre of Excellence and for the Trinidad and Tobago Football Federation, which Warner controlled.

The center also served as a pipeline for influence. Anyone wishing to curry favor with Warner could organize a trip to Macoya and book travel through his family company Simpaul at grossly inflated costs. In September 2010, while England was clamoring to become the 2018 World Cup venue, the David Beckham Academy, run by the London-born superstar, conducted a six-day training session for boys at the center. Beckham told the media he wasn't certain how much the operation cost and didn't really care as "long as the kids are happy," adding:

"Hopefully, if we do get a World Cup, it would continue." England did not, and the sessions ceased.

That same year, Australia's bid committee for the 2022 Cup agreed to contribute $485,000 to upgrade the Marvin Lee Stadium at the center two months before the votes on the 2018 and 2022 World Cups. The check was supposed to be processed through CONCACAF, but the Australians were directed by Warner's office to send the funds to a particular account in the Bahamas. Warner controlled at least four different accounts with slight variations in names, a shell game to cache diverted funds, investigators for the integrity committee discovered. When Blazer reached out to Australian bid committee chairman and shopping mall magnate Frank Lowy, inquiring about the promised money, the men realized it had been hijacked by Warner into one of his own accounts. "Please don't let this information get out," Lowy pleaded in an e-mail to Blazer. "It won't look good for us."

Lowy later denied the money was intended as a bribe. "We ran a clean bid," Lowy said in a letter to his football association. "But did we make mistakes? Yes. Were we naïve? In some cases, yes. Would we do things differently in future? Absolutely." Lowy said he never met with Warner to negotiate a deal for his vote. But he also told Sky News that he was hoping to influence Warner's vote. "We were trying to influence the whole world. He [Warner] was one who we would hope would vote for us," said Lowy.

The contribution that made the US indictments involved South Africa's bombshell $10 million donation to the center, which was touted as a soccer development site for the needy among the Caribbean's African diaspora, a term Warner used repeatedly to tout the social benefits of his complex. US officials called it a bribe. Blazer "understood the offer to be in exchange" for his and Warner's FIFA Ex-Co votes backing South Africa's bid to host the 2010 Cup, according to the federal indictments.

When CONCACAF investigators finally discovered in 2012 that Warner was the legal owner of the center, he insisted the facility had been intended all along as a "gift for the Caribbean and Jack Warner" by his conniving mentor, Havelange. "There is no ambiguity," he announced. Warner claimed he had been given an initial $6 million grant for the center in exchange for a promise to Havelange that he would deliver CONCACAF votes to Havelange's chosen successor as association president, Sepp Blatter. "Blatter was Havelange's candidate to succeed him for the FIFA presidency," Warner said in a 2013 statement. "Blatter had been at this time the most hated FIFA official by both the European and African confederations, and without my CONCACAF support at the FIFA elections, Blatter would never have seen the light of day as president of FIFA."

With CONCACAF's votes, Blatter did indeed beat his rival, UEFA boss Lennart Johansson, by a 111-to-80 count. Haiti's vote was cast at the CONCACAF Congress by the girlfriend of Warner pal Horace Burrell, head of the Jamaican Football Federation (JFF), even though she wasn't an official delegate. The switch was arranged by Warner after Haiti's delegate failed to show.

Warner's defense of the Centre of Excellence sham was something out of New York City's Tammany Hall political machine of the nineteenth century: He stole it fair and square. "There was no uncertainty. There was no secret in my dealings toward Dr. Havelange and the Centre of Excellence," Warner emphasized in his statement. "The center was built first by a loan that was given to Jack Warner that was converted into a grant—and by further assistance from Dr. Havelange, after whom I named the center."

It was this kind of breathtaking flimflam that helped turn an impoverished Trinidadian boy into a multimillionaire. If Chuck Blazer was the quintessential American huckster, Jack Warner was the other side of this counterfeit coin: a scrappy island striver. Together these two very different men would make corruption history.

While Blazer's upbringing was solidly middle class, Warner's was far more desperate. He was one of six siblings raised largely by his mom, Stella Warner, in the village of Rio Claro in southern Trinidad.

His heavy-drinking dad, Wilton, dropped into their lives only occasionally. Stella was a devout Catholic who attended Mass without fail every Sunday. She was also a strict disciplinarian, "never one to spare the rod," according to Warner's biography *From Zero to Hero*, written by journalist Valentino Singh. (It's coauthored by Warner even though the book refers to him in the third person.)

Warner's mom did cleaning and took in laundry for a number of Jack's classmates' parents, and his peers sometimes used this to embarrass him, a teacher recounted in the book. When the children later lived for a time with an aunt in another community, Warner and his siblings faced a new discrimination: racism. Rio Clara was "dominated by Afro-Trinidadians, now he found himself surrounded by Indo-Trinidadians" in a community where people's "complexion often dictated how they were treated." Even his aunt, whose children had lighter skin, treated her nieces and nephews differently. Warner compared his experience to Cinderella. "No one could possibly understand what we went through," he recalled in the book. "We were treated like outcasts and it was almost as if we were brought there to look after my aunt's children. We were made to do everything, while those children lived like royalty."

His struggles with poverty and humiliating discrimination would drive Warner to succeed. It also shaped an angry adult who would rail against unjust persecution whenever he was accused of criminal activity. "It's not a crime to be successful, even for people like me," he complains in *From Zero to Hero*. "But no one should attempt to impute improper business practices to me . . . when the reality is that I have selflessly given to the cause of football." (Warner's book includes a promotional blurb from Blazer saying his boss "is a measure of reality for those who like bullshit.")

Warner's attitude about himself was markedly different from Blazer's. The Trinidadian believed that he deserved all the fruits of his hard if less than legal work. But the Queens native, having conned his way through much of his life, thought he was lucky to be at the top of the soccer pyramid. He believed that it was only a matter of time before people discovered he had no business being there.

Warner was a bright, industrious student whose good grades earned him scholarships to some of Trinidad's most rigorous schools. He attended the College of St. Philip and St. James, and later earned a degree in international relations from the University of the West Indies. Eventually he became a history teacher at the island's prestigious Polytechnic Institute, where he met his future wife, Maureen Matthews, who also taught at the school.

Like Blazer, Warner began his life in sports politics through working with local soccer groups. He played soccer, but not very well. He loved the game, though, and was drawn to participate in the life of the sport on his island in any way he could. He initially served as the general secretary of the Central Football Association and the Central St. George Football Association, rising to become the secretary and head of the main Trinidad and Tobago Football Federation, and, eventually, the head of the Caribbean Football Union.

The combination of Warner's cunning and his hardscrabble background served him well among the varied demographics of Trinidad and Tobago's soccer associations—and, later, island politics. "He's a chameleon," noted island journalist Lasana Liburd, who has covered Warner for decades. "He can be a man of the people or fit in with the rich. He can be surrounded by locals on a street corner calling him 'Uncle Jack' in the morning, and turn up at a theater opening that night." He seldom put on airs, noted Liburd, either by condescending to the people he grew up with or reveling in ostentatious cars and homes he could have easily purchased with his dirty money.

Warner's relationship with Blazer thrived for years. The two improbable pals had a similar sticky-fingered approach to the soccer business and plotted to keep their various schemes well hidden as CONCACAF boss and the general secretary in charge of the accounts. Warner traveled often to New York to meet with the staff and help plan various events, including the Gold Cup. He often stayed at Le

Parker Méridien in Midtown, and expected a room outfitted with a variety of snacks, a bottle of Johnnie Walker Black, and a wide selection of mixers (until his doctor advised him to cut back on his drinking).

On most visits, he also handed Blazer a list of electronics he wanted for his Trinidadian staff, relatives, and friends: from iPads, to laptops, to cameras. Fulfilling the "shopping list" was the job of Blazer's assistant Adriana Martinez, and everything went on CONCACAF's bill. One Christmas Warner had a special list for his fellow parishioners, explaining to Martinez that he was a "devout Catholic" and the community of churchgoers was very important to him. Again, CONCACAF played Santa Claus. Blazer once quipped to a confidant: "I don't know how that works. You're a devout Catholic one day, and thieving the other six days." Warner rarely missed going to Mass each Sunday, even when it was difficult to find Catholic churches in Muslim countries during his travels for FIFA.

There were other transgressions on non–holy days. Both Warner and Blazer reveled in their reputations as womanizers: the two self-imagined studs enjoyed boasting to each other about their "dates." The men sometimes entertained women together as they stayed in apartments they rented on CONCACAF's dime on Miami's south shore and in the Bahamas.

Warner's wife, Maureen, stuck by her husband despite his infidelity, once telling a friend, "Sometimes you have to do what's best for your children." When her sons were young, Jack confessed to Maureen that they had a secret half brother, Jamal, who lives in the United States. "I know that it would have caused some anxiety and grief within the family, but I had to let them know," Warner quotes himself in *From Zero to Hero*. "Once Jamal was born, I made up my mind that I was not going to leave him out of my life or that of my family." By all reports, Jamal has had little to do with the Warner family and no connection to his dad's network of shady CONCACAF and FIFA dealings. Warner's sons Daryll and Daryan, however, pled guilty in 2013 to a number of charges, including wire fraud linked to World Cup ticket sales, and both cooperated with US investigators.

Warner's and Blazer's convivial relationship was fading by 2003. They still watched each other's backs assiduously, but tensions were becoming obvious. With CONCACAF headquarters in New York, it was often difficult for Warner, the de facto boss, to get the staff to carry out his wishes from Port of Spain. Blazer was calling the shots in Manhattan. "You often felt like you were in the middle of a tug-of-war," recalled Jill Fracisco. "Chuck had his pet projects, and Jack his, and they wanted us to work for them all the time."

Blazer also suspected that Warner was growing jealous of his increased power on the Ex-Co, as he was placed in charge of more committees. Blazer was widely regarded as the shrewder businessman, more likely to fill FIFA's bank accounts with savvy television and marketing deals. He was also a more eloquent, powerful speaker than Warner, who has a speech impediment: his tongue is slightly too big for his mouth, which sometimes makes him difficult to understand.

Warner's envy was further piqued after Blazer helped arrange a FIFA Congress in the Bahamas in 2009, and Bahamian prime minister Hubert Ingraham thanked him profusely from the podium, failing to mention the president of CONCACAF.

Few members of FIFA's executive committee have a soccer history as controversial as Warner's. Printing fake tickets and failing to pay players at the 1989 World Cup playoff was just the beginning. The Warner family company Simpaul Travel spun Jack's 1989 playoff ticket operation into a new, even pricier version by selling hundreds of black market 2002 World Cup tickets packaged in expensive trip deals at a $350,000 profit, FIFA investigators discovered. There were no FIFA sanctions because the association had no ethics rules until 2004. For the 2006 Cup in Germany Simpaul made at least a $1.7 million profit selling $30,000 ticket-and-trip packages, which was by then against the rules—and the law, according to US charges filed against Daryan

Warner. As a penalty, FIFA ordered Warner and his family to make a $1 million donation to a charity, but only $250,000 was paid. Warner also agreed to sever all family ties to Simpaul. But Daryan remained a director.

Media rights giveaways from FIFA presidents to Warner in exchange for his crucial support also made him a fortune. Former President Havelange "sold" Caribbean broadcast rights to the 1990 and 1994 World Cups to Warner for $1 each so that Jack could resell them for millions of dollars. The profits were supposed to be spent developing the sport in the region, but Warner was free to use the proceeds as he saw fit. By Warner's own admission, Havelange and Blatter arranged the same deal with the 1998 rights to reward Jack for his support in getting Blatter elected FIFA president in his tight race against Johansson.

Evidence emerged in 2015 that Blatter sold Caribbean broadcast rights for the 2010 and 2014 World Cups to Warner for a total of $600,000, according to a contract uncovered by Swiss television station SRF. Warner sublicensed the rights to his own private company J&D International (JDI), registered offshore in the Caymans, which in turn sold them to Jamaica SportsMax TV for as much as $20 million. Warner claimed that Blatter also gave him steep discounts on rights for the 2002 and 2006 Cups. His JDI company resold the 2006 World Cup rights for $4.25 million. No one but Jack knows where the money ended up.

Ticket and media deals were augmented by bribes and outright theft, according to federal law enforcement authorities and some soccer leaders. Lord David Triesman, the former chairman of the English Football Association and head of England's bid for the 2018 World Cup, accused Warner in 2011 of soliciting almost $4 million in return for votes. Funds were supposed to be filtered—again—through the Centre of Excellence. Warner called the accusations a "piece of nonsense" and claimed to have "laughed like hell" over the charges. He said he merely showed the British bid team where it could "put in a playground" in Trinidad. "I hold my head tall because I can stand up and tell the world I never accepted anything," he told a local newspaper. Blatter vowed to look into the accusations, but said he couldn't be responsible for what everyone on the Ex-Co did, saying that members "might be angels or they could be devils."

Some $750,000 paid to TTFF by FIFA and the South Korean Football Federation intended for victims of the catastrophic earthquake that struck Haiti in 2010 vanished while Warner was special adviser to the Caribbean association. TTFF officials said the money landed in an account controlled by Warner.

Warner operated under a different corruption etiquette than the Europeans or his American general secretary. He thought nothing of pressing targets for money loudly and pointedly—in front of witnesses. He even badgered the Queen of England while having tea with her at Buckingham Palace as part of her nation's bid to host the World Cup. Warner berated Her Excellency for not spending money to cultivate soccer in Trinidad and Tobago. When representatives of Russia gathered for an early meeting concerning their 2018 World Cup bid at CONCACAF offices in Trump Tower, Warner blurted out at the end of their presentation: "What's in it for me?" Blazer told friends he was mortified.

In 2004 Scottish Football Association president John McBeth accused Warner of demanding that money owed to the TTFF from a match between Scottish and Trinidadian teams that year be sent to Warner's personal account. "I said, we just don't do that," McBeth told the British newspaper the *Telegraph*. "I heard later that he went around to my staff members and hit them up for money."

McBeth was forced to step down in 2007 from a new position as vice president of FIFA after he was accused of racism by Warner for complaining about corruption in the Caribbean and African federations. McBeth then called Blatter a "tricky customer" and said some African representatives have different ethics from the British "fair play" attitude. "I know two or three [at FIFA] whom I'd want to count my fingers after shaking hands with them," he said. "As soon as you hit Africa, it's a slightly different kettle of fish. They're poor nations and want to grab what they can. I presume the Caribbean is much the same—they just come at it in a different way."

CONCACAF sent a letter of condemnation to FIFA over the remarks. "Why did he only mention African and Caribbean countries? To me, that smacks of racism of the worst kind," said Warner. "We all feel deeply insulted, and we will support any moves to send him back to Scotland where he belongs."

The "culture of business" doesn't follow the same rules from nation to nation, noted governance expert and longtime FIFA watcher Michael Hershman. "A lot of people in Africa consider Warner a hero for bringing the World Cup to South Africa. They don't care how he did it," he said. "And they believe he deserves every penny he took getting it done."

But journalist Lasana Liburd doesn't buy the "corruption gap" argument. Wealthy countries like the US may have more laws against corruption and insist on transparency but that hardly means they're off the hook. Commercial bribery is illegal in the United States, and American companies are forbidden by the Foreign Corrupt Practices Act from making bribes in foreign countries where they do business. Someone should have reminded Traffic Sports USA about that two decades ago—and both Zorana Davis of International Soccer Marketing in New Jersey and Roger Huguet, CEO of Media World in Miami. All have pled guilty in the US indictments.

Liburd blames sports administrators and sports marketing companies of richer nations for not only nurturing but also instigating corruption in other countries to get what they want. He calls it "financial doping." Those "superpowers are happy to hand over the money without appropriate penalties for misuse or in a manner that makes misuse likely, and then feign surprise or frustration at mismanagement," he said.

Liburd also complained that by helping to prop up corrupt leaders in developing countries, affluent nations end up turning the rogue officials into "demigods" in their communities: "There are photos of Jack Warner meeting Barack Obama in the White House, as well as being a guest of prime ministers and presidents from Britain to Russia to Australia to South Africa. Such meetings help people like Warner to launder their reputation and shore up the idea that what he is doing cannot be wrong if the United States treats him like a dignitary. Corruption exists in the 'developing world' in large part because the 'developed world' is happy for it to do so."

Warner was insulated from wider-scale criticism for years, tucked away in the Caribbean, far from the ravenous British press. Uncle Jack felt even more invincible as his island popularity continued to climb into Trinidad's political arena, and he was appointed Trinidad and Tobago's national minister of security. In 2007 Warner was elected co-chairman of the opposition party, the United National Congress-Alliance, and became a member of Parliament for Chaguanas West when the party grabbed fifteen of forty-one seats in the election that year. He won again in 2010 and vowed to enforce capital punishment by hanging to crack down on crime and corruption (there hasn't been a hanging in the nation since 1999). For someone who was popularly elected, Warner had a limited use for democracy. According to his biography, *Upwards Through the Night*, he described it as "a luxury which could not be afforded at all times."

The ultimate distribution of the $10 million bribe that Blazer testified he and Warner solicited from South Africa to host the 2010 World Cup—disguised as a donation to the Centre of Excellence—is stark testament to Warner's outsized greed and the collapse of his relationship with his general secretary. Blazer thought it was "Mandela's turn" to get the Cup, and he was unhappy that the Nobel Peace Prize winner was being "gouged," he told a confidant. Still, despite those feelings, Blazer nevertheless expected his $1 million "commission" from the bribe. The CONCACAF boss eventually coughed up three payments totaling $750,000. This lack of honor among thieves was one more fraying thread in the unraveling of Blazer and Warner's relationship.

The growing distance between the two men ended up serving Uncle Jack's ends—until it didn't. CONCACAF's increasing disaffection with Warner played into Jack's martyr narrative, the one he liked to present to his constituents. He was a poor minority man on a tiny island, facing nearly insurmountable challenges in his life and up against powerful, unjust detractors in Europe—and now the United States. Warner positioned himself as an island Robin Hood trying to cadge a few pennies to grow soccer and do some good for his people. He insisted that he had used nearly $1 million of his own funds for years to keep the local leagues afloat. (Warner also maintained that Blazer's business consultant wife had paid the Trump Tower office rent in the early days of CONCACAF in New York. Both men would claim, after they were accused of corruption, that they were actually *owed* money.)

"Jack is very good at his narrative," said Trinidadian journalist Liburd. "He is the put-upon, misunderstood minority martyr. Some people buy that."

Warner allied himself with people and countries that he considered rebuffed by the old, white, Western world of FIFA power brokers. He repeatedly emphasized his nation's part in the African diaspora and embraced bin Hammam as his "brother"—something he had never called Blazer. He felt that the Mideast had been as disrespected by FIFA, as had the Caribbean, and portrayed his indictment as persecution by the spoiled Americans, who were miffed because they had missed out on hosting the World Cup. "The country that bid for the World Cup and failed is America," Warner said in a videotaped news conference. "They are the ones who are angry, and we have seen that this has to be some kind of evidential witch hunt. America believes that it has some divine right to get the World Cup, and they don't believe that a country like Qatar, a small country—a Muslim country—has a right to a World Cup."

His position resounded with some, but it's difficult to know for certain how popular Warner was; he has been known to pipe in the sound of cheering crowds at his rallies.

Warner's reputation as a cunning giant slayer took a major hit after his indictment, when he mistook an article in the satirical *Onion* newspaper as legitimate American journalism. Under the "Fantasy Sports" department, the tongue-in-cheek paper headlined the piece "FIFA Frantically Announces 2015 Summer World Cup in United States." The article, with a Zurich dateline, reported that "visibly nervous officials from FIFA held an impromptu press conference to announce that the United States has been selected to host this summer's 2015 World Cup . . . with matches set to kick off today . . . in Los Angeles." A smiling Sepp Blatter unveiled the tournament's official logo, a hand-drawn stick figure kicking a soccer ball with "USA 2015!" scribbled hastily in black marker above its head, according to the ersatz story.

Warner immediately posted a video to his Facebook page holding up the *Onion* article and asking incredulously, "If FIFA is so bad, why is it that the USA wants to keep the FIFA World Cup?"

Far more entertaining was Warner's hilarious faceoff with British comedian John Oliver on Oliver's late-night HBO talk show *Last Week Tonight*. Warner first appeared in a paid political ad on Trinidad TV, denouncing his indictment. He vowed to provide evidence proving a link between FIFA officials and the 2010 Trinidad presidential election. "Not even death will stop the avalanche that is coming," he said in the bizarre announcement. "The die is cast. Let the chips fall where they fall."

All faux outrage and concern, Oliver paid for a spot on the same Trinidad station to run a portion of his comedy monologue answering Warner. He urged the Trinidadian to abide by his promise to lay bare FIFA's disgusting secrets, insisting that the "mittens of disapproval are off"—a goofy dig at Warner's threat that the "gloves are off." Oliver concluded: "I've been looking through the indictment. Good luck with that."

Warner's response was once again clueless. He gravely attacked Oliver for "embarrassing" the citizens of Trinidad and Tobago. He also criticized a local TV station for allowing the British comedian—whom he called an "American foreigner"—to purchase the spot. "I don't need any advice from any comedian fool," he grumbled. The Warner video made Oliver positively giddy. He crowed on his program the next night that he was adding "comedian fool" to his business card. Oliver, surrounded by bursting columns of flame, challenged Warner to an epic throwdown. "If you really want to trade shit-talking videos with increasingly high production elements, challenge accepted, my friend," he preened.

By then, someone had convinced Warner to keep his mouth shut. But it was way too late.

SEVEN

LIFE WAS GOOD

IN 1996, WHEN BLAZER ASCENDED TO THE ALMIGHTY FIFA EXECUTIVE COMMITTEE, A NEW world of excess and exploitation opened to him. The Ex-Co was the very top of soccer's economic pyramid, and, just like the world's economic pyramid, those living at the bottom—players scraping out a living in the lowest professional rungs, from Azerbaijan to Argentina—toiled in relative poverty compared with those at the pinnacle. FIFA brought in billions, and while some of it trickled down to the game's actual participants, Blazer found himself at the big-money trough of World Cup marketing deals and bid-rigging schemes. According to his indictment, Blazer admitted to a vast array of crimes that redirected millions into secret bank accounts in tax havens in the Cayman Islands and the Bahamas.

The 161-page document, while rich in detail about criminal behavior, did little to describe the golden existence of the twenty-four members of the committee that controls the world's most popular sport. Oh, there were the "small" things: up to a half million in salary and bonuses along with the extra money for sitting on any committee. There were the regular trips to Zurich for meetings at the mammoth $254 million glass-encased FIFA headquarters. Fittingly, two-thirds of the building sits belowground, a virtual bunker in the Zurichberg woods where hush-hush deals are sealed in aluminum-walled meeting rooms accented with American walnut and Brazilian shale. The heavily secured complex includes a marble meditation room, a regulation-sized soccer field, a fitness center, and an onyx-paneled prayer room that glitters like a diamond. Chefs from the world's finest restaurants prepare lavish dinners for Ex-Co members and their companions, who stay at the exquisite five-star Baur au Lac Hotel on the shores of Lake Zurich, where suites go for up to $6,500 a night.

The Baur au Lac is the location of the notorious raid by Swiss police that unfolded in the early hours of May 26, 2015. Until that morning, the hotel was also the scene of the many backroom deals and shakedowns that Blazer would spend four years describing to FBI and IRS agents.

The routine rarely changed: Ex-Co members, upon arrival of their first-class flights, were met by a waiting limousine that delivered them to the famously private hotel's front door, an obscure opening off the street, marked by a uniformed doorman and a parked Rolls-Royce at the ready.

The hotel rooms are decorated elegantly in ivory gold brocade, the heavy, lined drapes covering louvered metal shades that shutter the windows with the flick of a switch, creating a claustrophobic blackout described by Blanks as "like being in a vault." The maid service was exceptional and relentless. On the coffee table was a plate of perfect peaches, kiwi, plums, apples, and grapes, refreshed daily. Fluffy Egyptian towels lined the racks of the huge bathroom, which featured a deep Jacuzzi bath and a walk-in shower for Blazer, who was unable to swing his 450 pounds over the edge of a tub.

Blazer and Blanks always stayed in the same room: a suite on the second floor near the elevator and facing the domed roof of Le Hall, the grand lobby and main meeting room of the hotel, where the Ex-Co members gathered on the settees and chairs arranged around the perimeter, small coffee tables in front of each. Waiters took their cocktail orders as they nibbled on hors d'oeuvres and discussed their voting strategies and alliances. The members viewed Le Hall as a kind of permanent FIFA lounge; an exclusive clubhouse where deals were the lingua franca.

Many of Blazer's criminal conspiracies were consummated in Le Hall, or at the pop-up lounges that were assembled for Ex-Co members in other cities. Often conducting the discussions in Spanish, which he had mastered while dating a Colombian girlfriend years earlier, Blazer huddled with Julio Grondona of Argentina, Nicolás Leoz of Paraguay, Ángel María Villar Llona of Spain, or Ricardo Teixeira of Brazil, each of whom has been either named in the indictment or is under investigation by the US government or FIFA's ethics committee.

Sepp Blatter rarely made an appearance at Le Hall. He routinely attended dinners at the Pavillon, the hotel's gourmet restaurant, and held a reception there for Ex-Co members in 2002 when he married Graziella Bianca, a dolphin trainer who was a classmate of his daughter's. Blatter, who had once been a wedding singer, charmed his audience that night. His new wife took the microphone and gave a thank-you speech in five languages. Glasses were raised, and toasts were made. The marriage, Blatter's third, didn't last—the couple divorced just two years later—but the dinner was delicious.

Perhaps Blatter considered Le Hall off-limits, a refuge for his cronies where they could speak freely without being scrutinized by the boss—although everyone there watched everyone else, always looking for a cue to begin the negotiation dance. Or Blatter might simply have felt that it was too obvious a place for a man of his stature to conduct business. Instead, he summoned Blazer for meetings at his office in the FIFA bunker, often joined by his top lieutenant, Jérôme Valcke.

By late September 2015, Blatter himself had been officially added to the burgeoning list of suspects, as well as named as the subject of a FIFA ethics probe and the target of a criminal investigation by the Swiss attorney general. By October, he'd been suspended provisionally, accused by FIFA's ethics committee of funneling television rights to the 2010 and 2014 World Cups to Warner for a piddling $600,000 in 2005. Warner enjoyed a 323 percent return on his "investment" after selling the rights for $20 million

As the old joke goes, Ex-Co members had unlimited expense accounts—and exceeded them. No matter where they were traveling, members received a $500 per diem, even though all travel costs were covered. Then, beginning in late 2000, each committee member got to add a fully reimbursed traveling companion as well.

Like many things at FIFA, this perk, too, was born of intrigue. It was added after Charlie Dempsey, president of the Oceania Football Confederation and the Ex-Co delegate from New Zealand, abstained from the 2000 vote to decide the 2006 World Cup hosting rights. His abstention sensationally handed over the 2006 Cup to Germany instead of the favorite, South Africa, in a 12-to-11 vote. Andrew Jennings's book *The Dirty Game: Uncovering the Scandal at FIFA*, published in September 2015, alleges that Dempsey, who died in 2008, was paid $400,000 in New Zealand currency, or about $250,000, to abstain. That non-vote was critical because it avoided a tie that would have given Blatter the deciding vote, and Blatter was supporting South Africa. Without Dempsey, the victory went to Germany.

Following Jennings's accusations, Dempsey's friends and supporters came to his defense, denying impropriety. In 2015 his would-be biographer, Michael Brown, published an interview, conducted in 2003, in which the football administrator described the immense duress he was under in the days before the vote in Zurich. "I was taken to a room by four guys and pressured," Dempsey said of the night before the final vote. "I can't tell you who they were. I won't tell you who they were. That's where I am drawing the line. I wouldn't sleep at night if I named names."

Dempsey went on to describe what he was offered.

"Anything," he said. "You could almost pick what you wanted. It was for me personally. I came under a lot of pressure. I said I'd be consulting back to New Zealand and Oceania about what to do [with the vote]. I had dinner and went back to my room, and there was a letter under my door. It said if I voted for Germany and Germany got in . . . it would be very beneficial for me for years to come."

The letter was unsigned but had a phone number for Dempsey to ring. He didn't make the call, he said, phoning his lawyer instead. He listened to the attorney's advice: after supporting England, which lost in the second round, Dempsey decided not to vote in the final round. "He said I had a good name in football, and I shouldn't tarnish it."

In his blog, Blazer told a somewhat sanitized version of the story, writing a tribute to Dempsey on opening day of the World Cup in June 2006, saying that the Germans should "dedicate the games to Charlie Dempsey of New Zealand. More than any other man, Charlie assured the hosts that this day would finally come." Interestingly, Blazer added, "Charlie didn't do it by casting his vote for Germany six years ago; rather, he succeeded by not voting at all." He went on to say that Dempsey, who had supported England's bid, simply couldn't bring himself to vote outside of Europe despite pressure from his own federation to do so. "Even though the Oceania Confederation, in its Congress just months before the vote in Zurich, had directed their delegate to the FIFA executive committee to vote for South Africa following his support for England, he just couldn't do it," Blazer wrote. "For Charlie, that would be like breaking marriage vows."

Blazer explained that Charlie had been getting calls through the night from South African president Nelson Mandela and German chancellor Gerhard Schröder, and was a nervous wreck. His wife, after all, hadn't made the trip and couldn't field the calls and run interference for her husband. For Dempsey, the only answer was not voting for anyone after England's elimination, therefore sending the Cup to Germany by default.

There was no mention of any funny business, but after that debacle, FIFA's answer to the problem was to allow every Ex-Co member to bring a companion to reduce the stress of the meetings in Zurich and the incessant travel to tournaments and bid cities. Naturally Blazer took advantage of this change by double-billing FIFA for travel, generating an extra $17,000 per trip plus the $250 per day stipend for his "assistant": either Blanks or his personal aide, Adriana Martinez, or a business associate—or even one of his New York strip-club buddies.

For Blanks, travel was a daunting task, considering that she was in charge of a 450-pound man, his ubiquitous BiPAP machine to help him breathe, and as many as fourteen suitcases. The transatlantic routine rarely changed, whether they were headed to Zurich or London or the North African Coast. They would settle into their first-class seats and await takeoff. The pilots would not allow Blazer to plug in his BiPAP until they were in the air, but the second they turned off the Fasten Seatbelt sign, Blanks would begin assembling the machine and plug in Blazer's laptop and any other gadgets. Chuck rarely slept on the long flights. Too fat to reach into a carry-on bag but always nervous about losing power, he would wake Blanks halfway through a flight and have her charge the emergency batteries in his "breather," as he called the BiPAP.

Blazer spent the time eating, despite the machine. He timed his breathing so that he could swallow without taking off the mask, the smacking plus the clicking of the BiPAP audible throughout the otherwise still cabin. Part of Blanks's job was to regularly clean Blazer's hose and mask. Having spent ten years around circus elephants while working for Ringling Bros., it was hard for her not to notice the similarities.

No matter his destination, Blazer always traveled with someone in tow, and they were leaned on to handle more than the luggage. According to Blanks, some of the traveling partners helped him haul back the $20,000 in cash payments he routinely picked up in two envelopes from the FIFA finance department, which usually set up shop in the hotels where the Ex-Co members were staying when not in Zurich. Before heading to the airport, Blazer would put $9,900 in each envelope and make sure that he and his travel buddy carried no other cash in order to avoid having to declare the money as they went through customs. There is no requirement to declare an amount under $10,000, so the cash was never reported, and no laws were broken. On one trip, though, Blazer realized that he was over the limit, so he rushed to an airport gift shop and purchased a $3,000 pearl necklace to get in under the wire. Once the money was safely in the United States, Blazer would stash it in a locked file cabinet in a closet in the back bedroom of the cat apartment.

For seventeen years, Blazer and the other Ex-Co members were treated like visiting heads of state by tycoons, prime ministers, crown princes, and queens. He was feted by Russian president Vladimir Putin, the Queen of England, Nelson Mandela, and British prime minister David Cameron. All were motivated by the golden ticket: the World Cup.

The road trips were especially swell when the Ex-Co members were scheduled to choose the location of an upcoming Cup, usually six years in advance. When members and their wives arrived at a bid city, they'd sometimes find swag bags of pricey gifts in their hotel rooms. The haul might include cameras, perfumes, luxe lotions, and watches worth thousands of dollars, usually made by Hublot or Bulgari. There were Louis Vuitton garment bags and carry-ons.

The FIFA ethics committee limited "gifts" to those of "symbolic or trivial value," but that rule was met with a wink and a smile. When FIFA Ex-Co member and UEFA president Michel Platini was told, along with the other members, to return a $27,000 World Cup Parmigiani Fleurier watch given to them by the one of the sponsors of the Brazilian Football Confederation ahead of the 2014 World Cup, Platini initially refused and claimed he would donate the value of the watch to charity. "I'm a well-educated person," he said. "I don't return gifts. We receive many watches." As the FIFA scandal escalated, Platini apparently had a change of heart, and along with other FIFA members who had attended a FIFA congress in São Paulo before the Cup, returned the watches at the insistence of the FIFA ethics committee. The watches were then donated to the Streetfootballworld charity, which planned to funnel the $1.4 million in proceeds to Brazilian soccer projects.

For ten years, Blanks accompanied Blazer on his many FIFA trips. Besides the regular stops in Zurich, they flew, often on private jets, to Paris, Tokyo, Munich, Moscow, London, Sydney, Johannesburg, Doha, and the other cities around the world casting covetous glances at the World Cup. On the ground, a car and driver whisked them to audiences with the local dignitaries: breakfast with Mayor Boris Johnson in London, lunch with the governor of Kazan, Russia, not to mention the private meeting with Putin followed by a cruise on the Volga River. In the Black Sea city of Sochi, site of the 2014 Winter Olympics, they stayed in a vast apartment nestled in the foothills of the Great Caucasus Mountains. The glass-walled living room overlooked the sea, and the rooms were decorated in black fabric and dark wood. Even the toilet paper was black.

Russia's World Cup bid, like the country's successful effort to bring the Olympics to Sochi, was a top priority for Putin. In Moscow, he met alone with Blazer while hundreds of wildfires, ignited by record-high temperatures and a devastating drought, consumed the country. As Putin wooed Blazer, a phalanx of ministers cooled their heels in the hallway outside their boss's Kremlin office. Putin charmed Blazer, noting his remarkable resemblance to Karl Marx, high-fiving him, and suggesting he change the name of his blog from *Chuck Blazer* to *Chuck Blazer and Friends*, apparently including himself in that category.

In Kazan, the capital of the Republic of Tatarstan, in southeastern Russia, officials gave Blazer a huge silver coin. In Sydney, at the home of Frank Lowy, the head of Australia's bid for the 2022 Cup, large pearl teardrop necklaces awaited the wives at their place settings for dinner, while the men were given pearl cuff links. Those particular gifts, handed out when Australia hosted a 2008 FIFA Congress before the bid was officially announced, raised eyebrows once the inevitable investigations into the bids began.

In Qatar, the FIFA contingent was driven across a pebbly desert to a farm about an hour outside Doha, where the party was seated at big round tables in an open courtyard, the sky ablaze with stars. The food had been shipped in from Germany or Switzerland along with the waitstaff. When a cold desert wind kicked up, the wives donned their husbands' suit jackets or linen covers from the chairs.

Blazer, and a friend he was traveling with, would describe an especially surreal scene to Blanks that they claimed occurred during the 2002 World Cup in Japan—two years before FIFA would institute the first of its so-called ethics rules. In the telling, Blazer said the friend was stunned by the "boxes of cash" that littered Blazer's hotel room. The boxes contained stacks of $100 bills, he said, the proceeds from the sale of World Cup tickets, perfectly legal under FIFA's guidelines at the time, he said. The friend helped Blazer count the money.

There were nights in the Ritz in Paris, the Grand Budapest in Hungary, and the Dorchester in London, but the most over-the-top hotel was the Burj Al Arab in Dubai. A spiral staircase led to the bedroom level, where floor-to-ceiling windows looked out on the Persian Gulf. The amenities were Hermès, the bathrooms marble. A butler stood outside the suite's entrance twenty-four hours a day.

When FIFA celebrated its hundredth anniversary in 2004, members of the Ex-Co were invited to Buckingham Palace by Queen Elizabeth II and Prince Philip. As they mingled in a ballroom sipping champagne and cocktails, the Queen slowly worked her way through the group, greeting each cluster of members and their wives and listening intently to their responses to her questions about where they were from and what they did. She spoke five languages: English, of course, with Blazer and Blanks; French with the Platinis; German with the

Gerhard Mayer-Vorfelders; Spanish with the Villar-Llonas; and Russian with the Vyacheslav Koloskovs.

After the Queen had spoken with the two Americans, Blazer asked Blanks for her cocktail glass. She thought he was being polite—until she saw him slip both glasses into the outer pockets of his jacket. He told an appalled Blanks that he wanted a souvenir from his visit with the Queen. When they returned to New York, Chuck displayed the glasses in his red Chinese liquor cabinet in apartment 49J, showing them proudly to friends.

There were hundreds of other brilliant dinners in showy ballrooms, often just for the executive committee and wives. On those occasions, the dinner music was either by Franz Lambert, the German composer of the FIFA anthem, or a string quartet or harp. Blatter would begin by welcoming everyone, "Especially the lovely ladies," he would always say, and ask the men to applaud their beautiful wives. When he finished speaking, dinner would be served. No one could leave the table before Sepp, but when he did, Jack Warner was always the first out the door behind him.

Every major FIFA function had a Ladies Day Program, open only to the wives or partners of the committee members. During World Cups, there were Ladies Days in every city, often scheduled on a day when the men were in meetings. For the Ex-Co members, these women filled a critical role, lending decorum and propriety to the official functions. But Ladies Day was theirs. They could wander the streets of foreign cities, visit the museums and landmarks, sip Russian vodka or French champagne, and share their secrets with one another. The only rule was that the women had to be back to the hotel in time for cocktails and dinner.

In Dubai, the Ladies Day Program included a desert safari in SUVs: three cars loaded with the wives roaring up and sliding down the endless sand dunes. In Moscow, there was a private tour of the Kremlin, arranged by Dr. Tatiana Koloskov, the deputy director of the Historical Museum at the Kremlin and the wife of Vyacheslav "Slava"

Koloskov, a Russian member of the Ex-Co. Blanks had gotten to know Dr. Koloskov on Mary Lynn's first FIFA trip, a Ladies Day program in Toledo, Spain, where they walked the cobblestone streets and shared their guidebooks. In Japan, the women were taken to a Shinto shrine and treated to a private tea ceremony and ikebana flower-arranging lessons.

Not every Ladies Day Program met FIFA expectations. In the Bahamas, the wives were taken on a bus tour of Nassau. The bus was small and hot, and the driver blasted gospel tunes. When the vehicle ruptured a tire, the women stood on the side of the road for about an hour until another bus was dispatched. After ten minutes in the second bus, the engine blew. Finally, limos from the Atlantis Resort were called, and the tour wound up at the bar, where the drinks were on the house.

EIGHT

PAY TO PLAY

THE BUSINESS OF THE BRIBES THAT CHUCK BLAZER AND JACK WARNER EXTRACTED FROM Morocco, Egypt, and South Africa for the right to host the 2010 World Cup is described in almost farcical terms in the attorney general's 2015 indictment. Yet their crass, cruel exploitation of eighty-five-year-old former South African president Nelson Mandela, the preeminent historical figure of our time, was near tragic.

Blazer and Warner, along with other members of the Ex-Co, had kicked off an April 2004 inspection trip to Marrakech, Morocco—just as they had in 1992, in advance of voting for France to host the 1998 World Cup. Back then, Blazer "facilitated" a bribe to Warner—which he in turn shared with Blazer—in exchange for a vote for Morocco by insinuating to certain Moroccan officials that pay for play was the FIFA way. And, of course, it was. Spectacularly so. Now, twelve years later, the president and the general secretary of CONCACAF were thoroughly emboldened and out to make a much larger score.

Nelson Mandela's fragile health was the least of their concerns.

On the first stop of the bid junket, Warner, who in the weeks preceding the African swing had tried unsuccessfully to wring a $7 million bribe out of Egypt, was offered $1 million by a representative of the Moroccan committee. Nice, but not nearly enough. During the weeklong courtship in Marrakech, Warner confided to Blazer that high-ranking FIFA officials and the South African bid committee had arranged for that country's government to pay $10 million to the Caribbean Football Union in exchange for three votes: Warner's, Blazer's and one belonging to a man identified in the Lynch indictment as "co-conspirator number 17." The alleged bribe (and South Africa still disputes any allegation that it paid one) would come under the guise of support for the African diaspora—shorthand for greasing the money into a Caribbean account controlled by Warner and used for whatever purpose he deemed appropriate. And Warner always found it appropriate to divert money into his own bank accounts. He told Blazer he would cut him in for $1 million—Chuck's 10 percent.

Marrakech was just the first stop on the 2004 bribe-a-thon. Blazer, Blanks, and her ten-year-old son, Nick, checked into a suite overlooking an orange grove in the La Mamounia hotel, the place where Winston Churchill famously came to paint landscapes when depressed, and where Alfred Hitchcock filmed *The Man Who Knew Too Much*, starring Jimmy Stewart and Doris Day. Every morning, there were Moroccan breakfasts of fruit, fresh bread, assorted sliced meats and cheeses, poached eggs, and lamb shish kebab. At dusk, frogs submerged in the tiny ponds scattered around the hotel grounds would begin to croak, gradually building to a mystical musical cacophony.

Ex-Co members gathered at the palatial home of the president of the Moroccan bidding committee, Saad Kettani. There, Blazer and Warner met privately with Kettani, known among the Ex-Co as "the money guy," and the bid's hired gun, American attorney Alan Rothenberg. The competing countries spared no expense to sway the Ex-Co voters. The swag that each member accepted happily would, in the future, become the bullets fired by various ethics investigators, and the most-remembered passages in the many exposés that would haunt FIFA for years to come. On that April visit to Marrakech, Ex-Co delegates were given twenty-four-piece china place settings for twelve—and in Blazer's case, three premium wall-to-wall room-sized Moroccan rugs. (Once Morocco lost the bid, however, officials shipped cheaper rugs to apartment 49J at Trump Tower.)

In Cairo a week later, the $10 million South African bribe had already been settled, but the Egyptian bid committee didn't know that. Although Egypt's Football Association president, El-Dahshori Harb, had turned down Warner's demand for $7 million, the full-court press was on.

The Ex-Co made its Cairo entrance in a fifty-car motorcade. The private tours for each member included a dramatic sound and light show at the pyramids. For Blazer's appearance, the voice-over emerging from the mouth of the Sphinx was programmed to say, "I have waited thousands of years for the FIFA World Cup to come here." Pretty impressive, being pitched by the Sphinx, but at FIFA, money talked, not ancient history. Blazer had to give Harb the bad news: As wonderful and committed as its bid was—he thought it the best of the three—Chuck couldn't vote for Egypt because, he said, it was Mandela's turn. That was actually a plausible explanation.

The next trip, to Johannesburg, was physically taxing on Blazer, and by the time the group arrived, he needed a supplemental oxygen tank strapped to his BiPAP machine to cope with the sprawling city's 5,751-foot altitude. But Blazer was game for a dramatic helicopter ride from Joberg to the MalaMala Game Reserve for a three-day photo safari. Early each morning and late in the afternoon, the Ex-Co contingent rode in a big, open Land Rover, accompanied by a driver and an armed guide. They also toured the game reserve at night, when the hyenas and lions came out to dine beneath the inky African sky. They saw elephants and giraffes, and a leopard devouring a gazelle in a tree. They slept in huge safari-chic beds in a lodge at MalaMala Main Camp, an elegant cluster of native structures, each with a rustic balcony overlooking the Sand River, where animals would gather at dawn and dusk.

The South African bid was led by Danny Jordaan, the head of the SA Football Association, but Mandela, along with Bishop Desmond Tutu and Mandela's old prison cellmate, antiapartheid activist Tokyo Sexwale, also pressed for their country to be given the opportunity to host the Cup for the first time. South Africa had lost the 2006 Cup to Germany under suspicious circumstances, and the overwhelming sentiment within soccer was that the next World Cup was something Mandela and Africa deserved.

Warner had begun to cultivate South African officials around the time of the 2000 vote and in the early 2000s, according to Attorney General Lynch's indictment, and had arranged for his son Daryan to use his father's contacts to organize friendly matches for CONCACAF teams to play in South Africa. That was a legitimate endeavor on its face, except for one telling incident: according to Lynch, Warner directed Daryan to then fly to Paris and collect a briefcase filled with bundles of US currency in $10,000 stacks from a "high-ranking South African bid committee official." Hours later, Daryan Warner boarded a return flight to Trinidad and delivered the briefcase to his father.

No one was more acutely aware of Mandela's worldwide influence than Jack Warner, who put relentless pressure on the bid committee to send the already infirm leader—who had spent thirty years imprisoned at Robben Island—on a visit to Trinidad. Warner, who held a variety of government posts, including security minister and member of Parliament, was often in need of some political capital. He made it clear that—$10 million or not—his World Cup vote hinged on Mandela making the trip.

"Jack bluntly told us that if we wanted his vote, we must bring Mandela to the Caribbean," Irvin Khoza, the chairman of South Africa's organizing committee, told a university forum in Johannesburg in 2009. Jordaan pressed Mandela to go, even though Mandela's doctors advised against the long flight over the belly of the earth. Sexwale, former premier of South Africa's Gauteng Province and then running a diamond mining empire, pushed too, finally persuading the tired and frail "Madiba" to fly to Trinidad.

On April 28, 2004, Mandela boarded a Gulfstream V for the twenty-two-hour flight to Port of Spain. He was accompanied by Minister of Sport Ngconde Balfour, Sexwale, Mandela's personal assistant, Zelda La Grange—and Mary Lynn Blanks and Chuck Blazer.

In what became a bizarre tug-of-war, Warner, Blatter, and Patrick Manning, the prime minister of Trinidad and Tobago, argued over who would greet Mandela first upon his arrival. When the G5 touched down at Piarco International Airport, and he stepped off the plane, an honor guard stood on the tarmac, and an eager crowd of politicians and civilians greeted him with shouts of "Madiba! Madiba!"

Mandela hadn't wanted the fanfare and was too weak to climb the steps of a podium where he was to address the adoring throng. Instead, he smiled and told them simply that he had come "for two reasons: because I love you very much and because it is not easy to love an old man. So I urge you to love South Africa and this old man."

Mandela had barely slept on the flight, and La Grange, his assistant, was upset that he was seated in the front of the plane, where anyone wanting to use the lavatory had to walk past, disturbing him. She had advised against the trip, and later wrote in her book *Good Morning, Mr. Mandela: A Memoir*, that she had tried to minimize Mandela's appearances, to little avail. "When we landed, I looked through the aeroplane window and saw that the government had put out a full guard of honour for Madiba's arrival, when we had asked them not to," she wrote. "Tokyo and I had words, and I asked him to step in. He himself could see that Madiba was tired, so he called Jack Warner, the FIFA member in Trinidad who obviously wielded power in that country, on board the plane to meet us. We were told that the guard of honour was simply a receiving line and that Madiba would be free to depart from the airport immediately. The entire visit was a battle."

Blazer and Blanks had sat across the aisle from Mandela, whom they found to be an unfailingly charming man as he sipped tea and told stories about trying to counsel Bill and Hillary Clinton during their times of trouble. Blanks also chatted with Sexwale, who told her the great love story of how he had met his wife, a paralegal named Judy van Vuuren, when he was imprisoned with Mandela on Robben Island. The story would not have a happy ending, alas, as years later, Sexwale and van Vuuren would engage in a nasty divorce.

In 2015, as the FIFA scandal deepened, Sexwale announced his candidacy for the presidency. He was joined in the race by Prince Ali bin al-Hussein of Jordan, former Trinidad and Tobago midfielder David Nakhid, ex–FIFA official Jerome Champagne, UEFA general-secretary Gianni Infantino, and—until he announced that he was withdrawing from the race to concentrate on his appeal of the eight-year ban FIFA slapped on him in December—Platini. Sexwale received an endorsement from the German great Franz Beckenbauer, who also said that the German Football Association would back the former antiapartheid activist and FIFA adviser. "He has the smell of neutrality, and that's why I think he would be a good solution," said Beckenbauer, who failed to mention Sexwale's role as a major player on the 2010 South African bid committee—a part that led to his December 17 appearance as a witness before the Eastern District grand jury. "One of their [grand jury's] attorneys . . . indicated to me that 'Mr. Sexwale, you are not a suspect in anything, you are not our target, but you were at the crime scene, so if you were at the crime scene, you will be called,'" Sexwale told local media following his appearance. "I am very happy that as FIFA presidential candidate, I responded . . . because there is nothing to hide."

Mandela's stay in Trinidad was brief. He was called home less than two days later for the funeral of his first wife, Evelyn Mase, but not before attending a $1,000-a-plate dinner at the now infamous Dr. João Havelange Centre of Excellence, the $26 million boondoggle in a hard-to-reach dusty wasteland eleven miles east of Port of Spain. On the evening of April 29, it hosted a gala honoring Mandela, with the cracks in the walls covered by screens and curtains. No children were playing on the soccer fields or swimming in the pool, but Warner had made his point, wringing political gain from a sickly icon under the guise of bringing the CONCACAF vote to South Africa.

To the outside world, Mandela's courage, charisma, and place in history were the reasons for South Africa's 14-to-10 winning vote over Morocco and Egypt, announced two weeks later in Zurich. Eleven years later, Attorney General Lynch would shatter that perception, making it clear that the three tainted votes Warner had delivered were the real difference. "Around 2004, bidding began for the opportunity to host the 2010 World Cup, which was ultimately awarded to South Africa, the first time the tournament would be held on the African continent," she said. "But even for this historic event, FIFA executives and others corrupted the process by using bribes to influence the hosting decision."

As South Africa *Daily Maverick* newspaper columnist Stephen Grootes wrote after the indictments: "We didn't know then the cost. And particularly the cost to Nelson Mandela, shipping around the world to satisfy the craving of some two-bit crook, who just happened to hold the balance of voting power."

That was perhaps a little unfair to Warner, who was much more than a "two-bit" crook. After all, he'd already stolen more than $25 million from FIFA, from CONCACAF, and even from his own friend and criminal partner, Blazer.

NINE

A HUNDRED AND FIVE
IN THE SHADE

AS DUSK FELL ON THE EVENING OF DECEMBER 2, 2010, THE WIVES OF THE EX-CO MEM-bers entered the darkened auditorium of the Zurich Messe convention center, where the men would soon make the red carpet entrance that typically accompanied the committee's big announcements.

And this one was big: the unveiling of the hosts of the 2018 and 2022 World Cups. The bidding had been a heavily financed, acrimonious battle among nine countries vying for the honors. England, Russia, Spain and Portugal, and Holland and Belgium were going for 2018; for 2022, the contestants included the United States, Australia, Japan, Korea, and, incongruously, the tiny, fabulously wealthy but soccer-bereft Gulf state of Qatar.

Sepp Blatter was already on the stage as the Ex-Co members settled into their seats below him—Blazer's chair often had to have the arms removed to accommodate his girth. Mary Lynn Blanks took her place in the first row of wives; behind her sat Ann Thompson, the wife of Ex-Co member Geoff Thompson of England.

Everyone had checked his or her cell phone with security officials before entering, and the members of each country's delegation huddled quietly while awaiting the verdicts. As she entered the room, Blanks took a photograph of Blazer, who was seated next to Mohamed bin Hammam; the Qatari reportedly kept a notebook with a list of those he believed would vote for his country. A light fell on Blazer's head as Blanks snapped the picture, and she caught a glimpse of his solemn face. "I was looking at him like, 'What's the vote? Who won?'" she would say later, hoping for a signal, "and I knew then it wasn't going to be good for the US."

In his usual theatrical fashion, Blatter ripped open the envelope and pulled out the slip of paper containing the name of the 2018 World Cup host. "And the winner is . . . Russia!" Blatter proclaimed. That first announcement raised eyebrows, and shocked and angered England. Soccer's ancestral home had made Prince William and David Beckham the hood ornaments of its bid effort and expected a much different outcome.

The second announcement, however, would truly raise hell: Blatter tore open the envelope and yelled out, "Qatar!" Blanks, not to mention millions of fans around the world, knew the tipping point had finally come for the rulers of the beautiful game. She turned around to Thompson and, in a loud voice, made a prescient pronouncement: "That'll be the end of FIFA." Not missing a beat, Thompson had her own reply: "I do believe you're right, Mary Lynn."

The outrage was instant, and while it would take four and a half years to manifest in the US attorney general's shocking indictment, the wheels of the American justice system would start to roll. At about the same time, journalists in Britain would launch a series of damning investigations into corruption surrounding FIFA's World Cup bidding procedures; and the United States and Australia reportedly hired teams of private investigators to ferret out witnesses and obtain documents in a search for proof of bribery. An investigation by the FBI's Eurasian Organized Crime Squad was also under way, according to government sources and media reports. "The investigation was no doubt driven by American commercial and political interests after the US was cut out of the Cup," said a source involved in a parallel investigation. "That vote was the impetus for everything that was to follow."

The central question: How could Qatar have possibly won the vote without large amounts of cash changing hands? Russia, despite its political liabilities and human rights issues, at least had a soccer tradition, a competitive national team, and club success in European tournaments, as Blazer would tell people who complained about that selection.

Qatar, on the other hand, had no soccer pedigree and lacked a single world-class stadium. It was also an oppressive state with no political parties or elections, a history of horrific human rights violations, a nineteenth-century view of women, and a constitution that follows the tenets of Sharia law, meaning that punishments such as beheading, flogging, and stoning are still acceptable for certain offenses.

It also gets very hot in Qatar. In the summer, when the World Cup is traditionally held, temperatures soar to 122 degrees Fahrenheit, broiling Doha and the parched desert plains around the capital city, and creating what a FIFA evaluation report described as a "potential health risk for players, officials, the FIFA family and spectators, and requires precautions to be taken."

By 2015, those conditions—well known to the Ex-Co—forced organizers to move the tournament from June and July to November and December, and to shorten it by four days to prevent a potential catastrophe. That meant the World Cup had to be rescheduled around the Champions League and other lucrative tournaments played in Britain and on the Continent, further alienating European fans and officials already angry over the entire 2010 vote.

At the time of the dual bid announcements, Qatar met almost none of FIFA's exhaustive list of requirements to host a World Cup and, in fact, had the worst ranking in the internal bid evaluations based on risk assessment. It was next to last in a FIFA-commissioned report by McKinsey & Company management consulting firm ranking each country's ability to produce revenue.

When Qatar presented its bid, the country had all of three existing soccer stadiums, none of which met FIFA's standards. (The FIFA constitution calls for twelve World Cup stadiums, a requirement that was later amended to eight to help Qatar meet its ambitious goals.) Qatar had about twenty thousand fewer hotel rooms than the sixty thousand required to accommodate the fans who would theoretically flock to the recently opened Hamad International Airport, where handling World Cup–volume traffic also presented an issue, as did the country's basically nonexistent rail system. Even the cities where the necessary stadiums were to be built were underpopulated.

Almost all of Qatar's bid for the 2022 Cup was based on spec. Stadiums and training facilities would have to be built, hotels added, high-speed rail links and a new highway network and bridge linking the airport to the Doha city center constructed—largely on the backs of migrant workers living in squalid, overcrowded conditions, exposed to sewage and with no running water.

There were nine dog-and-pony shows staged by Australia, Korea, Qatar, the United States, Japan, Holland-Belgium, Spain-Portugal, England, and Russia, held over the two days prior to the announcement. Prince William and David Beckham spoke up for England; the former supermodel Elle Macpherson, for Australia; and former president Bill Clinton and actor Morgan Freeman for the United States. Each nation made its pitch to an audience limited to a few Ex-Co members and their wives in a mostly empty FIFA House auditorium. The presentations weren't open to the public. Even some of the Ex-Co members failed to show, or if they did, left early.

Theoretically, that lack of interest should have been a good thing for the United States, since its presentation was less than impressive. Clinton's charm was in evidence, but he rambled on, shooting from the hip, according to one soccer executive who watched the show via a television feed, and Freeman stumbled through his speech, at one point skipping an entire page. The video pitch was equally lame, a montage of New York street vendors pointing hot dogs at the camera and reciting the slogan "The Game Is in US."

The Australian offering was weak too, featuring a movie in which *Crocodile Dundee* star Paul Hogan chased an animated kangaroo around Australia after it had snatched the World Cup from FIFA's headquarters, finally catching the critter at Sydney's Olympic Stadium. Social media reviews were less than flattering. "Worst freaking movie ever. It was a joke," said one observer on Facebook. "I will not be surprised if we are banned forever from hosting FIFA." Neither England nor Belgium did much better.

The Qatar show, on the other hand, was stunning; the video of space-age, air-conditioned stadiums and steel-and-glass hotels nothing short of spectacular—never mind that most of the structures had not been built yet. The highlight came when Sheikha Mozah bint Nasser, the glamorous wife of Qatari emir Hamad bin Khalifa al-Thani, began speaking. Wearing a burgundy satin evening gown and matching turban, the tall, slender sheikha began her presentation by asking in a soft voice, "The time is now. If it's not our time, if not now, when?" Her voice rising, she continued to ask "When? If not now, when?" By the time she left the stage, the few spectators in the audience were clapping and cheering. "It was fantastic," said one soccer executive. "They nailed it." Nevertheless, the United States had an unquestionable capability to host the tournament, as it had proven in 1994. And England, one of the world's most popular tourist destinations, would demonstrate its hosting prowess rather well at the 2012 Olympics.

Clinton, the honorary chairman of the American bid, had spent two years traveling the world courting the members of the Ex-Co. He was stunned and angered by Qatar's victory. "Clinton was fuming," the *Telegraph* reported, quoting a source. "He felt humiliated and felt the decision did not make sense." There were media reports that the former president returned to the Savoy Baur en Ville Hotel in Zurich following the announcement, picked up an ornament off a table, and hurled it through a wall mirror. The incident made for a delicious image, to be sure, even though it would be disputed by at least one official present for the vote. A disgusted Clinton didn't stick around long enough to hurl anything, said the official, and instead headed directly to the airport.

Once US District Attorney Lynch's indictment dropped in May 2015, by which time she had ascended to the position of US attorney general, and the ethics committee had riddled the Ex-Co with suspensions, it would become apparent that the presentations, and the costly bid evaluations, had little to do with winning the rights to host the 2018 and 2022 tournaments. Blazer and Warner had set the price for delivering their votes long ago. Two other members of the Ex-Co had already been suspended in November 2010 and banned from the election, after being accused of offering to sell their votes. They were caught in a sting set up by London's *Sunday Times*. The newspaper secretly recorded Nigerian Dr. Amus Adamu and Tahitian Reynald Termari, the Oceania Football Confederation president, allegedly asking reporters posing as American soccer lobbyists for payments in exchange for votes.

Blatter himself would confirm that Qatar and the Spain-Portugal combo hatched a plan to trade votes for their respective bids despite an earlier FIFA investigation that concluded there had been no vote swapping. "I'll be honest: there was a bundle of votes between Spain and Qatar," Blatter would tell the BBC. "But it was a nonsense. It was there, but it didn't work, not for one and not for the other side."

In the US indictment, Chuck Blazer wasn't implicated in vote rigging for the 2018 and 2022 Cups, but he had to be aware that December evening of the implications of awarding the tournaments to Russia and Qatar. The elections unfolded in rounds, with twelve votes needed for an absolute majority and the right to host the Cup. For 2018, England got just two votes in the first round; the Netherlands-Belgium, four; Spain-Portugal, seven; and Russia, nine. This threw the election to a second round and eliminated England. Russia won that round with thirteen votes.

The 2022 vote went four rounds before reaching the final tally: Qatar, fourteen, and the United States, eight. Australia received just one vote. Their lousy movie notwithstanding, the Australians would demand a $50 million refund from FIFA once the allegations started to flow.

According to Blanks, even in the hours before the vote, Blazer didn't seem to know who would win. It was often difficult to tell how the members had actually voted in the secret ballots—even hefty bribes couldn't absolutely secure a ballot. Blazer said publicly that he had voted for Russia and the United States, and had told Blanks the same privately. There were whispers that Blazer had seen Warner's name on bin Hammam's notebook tally, and even though Warner would later insist in interviews that he had voted for the United States, Blazer suspected otherwise. Those suspicions would further threaten what remained of his relationship with Warner.

There would be disagreement among investigators about bin Hammam's actual role in landing the Qatari bid. The *Sunday Times* would view millions of pages of leaked documents showing bribes paid to Ex-Co members in a plot allegedly organized by bin Hammam, then the head of the Asian Football Conference (AFC) and Qatar's most senior football official. The *Telegraph* would also report that soon after the vote, Warner received $1.2 million of a nearly $2 million payment from a Qatari company once owned by bin Hammam.

Although not part of Qatar's official bid team, bin Hammam was reported to have used secret slush funds to make payments to senior African football officials who could lobby that continent's Ex-Co voters to choose Qatar. Bin Hammam would be banned for life by FIFA in 2011—a decision that was overturned in 2012 by the Court of Arbitration for Sport—and then banned again in 2012 after conflicts of interest were identified by the ethics committee. A book published in April 2015 by *Sunday Times* reporters Jonathan Calvert and Heidi Blake titled *The Ugly Game: The Corruption of FIFA and the Qatari Plot to Buy the World Cup*, describes how bin Hammam was a pivotal figure in a shadow campaign to bring the Cup to Qatar. There is no question that he played a huge role in the downfall of Blazer and Warner, but he also had his defenders.

"I'm not saying he was a saint," said one person who followed the investigations. "He spread money around, but he gave away his own money, too. I'd take bin Hammam any day over the others." Not exactly a good-citizen endorsement, but on the executive committee, everything was relative. "He perfected the art of gift giving," said another soccer executive. "If you live in an Asian culture, you have to give a gift. He was a passionate football guy."

Blatter managed to take much of the heat off bin Hammam when he alluded in a blatantly self-serving October 2015 interview with Tass, the official Russian press agency, to a 2010 agreement among the Ex-Co members that the World Cup would go to Russia in 2018 and the United States in 2022. Except, he said, the pact was sabotaged by the current Qatari emir, Sheikh Tamim bin Hammad al-Thani, Hamad's son, in a meeting with former French president Nicolas Sarkozy.

"In 2010 we had a discussion of the World Cup, and then we went to a double decision," Blatter claimed. "For the World Cup, it was agreed that we go to Russia because it's never been in Russia, Eastern Europe, and for 2022 we go to America. And so we will have the World Cup in the two best political powers. Everything was good until the moment when Sarkozy came in a meeting with the crown prince of Qatar. And at a lunch afterward with Mr. Platini, he said it would be good to go to Qatar. And this has changed all pattern. There was an election by secret ballot. Four votes from Europe went away from the USA, and so the result was fourteen to eight. If you pull the four votes, it would have been twelve to ten. If the USA was given the World Cup, we would only speak about the wonderful World Cup 2018 in Russia, and we would not speak about any problems at FIFA." In 2012, as part of Blatter's so-called anticorruption measures, FIFA commissioned Michael Garcia, the former US attorney for the Southern District of New York, to conduct an independent investigation of the 2018 and 2022 bids, and appointed German judge Hans-Joachim Eckert as the chairman of the ethics committee's adjudication chamber. They were also given the authority to investigate old charges.

Much of Garcia's report coincides with what is found in Lynch's indictment, but Garcia is not believed to have linked bin Hammam directly to securing the 2022 Cup for Qatar. Garcia filed his much-anticipated report in September 2014, calling for it to be made public. He resigned his position three months later in protest of a forty-two-page summary released by Eckert that Garcia called "materially incomplete," with "erroneous representations of the facts and conclusions."

He would also say that FIFA's "investigation and adjudication process operates in most parts unseen and unheard . . . That's a kind of system which might be appropriate for an intelligence agency but not for an ethics compliance process in an international sports institution that serves the public and is the subject of intense public scrutiny."

Blazer's name wasn't in bin Hammam's notebook, although somehow the names of fourteen of his fellow Ex-Co members got there. Blazer would joke privately that he felt slighted being the only one Qatar hadn't tried to bribe. The Qataris clearly figured he was untouchable because he wanted the tournament in his home country. "Blazer voted for the US," said one source familiar with the investigations that would dog FIFA in the wake of the 2010 votes. "He would have been the king if the World Cup came to the United States."

Blazer had some sympathy for England, too. After the Russian delegation had taken the stage to accept Blatter's congratulations, and Sheikh Mohammed bin Hamad al-Thani, the Harvard-educated son of the emir and head of the Qatari bid team, thanked the Ex-Co for "believing in change, for expanding the game, and for giving Qatar a chance," Blazer declined Russia's invitation to celebrate back at the Baur au Lac. Instead, he commiserated with England's "losing party."

"I think I need to stay here," he told Alexey Sorokin, the head of the Russian organizing committee. Putin had been rumored to be hiding at the hotel as the vote was cast and had shown up at the party, although the official version was that he had remained in Moscow, ostensibly to avoid humiliation if Russia lost. Either way, he was in Zurich the following day to accept congratulations and address the worldwide media.

While the US indictment didn't explicitly explain how and why the United States got so deeply involved in cleaning up "a culture of corruption and greed that created an uneven playing field for the biggest sport in the world," there were hints. In her press conference, AG Lynch made it clear that the investigation into FIFA was ongoing. As the New York *Daily News* reported, the document described rampant bribery influencing past World Cups, including the 1998 and 2010 tournaments that Blazer and Warner helped corrupt. "It started with the 2010 World Cup bids," one source familiar with the investigation would say. "No one could believe Qatar and Russia. What was going on?"

TEN

PIRATES OF THE CARIBBEAN

MONTHS AFTER FIFA'S EX-CO CHOSE QATAR AS THE SITE OF THE 2022 WORLD CUP—A selection that stunned fans and players around the world—Mohamed bin Hammam acted to capitalize on his nation's new soccer clout. He announced in March 2011 that he was running to unseat Sepp Blatter as FIFA president.

Bin Hammam campaigned on a "Clean up FIFA" platform, vowing to battle corruption and increase financial transparency—while at the same time arranging to offer cash to voters in the Caribbean with Jack Warner's help. It would be a package deal, since Warner controlled twenty-five votes in his own regional Caribbean Football Union, plus an additional ten votes from the rest of CONCACAF, which always voted in a bloc.

That tally could clinch the presidency for bin Hammam. He was already counting on the 46 votes from his own federation, as well as the

54 of the Confederation of African Football (CAF)—an organization disposed to backing him, and whose votes were also influenced largely by Warner. The combined 135 votes would almost certainly hand bin Hammam the election in the 209-vote FIFA federation. A first-round win requires a two-thirds vote, but a simple majority wins on a second ballot. A nervous Blatter was also toting up bin Hammam's support and was convinced the Qatari had a solid chance of wresting away his presidency.

Bin Hammam aimed to pay a total of $1 million to leaders of the various CFU member associations in Trinidad, investigators would later find. Presidents of each local federation and their general secretaries were summoned by Warner in an e-mailed invitation to a specially called, all-expenses-paid meeting at the Hyatt Regency in Port of Spain on Tuesday, May 10. Their presence was requested by Mohamed bin Hammam, "a wealthy Qatari businessman and candidate for the presidency" of FIFA, Warner noted formally in the invitation.

First to arrive in Trinidad on the eve of the meeting was the Qatari billionaire and his nine-member delegation, who received a VIP welcome at Piarco International Airport and were allowed to skip standard immigration procedures. Bin Hammam had been issued a visa exemption by Subhas Panday, Trinidad and Tobago's minister of national security, whom Warner had asked to do so just days earlier. Warner, then the minister of works and transport for his government, arranged for his protocol officer to drive bin Hammam from the airport to the hotel. The following day, CFU's general secretary, Angenie Kanhai, retrieved a suitcase packed with envelopes of cash from Warner's office, she would testify. Bin Hammam was used to splashing cash to get what he wanted. "Did bin Hammam pay bribes? Oh God, yes. He always had a man standing by with bags of cash," said one investigator. "At least it was his own money."

CFU representatives gathered the morning of May 10 at the Hyatt, a sleek, modern compound at the edge of the vast turquoise Gulf of Paria. They ate breakfast in a conference room where bin Hammam presented a forty-five-minute speech explaining why he would make an excellent FIFA president. If elected, bin Hammam promised that the associations would have "more say, more support, and more pay."

At a luncheon later, Warner thanked everyone for attending and instructed them to go to one of the hotel conference rooms and collect their "gift," as Fred Lunn, a former pro soccer player who was vice president of the Bahamas Football Association, would explain in an affidavit. When Lunn arrived at the conference room, the door was locked; he was told by CFU administrator Debbie Minguell to wait as others were being "processed." When he was ushered into the room, Minguell asked him to sign a registration form. Lunn added in his affidavit:

> She then handed me a manila envelope with "Bahamas" written on it. I opened the envelope, which was stapled, and stacks of hundred-dollar bills fell out of the envelope and onto the table. I was stunned to see this cash. I asked them what it was, and they told me that it was forty thousand dollars. They said it was a "gift" from the CFU, and I could count it if I wanted. I told them that I had not been authorized to accept such a gift and that even if I had, I could not possibly take such a gift with me, since I was flying through the United States on my way back to the Bahamas. Debbie suggested that maybe I could mail it to the Bahamas. I recall saying, "Are you kidding?" during this exchange. Debbie reiterated that it was just a gift, and I should accept it. She also told me not to tell anyone about the money.

Lunn covered the package of money with his jacket "so that no one would see it, as I had been directed," and returned to his room to contact his association president, Anton Sealey, another former pro player. Sealey told Lunn that under no circumstances would the Bahamas Football Association accept such a gift and to immediately return the money and make certain that Lunn's name was removed from any registration list. Sealey suggested that Lunn take a photo of the cash for documentation, which he did.

This time, Lunn stuffed the money in his trousers—he had been instructed by Sealey not to let anyone see the cash—and returned to the conference room. Many of the delegates looked at him aghast, apparently believing he was back looking for seconds.

Sealey said in his own affidavit that after he heard again from Lunn, he sent him a text "sharing my disappointment over this matter." Sealey then called Chuck Blazer, knowing that he couldn't report the payments to Warner, the man who had helped arrange the handoff. Blazer "indicated that he was not aware of any payments and that he had not authorized any CONCACAF funds to be distributed as cash gifts," Sealey recalled in his affidavit. At least four other CFU officials—from the Bermuda Football Association, the Cayman Islands FA, and the Turks and Caicos Islands Football Association—also refused the money. Eight federations would ultimately either reject or return the bribes.

Sealey and Lunn continued to text about the cash, with Lunn noting that having witnessed the payments was "particularly troubling" because at that exact moment, CNN stories were being broadcast on television screens in the hotel lobby about suspicions that bribes were responsible for the decision to award the 2022 World Cup to bin Hammam's home country of Qatar. Lunn asked Sealey if he should save the photo of the cash. Sealey texted: "Of course. I have never seen that amount of money. I need to see what it looks like. LOL." Lunn texted back: "It hurt to give it back. What bills it could pay." Sealey said he was "disappointed, but not surprised" about the payoffs, adding, "It is important that we maintain our integrity when the story is told. That money will not make or break our association. You can leave with your head high."

Before reporting the situation to FIFA, Blazer sent Warner an e-mail warning him, in code, that "MBH's ATMs"—Mohamed bin Hammam's payoffs—"were doing some damage, and we need to talk."

Blazer later explained, in his own affidavit: "I told Jack that people were asking questions, and I didn't know how to respond." Weeks later, Warner would express astonishment that anything about the money would raise concern. "It's not unusual for such things to happen, and gifts have been around throughout the history of FIFA," he said.

The day after Sealey called Blazer, an angry Warner again summoned CFU members to a hotel conference room, first making certain that no reporters were present. His remarks were recorded by Kanhai, who had been talking secretly with Blazer ever since she had learned the meeting was being planned.

Warner expressed his extreme disappointment to CFU leaders that word of the "gifts" had leaked. "Before I came here this morning to explain to you, I saw a few of you rush to the office in New York, the CONCACAF office in New York, to talk of business before we had even talked of it among ourselves," he grumbled. "If you are coming in this room here, we cuss and disagree and rave and rant, but when we leave here, our business is our business. And that is what solidarity is about."

Warner insisted that both CONCACAF and FIFA knew about the payments, and that "any country that doesn't want the gift has the right" to return it to bin Hammam. "What I am telling you, even Mr. Blatter is aware of, no secret; I told Blatter also what he gets as well," said Warner. He explained that cash was simply the most convenient gift available; no need for any fancy wrapping paper. "So I am making the point here, folks, that it was given to you because he [bin Hammam] could not bring . . . some silver trinkets and so on, and something with Qatari sand. So I said put a value on it and give the countries." He was annoyed that his CFU members had tattled to Blazer. "Let me talk to New York to stop you running to New York and tell everything," he said.

Warner emphasized that the payments could be "used for any purpose": grassroots soccer programs or "whatever," a charity line that he used as cover repeatedly for the millions in kickbacks that he would soon be accused of accepting. "So I want to put clear and behind, and if there is anybody here who has a conscience and wishes to send back the money, I am willing to take the money and give it back to him at any moment," he said.

There was no pushback from the audience, Lunn recalled, and Warner dismissed any moralizing: "I know there are some people here who believe they are more pious than thou. If you are pious, go to a church, friends."

Later that day, Warner called Blazer to reassure him that he had informed Blatter about the money and that Blatter had no qualms about the payments.

Three days after Sealey called him, Blazer was again in his "office"—sitting on the edge of his bed, phone in hand—about to contact FIFA's general secretary to advise him of an apparent violation of the organization's code of ethics. Blazer couldn't see any way to avoid making the call. Too many people knew about the payments, and one of them had come to him directly with a complaint.

Warner was floored that his friend reported him to Zurich and appeared shaken in the days following the call, according to witnesses. But the hurt quickly turned to rage over Blazer's betrayal, and Warner vowed revenge. In the kind of threat that has now become familiar to the international soccer community, he promised to expose Blazer and unleash a "tsunami" of information that would hit FIFA in the "fullness of time."

Warner ripped Blazer's "ingratitude" as "worse than witchcraft," and blamed a "Zionist plot" against himself and bin Hammam, a clear attack on his Jewish general secretary. "The role of Blazer in CONCACAF will be exposed," Warner vowed in a published letter. "His addiction to the stock market and how this impacted on CONCACAF's finances will all be revealed. You will also be told why for some seven years I refused to sign Blazer's contract, and even today as I write to you, he has none. His wheeling and dealing will stymie the international football community . . . he is quite aware of what a five-year audit into CONCACAF will reveal about him. There is much to talk about that will make the sponsors of both FIFA and CONCACAF cringe with painful surprise."

In an unusual, lightning-fast response—one that ensured another term for Blatter in the June 1 election for president—FIFA suspended both Warner and bin Hammam from all soccer administration activities on May 29, and bin Hammam bowed out of the race for president. Some FIFA watchers sensed a conspiracy, believing that Blatter knew about the plot from the start and let it continue so he could expose—and oust—bin Hammam and Warner with Blazer's help. By June 11, FIFA had announced that Warner was resigning from all international football organizations, and barred bin Hammam for life from soccer activities.

Warner apparently got an extra push out the door from Kamla Persad-Bissessar, Trinidad and Tobago's prime minister, according to a confidential memo forwarded to Blazer by a former high-ranking CIA official working for a private security firm. Persad-Bissessar pressed Warner privately to step aside as part of an understanding with FIFA not to pursue an investigation into his dirty dealing, his corruption being "an issue within the government," noted the memo. Warner, then a member of Trinidad's Parliament, was a major fund-raiser for Persad-Bissessar and played a key role in forming the five-party coalition that boosted her to power as the country's first woman prime minister. Many in Trinidad, including some close to Warner, believe he spent millions of dollars of his bribe money over the years on political favors and to back candidates to realize his dream of becoming prime minister himself one day. He had already filled in as prime minister when Persad-Bissessar was out of the country.

"Persad-Bissessar sees Warner's activities not only as a source of embarrassment for Trinidad, but a threat to her role as a reformer," the memo stated. She was particularly concerned about any probe into the "problematic" money paid by Australia during its 2022 World Cup bid that was supposed to go to the Centre of Excellence but instead disappeared into the black hole of one of Warner's bank accounts. The Persad-Bissessar government worried, said the memo, "that any exposure of this activity will only serve to confirm the view that Trinidad is one of the most corrupt countries in the Western Hemisphere, and that this corruption is tolerated, and even sanctioned, by various ministers in the government." Yet, the memo went on, she "realizes the bulk of Warner's funds come from corruption."

Persad-Bissessar aimed to convince Warner to resign his soccer roles "before the investigation turned up dramatic evidence of corruption that could not be explained or ignored," said the report. Warner, nevertheless, would be permitted to keep government and party posts as a sort of parting gift, "which allow him to continue to profit from graft, but nothing on the scale of his activities in FIFA," according to the memo. Bizarrely, a year after Warner stepped down from FIFA, the prime minister made him minister of security.

Warner framed his resignation from FIFA and CONCACAF as an act of patriotism. "I told my constituents that whenever the time comes for me to make a choice between FIFA and country, I will have no problem, for I will choose my country," he wrote in his June resignation letter to the FIFA ethics committee. "I do believe that such a time has come." He likely thought he was home free—until the US indictments—because FIFA always dropped accusations when an official stepped down. "As a consequence of Mr. Warner's self-determined resignation, all ethics committee procedures against him have been closed, and the presumption of innocence is maintained," FIFA announced.

According to the security firm memo, Warner planned to spend his FIFA retirement "plotting revenge against Chuck Blazer, whom he blames for his downfall." He finally gave up his government posts and quit Parliament after the damning 2013 investigative report by the CONCACAF integrity committee. (Warner was reelected to Parliament just months later after forming a new party, but lost in 2015.) Persad-Bissessar, who would lose her 2015 bid for reelection to rival

Keith Rowley, hailed Warner at his resignation as a "highly industrious and productive member of the government."

As for bin Hammam, FIFA's ban would, astoundingly, be lifted just over a year after the cash-for-votes scandal by the notoriously lenient Court of Arbitration for Sport (CAS). The ruling was based in part on Warner's amnesia about events. He told the FIFA ethics committee that he had absolutely no knowledge of any payments at the Port of Spain special meeting and had nothing to do with them; the only gifts he recalled were laptops that FIFA distributed to CFU representatives. By the time the CAS ruling came down, Warner had been named the new minister of security by Persad-Bissessar, who lauded him as a man of action who would be effective in fighting crime. (In one of his early ministerial acts, Warner ordered police to stop releasing crime statistics, because he said that doing so upset citizens.)

"I felt it was wrong for FIFA to use Mr. bin Hammam's meeting to give delegates FIFA gifts, but, be that as it may, I [told members], 'You have to receive from FIFA a laptop and a monitor and sign for having received it.' That's the only mention of gifts," Warner testified to the FIFA ethics committee, despite what he'd said in his Port of Spain speech. "I sent President Blatter a report, an update, and I told him in the update, of course, how Mr. bin Hammam was grilled by members" during his candidate question-and-answer session at the meeting. "Members who receive a bribe don't grill you," he added.

CAS determined that Warner "appears to be prone to an economy with the truth" and was an "unreliable witness." Nevertheless, it lifted bin Hammam's ban. CAS ruled that bin Hammam was "more likely than not" the source of the cash and conceded that his and Warner's behavior "may not have complied with the highest ethical standards in sports." But it was a matter of a "case not proven"—because there was no specific physical evidence (serial numbers, for example) that directly linked the bills from bin Hammam to CFU leaders. The panel said it hadn't been presented with "any direct evidence to link Mr. bin Hammam with the money's physical presence in Trinidad and Tobago, its transfer in a suitcase or otherwise to Mr. Warner, and its subsequent offer to the CFU members for the purpose of inducing them to vote for Mr. bin Hammam. In particular, no efforts were made to trace the source of banknotes that were photographed." There were other possible explanations for the cash, the panel noted, such as bin Hammam giving $1 million to Warner "as a token of appreciation for setting up the meeting."

One intriguing aside in the ruling presaged serious trouble for Blazer: CAS noted that Warner had made a mysterious $455,000 payment to Blazer from a secret CFU account. Anton Sealey testified that he was unaware of any secret account. Later, federal investigators would link the cash to money paid by South Africa as part of its bid to host the 2010 World Cup.

Chicago lawyer John Collins, a former federal prosecutor whom Blazer had hired to investigate the Port of Spain payments, was stunned by the events. "I cannot believe the CAS decision. What more do they want?" Collins e-mailed Blazer shortly after the ruling. "A videotaped statement . . . by a coconspirator, pictures of the cash, no other possible source of the money, a rule that says cash gifts are not permitted in any amount. It does not get any better. Very, very sad."

Blazer responded, "They wanted a picture of bin Hammam handing the money over to Jack or the Trinidadian government or some other body with the power to track the funds to identify and link the serial numbers to MBH."

Collins answered: "Jack's comments are disgusting, and the press is ridiculously lazy . . . Oh, well, enough venting. Hopefully, Garcia will get him," he added, referring to the investigation by former US federal attorney Michael Garcia. In a sign of his profound new enmity with his old friend Warner, Blazer added, "Personally, I thought we had it right (and still do). It is disgusting watching Jack claim how this vindicates him . . . totally absurd."

FIFA reinstated the bin Hammam ban five months later for violations of FIFA's rules concerning conflicts of interest following the findings of a PricewaterhouseCoopers (PwC) audit commissioned by the Asian Football Confederation. The probe was instigated by Prince Ali bin al-Hussein, then president of the Jordan Football Association and the West Asian Football Federation, after bin Hammam's Caribbean caper was exposed. Ali complained to Blazer in a July 28, 2011, e-mail of "intimidation by BH" as bin Hammam pressed Ex-Co members in a battle to keep his position. "He is going all out. I am trying to keep all on the right road for what we want as a continent ethically," wrote Ali, not realizing that Blazer had been driving on the wrong side of the road for decades. "However, this guy will not give up. We'll get through this. We plan to have a complete outside audit and to set up an evaluation committee to reorganize AFC. BH is in total panic."

The PwC examination raised questions about bin Hammam's role, as president of the AFC, in possible bribery, tax evasion, and money laundering tied to negotiations for a $1 billion master rights agreement with Singapore-based sports marketing company World Sport Group (WSG). The auditors recommended that the AFC seek legal advice about whether to pursue a further investigation and possible criminal charges or civil penalties against bin Hammam—and to review its contract with WSG. The report was never released publicly, and the AFC denied news stories in 2015 that it was negotiating another contract with WSG. A WSG insider insisted the PwC report was "politically motivated."

The new head of the AFC, Sheikh Salman bin Ebrahim al-Khalifa, who replaced bin Hammam in May 2013, wasn't going to break any new ground in the transparency department. He refused to release the findings of the PwC audit, or a second one. FIFA would send another message to soccer fans longing for real reform in the aftermath of scandal: move along, there's nothing to see here, and particularly not if Al Khalifa could help it. In 2015 Al Khalifa was cleared by FIFA's ethics committee to run for the presidency of the organization.

ELEVEN

WHISTLE-BLOWING PAST THE GRAVEYARD

CHUCK BLAZER ENJOYED SEVERAL HEADY WEEKS HAILED AS A BOLD WHISTLE-BLOWER after he reported Warner's and bin Hammam's vote scandal to FIFA in May 2011. Soccer fans were angrily poring over every FIFA activity reported in the press, frustrated and infuriated by its maddening soap opera of corruption. They were especially hungry for a crackdown in the wake of the stunning decision—almost universally regarded as dirty—to let Qatar host the World Cup. Then in stepped Blazer with a timely tackle of Warner and bin Hammam. That added up to nine members of the Ex-Co accused of corruption over the previous twelve months.

Chuck was the man of the hour. "Blazer is witty, gregarious, and a whistle-blower," gushed an Associated Press story. "The only American on FIFA's powerful executive committee has spent thirty years promoting soccer and has shown before that he will step in when he feels the game is being shortchanged," noted the reporter. The story quoted John Skipper, then executive vice president of content for ESPN, which had recently agreed to pay millions to FIFA for the rights to telecast the 2014 World Cup. Skipper dubbed Blazer a "tireless advocate for soccer, not only in America but in this hemisphere."

News photos showed Blazer large, smiling, and confident, so very American. He appeared in a Sky News interview on a Zurich street on his way to an Ex-Co meeting talking of the scandal like the world's soccer dad: looming, ethical, sad, gravely disappointed by human venality—yet hopeful for the future. Asked if FIFA was corrupt, he responded: "No sir, people are." Pressed for a solution to that problem, he explained, "Do what I did. Expose it where it exists . . . punish those who transgressed." As for his relationship with Warner, he noted: "It's obviously been broken. I feel betrayed. Based on the risk and danger he put on members to expose them to this . . . jeopardy by accepting the gifts is unconscionable."

In one surprising answer, Blazer seemed to indicate that Blatter knew about the bin Hammam plot beforehand and warned Warner not to go through with it. Blatter had no culpability in the scheme, said Blazer, because "how do you say you have to report something before it's happened? I think he [Blatter] had every expectation that the advice he gave to Jack is that he wouldn't do it and shouldn't do it, and we're all quite shocked to find out what happened."

Any trepidation Blazer had about Warner turning the tables on him seemed to fade—at least temporarily—in the glow of the flattering media attention. Blazer almost gleefully played a video on his computer for Clive Toye that, Toye recalled, showed CFU leaders accepting the envelopes of cash in the Port of Spain Hyatt hotel. "It was shocking to see," said Toye. "All I could say was a four-letter obscenity—over and over." Blazer told Toye he expected to replace the soon-to-be ousted Warner as one of the two vice presidents of the Ex-Co and enjoy even more sway on the FIFA board.

The power struggle at CONCACAF turned ugly and crazy in the

weeks after Blazer reported Warner to FIFA and hired John Collins to investigate the bin Hammam payoffs on behalf of the association. Collins's probe, finished quickly by May 22, concluded that the cash exchange violated FIFA's ethics regulations barring bribery, and laid all culpability at bin Hammam's and Warner's feet. He praised Blazer's honesty and full cooperation with the investigation. Collins was convinced the scandal never would have come to light had Blazer not brought it to FIFA's attention, because the Bahamian whistle-blowers wouldn't have gone over his head if Blazer had dismissed their complaints. Blatter hailed Blazer's "civic courage" at a press conference.

FIFA provisionally suspended Warner—and bin Hammam—from all soccer activities as of May 29. CONCACAF's executive committee immediately appointed Lisle Austin, head of the Barbados Football Association, a CFU member organization, as acting president.

Austin's first official move, on May 30, was to order CONCACAF to "cease all contractual arrangements with the law firm Collins & Collins, effective immediately." He also demanded that Blazer explain, within forty-eight hours, "on what authority" he had the right to hire Collins. A press release revealing Austin's demands was distributed by Ann Dookie, a media officer who worked for Warner in his role as a member of Trinidad and Tobago's Parliament. By June 1, Austin had called Blazer's decision to hire Collins "inexcusable and a gross misconduct of duty and judgment"—and fired Blazer, telling him in a letter, "It is apparent that you are no longer fit to act as general secretary of CONCACAF."

Austin directed the heads of sixteen associations within the Caribbean Football Union to file a complaint with FIFA's ethics committee demanding an investigation into Blazer. They accused Blazer of breaching FIFA regulations by announcing at a CONCACAF meeting, before any formal charges had been leveled by FIFA, that CFU leaders had accepted bribes. Blazer "made statements of contempt and slander that served to impugn the integrity, discriminate against, and infringe upon the personal rights of officials of FIFA member associations," the letter stated. According to the complaint, which Blazer denied, the general secretary had announced that the president of the Jamaican Football Federation, Captain Horace Burrell, was under investigation for bribe taking, adding that "half of those who are speaking are under investigation . . . In fact, all of you are under investigation." The letter played the race card, saying that Blazer "discriminated against Captain Burrell and certain members of CONCACAF through his contemptuous and denigratory words, since all the persons who were singled out were of a specific race." FIFA would, in fact, later suspend Burrell and place him on probation for two years for the bin Hammam affair; twenty-nine other CFU leaders and staff members were also suspended for various terms for accepting the payoffs.

Austin—and Warner—were intent on characterizing Blazer's whistle-blowing as a Goliath-against-David US plot by Blazer and his Yankee lawyer Collins to seize control of CONCACAF from the Caribbean, a narrative that played well to many on the islands. But CONCACAF's executive committee stepped in to protect Blazer after he was fired by Austin, declaring that he would continue as general secretary with the "full authority of his office." By June 4, Austin had been booted—banned provisionally by CONCACAF and FIFA from soccer activities—and replaced with CONCACAF executive vice president Alfredo Hawit, an apparent peacemaker who expressed the hope that association factions could join together to move forward. Austin released a furious statement, blasting the "kangaroo court" of FIFA, an organization he characterized as a "corrupt cabal of arrogance and cronyism." He obtained an injunction against the firing from a Bahamian court, which ordered FIFA to stop "intermeddling" in the regional federation's affairs, but FIFA lawyers ignored the ruling, pointing out that the court had no jurisdiction over the organization's administrative matters. FIFA's ethics committee did, however, launch an investigation into Blazer's statements at the CONCACAF caucus. He was eventually cleared of any violation.

Blazer's new boss, Hawit, however, hardly ushered in a new era for CONCACAF. Within months of becoming acting president, he collected bribes in exchange for promising to award upcoming Gold Cup rights to the sports marketing company Full Play, according to the Eastern District indictment in December 2015. After Jeffrey Webb was elected president the following summer, he dutifully vowed reform. Then he and general secretary Enrique Sanz immediately arranged a $1.1 million bribe from Traffic USA in exchange for granting the company exclusive rights to market the 2013 Gold Cup and the 2014 and 2015 Champions League, according to federal investigators.

For the time being, following Warner's ejection, Blazer emerged from the mess unscathed, still appearing like a stalwart of ethical behavior, but legal forces were already moving against him. In June FIFA's ethics committee launched its own probe of the Port of Spain meeting based on the Collins report, hiring the investigative company Freeh Group International Solutions, run by former FBI director Louis Freeh, to examine the case. Warner refused to cooperate, characterizing the probe as part of the CONCACAF coup orchestrated by Americans. "I'm not going to back a complaint made by an American and investigated by Americans and an attempt to put it on American soil because the complaint is from Miami," he said. "I don't back this farce." Collins derided Warner's charge, telling the *Telegraph* that the "claim that Louis Freeh and I are somehow close because we are Americans is laughable. It is like saying I know and am close with all three hundred ten million Americans." Much of the Freeh probe was conducted in Zurich, at FIFA's request.

Blazer flew with Blanks to Zurich to attend a June Ex-Co meeting and was carefully questioned by Freeh in a FIFA office. Blazer went over the details of the bribe scandal again. He was affable, at ease, self-assured. But Blanks, who sat at Blazer's side throughout the interrogation at Freeh's request, found the grilling unnerving. Freeh asked his questions without any hint of emotion. Three other investigators working with Freeh sat stone-faced—and silent. One took notes, while the other two observed Blazer's and Blanks's faces and body language intently as Chuck recounted events. Blazer was supremely confident that he had nothing to worry about. Investigators, in fact, found him credible—about the bin Hammam scheme. He wasn't questioned about anything else.

On July 7, just over two months after the envelopes had changed hands in Port of Spain, FIFA issued Freeh's findings: there was "compelling circumstantial evidence" that bin Hammam and Warner had colluded to buy votes. FIFA banned the men from soccer for life. They became the most senior officials jettisoned from the Ex-Co for corruption in FIFA's 107-year history. As in all corruption cases in FIFA, expulsion was the worst penalty the men faced—until Warner would be indicted four years later.

Blazer praised the decision immediately. "I am very glad the ethics committee has confirmed that, regarding bribery, we have zero tolerance," he told the *Guardian*. "It sets a precedent, and one that I fully support. The fact we have suffered suspensions is sad, but it will send notice to anybody else that might be considering that type of corrupt activity that FIFA is not the place to try it."

But Blazer's moment in the sun dimmed quickly. He was attacked by sports bloggers who were either suspicious that he was somehow involved in the scandal, or angry that he had made trouble for CONCACAF. They began to criticize the over-the-top lifestyle he boasted about in his blog. "Once the issue of the elections and the Trinidad meeting became news, my blog became the source of pictures of a lifestyle that many bloggers found objectionable," Blazer wrote in August. "I was proud to know and happy to share those moments with you, the readers of this blog. Instead, others used them to poke fun at me and my family, and the pictures gave them a wealth of material to draw whatever fanciful conclusions they wished to make about many of the people found on these pages. I chose to avoid doing my normal writing . . . I had done my part. The ethics code required me . . . to report any evidence of violations of conduct to the FIFA General-Secretary . . . The cases brought on May 29th are closed. No longer am

I inhibited by those open issues . . . I look forward to filling the vacuum with real information."

Far more seriously for Blazer, a report surfaced in a London paper in July that he was hardly Mr. Clean. Britain was still miffed about having lost the 2018 World Cup bid to Russia, and its press was keeping a sharp eye on all things FIFA. The *Independent* was the first to reveal, in a story by investigative reporter Andrew Jennings, that the FBI was examining mysterious payments of $250,000, $205,000, and $57,750 made earlier in the year to a Cayman Islands account registered to a company owned by Blazer. The money came from the Caribbean Football Union, when it was still controlled by Warner.

Now it was Chuck's turn to play defense. He insisted to the *Independent* that the transactions were "legally and properly done in compliance with the various laws of the applicable jurisdictions," clearly referring to tax statutes. He said initially that the funds were repayment of a loan he had made to Warner, and a note dated 2009 on Trinidad and Tobago Football Federation letterhead with Jack Warner's signature appeared suddenly, acknowledging receipt of a $250,000 loan from the general secretary. Blazer conceded later that the money might have been linked to Warner's inappropriate, possibly even illegal, shuffling of CFU accounts. Some FIFA watchers speculated that Warner had deliberately made payments into Blazer's accounts to get him in trouble and then leaked the evidence to Jennings.

News of the checks was the beginning of the end for Blazer. This is exactly what he had feared: that his betrayal of Warner would turn back on him. But Warner didn't blow the whistle on Blazer, according to a source familiar with federal scrutiny of the men. Chuck's report of the bin Hammam vote scandal, however, did trigger meticulous tracking by government and organization probers of CONCACAF and Warner's financial dealings that led inexorably back to his partner.

The damning checks were uncovered by Simon Strong, owner of a Miami investigative firm called Tenacitas International, who was enlisted into the CONCACAF power struggle by Lisle Austin as he battled to retain the presidency. Strong had been hired to examine the association's books to obtain detailed financial information. Despite the perception among many FIFA and CONCACAF leaders that the new CONCACAF president was a Warner confederate, Austin insisted that he was truly out to obtain reliable information about CONCACAF's finances. Austin said he had doubts about the accounting since he'd first joined the CONCACAF board, even before Warner became president in 1990. "In all those years until I left the board in 2011, I never once saw any accounting of income for World Cup TV and sponsorship rights in the annual statements," he said. "I wanted to get to the bottom of that. Some kept me away from the finances because they thought I was working for Jack Warner. Others didn't want those figures to come out."

Blazer was determined to keep the transactions hidden. When Strong and Austin turned up at the doors of 725 Fifth Avenue, Trump security guards presented them with a letter advising the men they would not be allowed onto the elevators. Blazer even hired additional guards for the seventeenth-floor reception area to block Strong's crew if they managed to make it that far. But Strong's team had been tipped off by Manhattan CONCACAF workers to "look at the taxes," as in: they're not being paid, either by Blazer on his own income or on CONCACAF revenue. Strong was also kept out of CONCACAF's Miami offices.

Blocked from investigating CONCACAF in the United States, the Tenacitas probers turned to the Bahamas after Austin filed his lawsuit there against his ejection by FIFA. "We continued with our work, even though it was no longer an internal CONCACAF investigation," said Strong. "It was a turbulent time in the Caribbean as different factions, including some loyal to Blazer, battled for position, and documents came into our possession."

The information Strong had obtained would prove crucial to the case against Blazer—and, eventually, against FIFA. Strong discovered undisclosed contracts and checks made out by Warner to Blazer's off-shore company on the CFU account. "We didn't know what we had at the time, but we did have the canceled checks," said Strong. Two of the checks, totaling $455,000, would turn out to be part of Blazer's slice of a $10 million bribe Warner solicited from South Africa in return for votes for that nation to host the 2010 World Cup, Blazer would later testify. Warner had promised Blazer a $1 million cut but later told him he had spent most of that money, according to the Eastern District indictments. He paid Blazer only $750,000, in three checks, from December 2008 to March 2011, according to federal investigators.

It would have been a simple matter at that point for the IRS to determine if Blazer had reported the income. A little digging would reveal that Blazer had not declared any income for the previous nineteen years. It was the exposure Blazer most feared: a crime that could result in massive fines and prison. This was it. Federal officials finally had the leverage on an American citizen they could use to bust open a case against FIFA corruption. Just as with mobster Al Capone's bootlegging, Blazer's dirty house of cards toppled because he hadn't bothered to pay taxes.

Blazer's sense of impending doom on the day he'd reported Warner returned with the article by Jennings, who would later recount how he provided the information about the checks to FBI agents in London. By late summer, Blazer was noticeably agitated and meeting frequently with pal Shep Messing in a new set of offices he had rented in the Crown Building across from Trump Tower for yet another private venture he called BEST—Blazer Entertainment, Sports & Technology—that could serve as a safe landing spot. In the wake of the bin Hammam scandal, news about the mysterious checks, and Jack Warner's revelations in the press that CONCACAF was paying all of Blazer's living expenses, the association's executive committee was grilling Blazer about his compensation based on a long-expired contract. He was informed that he was finished as general secretary. In

October Blazer announced he would step down on the last day of the year, though he continued to use his CONCACAF office until the following April. When he informed his CMTV deputy Italo Zanzi that he was leaving, Zanzi quit immediately.

THE FEDS FINALLY COLLARED THE BIG MAN ON NOVEMBER 30, 2011, JUST AS BLAZER WAS looking forward to a meal out with Blanks and his pal Al Rothenberg. The lawyer said Blazer missed going to "Mama's"—what he called Elaine's, which had shuttered by then, after the trio had attended a memorial service for Chuck's beloved friend Elaine Kaufman a year after the restaurateur's death. They opted to eat nearby that evening. Leaving Trump Tower, Blazer was tooling west on his mobility scooter along Fifty-Sixth Street toward Uncle Jack's Steakhouse when he was stopped short by IRS agent Steve Berryman and FBI officer Jared Randall, one of whom called out behind him: "Mr. Blazer, may we have a word with you, please?" The agents escorted Blazer, alone, to the Trump Tower atrium, where he quickly agreed to cooperate in their investigation of FIFA's corruption—rather than be hauled off in handcuffs. Because of his weight and borderline diabetes, which he knew would cause complications in prison, the luxury-loving Blazer couldn't tolerate the thought of life behind bars.

The next days were a blur of closed-door negotiations and meetings in Chuck's conference room at his BEST offices. Blazer hired attorney Stuart Friedman, of Friedman & Wittenstein, who had represented Messing years earlier. Messing and Blanks kept vigil outside the offices while Blazer spent hours meeting with Friedman, his staff, and federal law enforcement representatives. At one point, as Friedman exited the room, an agitated Blanks asked the grim-faced attorney what was happening. "We're trying to keep him out of prison, Mary Lynn," he told her. Over the next days, Blanks continued to plead with Blazer to "just pay your taxes" and not betray everyone in FIFA, comparing the Ex-Co members and their wives to "family."

Blazer told her it was too late for that. "It wouldn't be enough," he said, explaining that the feds also had him cold on other charges, including fraud and racketeering.

The deal negotiated with the agents and prosecutors of the Eastern District called for Blazer to secretly record conversations with his FIFA and CONCACAF colleagues, asking questions or steering conversations into particular topics as directed by Berryman and Randall. Blazer's home phone would be tapped, and conversations with particular individuals would be recorded; other discussions would be taped during face-to-face meetings. CONCACAF's general secretary also agreed to plead guilty to arranging and accepting bribes, failing to pay taxes, and bank and wire fraud. The prosecutors said they would inform the judge hearing his case of Blazer's full cooperation. The information would likely result in a reduced sentence and financial penalty, but there were no guarantees.

Friedman, meanwhile, gave Blazer his own strict warning: his client had to tell the absolute truth to his attorneys and the FBI about hidden funds and any collusion in crimes, or the law firm would cease representing him. He also warned Chuck not to act like the smartest guy in the room. "The FBI doesn't like that," Friedman added. The advice wasn't taken to heart entirely. One investigator observed that Blazer "thought he was smarter than the average bear."

As law enforcement agents pored over his old-school Rolodex (or, at least the portion of the names Blazer turned over to them)—a who's who of the world's top soccer administrators—the feds fashioned a list of people who would be recorded in phone wiretaps or at meetings and meals. Those included changed as more information was collected over the years. Forty-four names made the initial list that federal officials presented to Blazer, including FIFA president Blatter and his nephew Philippe Blatter, lucratively employed by International Sports Marketing, a British company that had profited from millions of dollars' worth of contracts linked to FIFA. Other current and former Ex-Co members on the list included General Secretary Valcke, Belgian member

Dr. Michael D'Hooge, former general secretary Michel Zen-Ruffinen (driven out of office after producing a report in 2002 charging Blatter with mismanaging FIFA finances), and Botswana soccer administrator Ismail Bhamjee, who was banned from FIFA after selling 2006 World Cup tickets at three times their face value.

Current and former CONCACAF leaders and staffers included soon-to-be-president Jeffrey Webb; the whistle-blowers Fred Lunn and Anton Sealey; Horace Burrell (the booted president of the Jamaican Football Federation); Enrique Sanz, who would become Webb's general secretary and later a suspected government snitch; and CONCACAF's vodka-loving controller. Top Mexican soccer officials on the roster included Guillermo Cañedo White, a former CONCACAF vice president and onetime chief financial officer for Grupo Televisa in Mexico, and Mexico Football Federation president Justino Compean. Sunil Gulati, the head of US Soccer, who eventually replaced Blazer on the FIFA Ex-Co, also made the list, as did people linked to various World Cup bids, including Australian mall magnate Fred Lowy; banker Saad Kettani, who largely financed Morocco's bid; lawyer and former US Soccer Federation president Alan Rothenberg, who worked as a consultant for Morocco during its bid; and Danny Jordaan, who helped orchestrate South Africa's successful bid to host the 2010 World Cup. Businessmen Aaron Davidson, then president of marketing for the corporation Traffic Sports USA and chairman of the board of governors of the National American Soccer League, was also tapped. Davidson, a self-described "Tex-Mex Costa Rican Jew" from Florida, was a longtime friend and business associate of Blazer's who was involved with CONCACAF from the very first Gold Cup tournament. He was a guest at Blazer's Trump Tower home one year for Passover Seder. He would be indicted in the first round of Eastern District indictments on charges that he paid bribes to secure some $35 million in Traffic contracts. Four others on Blazer's "to-be-recorded" list would be indicted by December 2015: Jeffrey Webb, former CONCACAF president; Alfredo Hawit, who served as temporary CONCACAF president; Panamanian soccer president Ariel Alvarado; and former CEO of Traffic Sports USA Fabio Tordin. Webb and Tordin would plead guilty.

Blazer, fluent in Spanish, was often directed by the FBI to conduct phone calls with Mexican and South American targets in their native language. Because his home phones were outfitted for recording, he would often leave the seventeenth floor CONCACAF offices while still working there to return calls from his apartment. In a clear testament to Blazer's critical role in the investigation, all soccer administration leaders or sports marketing executives named in the 2015 indictments were from the Western Hemisphere, and most from Spanish-language nations.

As part of Blazer's agreement with the feds, Blanks (identified as Blazer's "significant other") and her two sons were deemed off–limits for the recording. So was Blazer's ex-wife, Susan; his kids, Jason and Marci (and their spouses); brother Barry; a niece, nephew, aunt, and cousins; lawyers, personal doctors, and his dentist; a priest pal; and some thirty-eight other friends, including Ruth Westheimer, as well as Shep Messing and his brother, Roy.

No one else in CONCACAF's circle other than Blazer appeared to be questioned by the FBI at the time, perhaps to more effectively protect Blazer's cover (though investigators did begin to question Trinidad's soccer players in a hunt for any information about Jack Warner, according to sources). The agents asked Blazer about Blanks's possible role in any of his lawbreaking, but he told them that she wasn't involved. He was asked if any jewelry he gave Blanks was worth $10,000—a value required to be reported to the IRS. "Jewelry isn't her 'currency,'" Blazer explained coldly to the agents. "Her 'currency' is her children." The comment was a chilling reminder of Blazer's ability to assess exactly how to reach—and manipulate—individuals to serve his own ends. In Blanks's case, he knew that taking care of her children was the way to keep her at his side.

From then on, Blazer belonged to the FBI. He continued to make appearances in his CONCACAF office until shortly after he stepped down and at his private offices for BEST across the street, but he functioned essentially as a federal employee. Initially, he was driven each day in an unmarked van to FBI headquarters at 26 Federal Plaza in downtown Manhattan. But he complained that the agents he knew and had socialized with at Elaine's might spot him, so meetings were shifted to his BEST office, various restaurants and cafés near his home, or simply inside the van.

Technicians realized that Blazer couldn't easily be outfitted in the conventional sense with a wire taped to his skin. His obesity made that impractical, and his sweat threatened to short out the electronics, so agents instead installed a tiny recording microphone in a small fob connected to his key chain. He was instructed to place the key chain on a table or desk while speaking with a target to record the conversation. Agents gave Blazer the key fob shortly before each mission and then collected it immediately after, presumably to guard against tampering. A clean fob was returned to him before his next recording session. When Blazer complained that placing his key chain on a table was too déclassé, the agents were not amused and reminded him sternly to follow orders. When he groused that he couldn't get any work done, he was told he no longer had outside work; activities at CONCACAF and BEST were merely a cover for his real job as a clandestine operative.

Blazer was initially nervous about becoming an informant, and appeared sad and despondent at home. But as the weeks rolled by, he became intrigued with the FBI operation and began to view himself as a savior of the beautiful game, much as he had been regarded after the bin Hammam scandal. He dutifully followed orders—usually—calling specific people at the behest of his handlers. He also gave agents advice as if he were one of the brains behind the operation. When agents ordered him to call back a South American target because he had failed to get the information they were after, for example, he argued with them, warning that it would make the target suspicious—and successfully won a delay. He was an effective undercover operative, according to an investigative source. Blazer used the same tactics that made him a popular, charismatic millionaire hailed for his business acumen while he was stealing money in bribes and kickbacks. He could be just as charming on the right side of the law as he lured people into incriminating themselves.

Blazer was fascinated with the FBI strategy and tried to figure out what cases they were trying to build, based on the targets he was ordered to pursue and the information agents pressed him to obtain. Clearly, they were after information about World Cup bids and possible bribes, particularly linked to campaigns by Russia, Qatar, Morocco, and South Africa. Blazer capitalized on his attendance at the 2012 London Summer Olympics to insistently pursue lunch and dinner dates—and recorded conversations—with people linked to World Cup bids. Before traveling to his lodgings at London's five-star May Fair Hotel, Blazer e-mailed Russian, Hungarian, Australian, and American soccer officials to arrange meetings the feds wanted him to secretly record.

He reached out to Alexey Sorokin, CEO of Russia's local organizing committee for the 2018 World Cup; Frank Lowy, in charge of Australia's bid for the 2022 cup; Anton Baranov, secretary for Russian sports minister and Ex-Co member Vitaly Mutko; and Vitaly Logvin, the president of the international charity fund For the Future of Fencing.

"Mr. Mutko was very glad to have this hearing from your side," Baranov responded to an invitation from Blazer. "He would definitely long to meet you during the London Olympics." By November 2015, Mutko was under fire following a decision by the International Association of Athletics Federations to suspend Russian track-and-field athletes after a World Anti-Doping Agency (WADA) report alleged "state-sponsored doping."

Hungarian Peter Hargitay, a special adviser to and media wrangler for Sepp Blatter and other top soccer officials, was also contacted for a sit-down. "Hi, Chuck," Hargitay wrote. "I am in London this week (until Thursday), then in Budapest at the F1 race, then back again as of August 2. Happy to have a drink with you."

Only one of Blazer's Olympic guests ended up in the federal indictments: José Hawilla. "Did Mr. Hawilla confirm his plans for the Olympics?" Blazer wrote innocently to an aide for Hawilla, the Brazilian owner of the Traffic Group, the sports marketing company eventually hit with a wall of charges. "I would greatly enjoy having dinner with him in London. Please let me know his plans." Hawilla would later plead guilty to racketeering, wire fraud, money laundering, and obstruction of justice linked to a series of bribes to CONCACAF and the South American federation CONMEBOL. On May 14, 2015, his companies Traffic Sports USA and Traffic Sports International pled guilty to wire fraud.

NOT EVERYONE ACCEPTED BLAZER'S INVITATION. ALAN ROTHENBERG, WHO LED THE BID to bring the World Cup to the United States in 1994, sent Blazer his regrets: "Chuck, I'm not coming to London. Let's talk when you come back. We, too, enjoyed our visit in LA. I look forward to seeing you again."

It was nearly impossible for anyone—outsiders or friends—to perceive any significant change in secret agent Blazer's lifestyle. He cut back on work for FIFA, but because he usually spent most of his time as a soccer administrator discussing deals and events over dinner and drinks, little seemed amiss to those around him. Living high on the fat of soccer business continued unabated. He kept gambling, dining out nightly, frequenting strip clubs, and traveling to Vegas, Miami, the Bahamas, and Zurich. During his undercover days, he coldly hosted a birthday party for one of the men on his FBI list: Guillermo Cañedo White. "Following a great dinner at The Dutch, a hot New York eatery . . . it was time for Guillermo to blow out the candles on his birthday cake," Chuck blogged in February 2012. "Accompanied by his wife, Adriana, and their three sons, Mary Lynn and I had a great time in-

Top ON THE UP AND UP: Blazer and FIFA president Sepp Blatter are bullish at the 2005 Confederations Cup in Germany, the dress rehearsal for the '06 World Cup.

Bottom LAUGHING ALL THE WAY TO THE OFF-SHORE BANK: Blazer *(right)*, Mary Lynn Blanks *(center)*, and Jack Warner are all smiles during one of the many banquets and state dinners held for the FIFA Executive Committee around the world.

All photos courtesy of Mary Lynn Blanks

LEFT TOP FAMILY PORTRAIT: Blazer's stash of family photographs includes a group shot *(left)* of his Russian-immigrant forbearers, and photos of his mother, Edna, and father, Abe.

LEFT BOTTOM WHAT A CARD: Always looking to make an impression, a 20-something Blazer used this joke business card to turn heads, especially Mary Lynn Blanks's, during his days as a marketer in the 1970s.

RIGHT TOP LEFT FLIGHT RISK: Chuck and Max, his cranky pet parrot, in repose, 2003.

RIGHT TOP RIGHT BIRD BRAIN: With his piercing squawk and vicious beak, Max was a constant, irritating presence at CONCACAF headquarters, wailing "Chuuuuuuck" whenever Blazer left the office.

RIGHT MIDDLE FAT CAT: Cosmo, one of two leaky pets that Blazer kept in a separate luxury apartment in New York's Trump Tower.

RIGHT BOTTOM A BENZ FOR HIS BABY: Blazer bought a vintage 1952 Mercedes Adenauer for Blanks during the 2006 World Cup in Germany. (The vehicle was never shipped to the United States and now rests six floors underground in the FIFA House garage in Zurich, signed over to the association by Blazer so he could park it there for free.)

TOP LOOKING FOR A HAND OUT: German soccer legend Franz Beckenbauer *(right)*, known as "der Kaiser" during his playing days, led his country's successful effort to land the World Cup in 2006.

BOTTOM SHOCKER!: The world was stunned when, in 2010, Blatter announced that FIFA had awarded the 2022 World Cup to the tiny desert nation of Qatar.

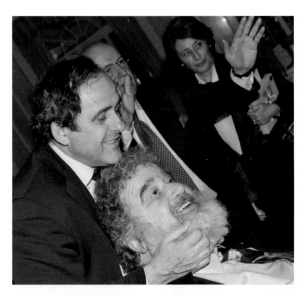

TOP CHIN UP: UEFA boss Michel Platini *(left)* and Blazer clown around in Japan during the 2007 Club World Cup. In December 2015, Platini would be banned from all soccer-related activities for eight years by FIFA's Ethics Committee, dashing his hopes to succeed Blatter as president.

BOTTOM LEFT PIRATE OF THE CARRIBEAN: Chuck and Mary Lynn dress as pirate and wench during at the CONCACAF offices on Halloween in 2009. He pillaged millions of dollars from the organization.

BOTTOM RIGHT YOU BETTER WATCH OUT: In December 2011, about a month after Blazer agreed to cooperate with federal authorities investigating FIFA corruption, he donned a Santa suit in the foyer of his Trump Tower apartment and carried a sack full of Christmas candy downstairs to the CONCACAF offices.

TOP FIRST CLASS: Blanks and Blazer spent 22 hours of quality flight time with Nelson Mandela on their trip from South Africa to Trinidad in 2004.

BOTTOM SHAMAN ON YOU!: Blazer offers the traditional greeting to a Maori wise man after receiving a native blessing during a trip to New Zealand in 2008.

TOP CAMPAIGN STOP: Blazer with then New York senator Hillary Clinton in Singapore in July 2005, during New York City's failed bid to host the 2012 Olympics, which were awarded to London.

BOTTOM ROYAL TREATMENT: Blazer and Prince William at a greet-and-grin session in Capetown, South Africa, during the 2010 World Cup. England was seeking the 2018 tournament.

GOTCHA!: Blazer and Blatter made the front page of the November 2, 2014, editions of the New York *Daily News* when the paper broke the tale of Blazer's cooperation in the federal government's secret investigation into corruption at the highest levels of international soccer. Two of the reporters responsible for that scoop are the authors of this book.

troducing them to one of the city's 'top ten' restaurants." Blazer also boasted on his blog about his reappointment as a member of FIFA's players' status committee. The sports administrator, who had admitted to bribe taking, money laundering, and conspiracy, was part of a panel determining if soccer players and teams were complying strictly with FIFA regulations concerning eligibility to compete in tournaments around the world.

One blog post the FBI refused to allow was a Blazer push for the United States to host an upcoming World Cup. The proposed missive, written in the form of a press release, was headlined "Blazer Launches Campaign for the World Cup 2026 in the USA." The "decisions of 2018 and 2022 are behind us. I believe we need to bring attention to the future and how the USA can be the best host to the world," Blazer said in the draft that was nixed by the feds. The agents were apparently uncomfortable with a crook touting a World Cup in the United States.

Despite his continued pursuit of the good life, Blazer was nearing the end of his remarkable run as a shrewd, rapacious, soccer moneyman. What the feds already knew—and suspected—about him, CONCACAF would soon make public. The association launched a wide-ranging investigation in June 2012, instigated by concerns about the bin Hammam fiasco and the information that emerged about the mysterious payments from CFU to offshore accounts controlled by Blazer. The probe was conducted by an integrity committee composed of Ernesto Hempe, retired partner in charge of risk management and ethics at PricewaterhouseCoopers InterAmerica; retired Washington, DC, federal judge Ricardo Urbina; and Sir David Anthony Cathcart, former attorney general and chief justice of Barbados. Their investigation uncovered decades of lies and front companies that hid millions of CONCACAF dollars "misappropriated" by both Blazer and Warner. Far from being a boy scout whistle-blower, Blazer starkly emerged as Warner's partner in crime. The scope and bald audacity of his scams were astounding.

Blazer's initial contract, written by him and signed by Warner, awarded his New York shell company Sportvertising Inc. (located in Trump Tower) 10 percent of CONCACAF revenue for television rights and sponsorship deals. In fact, Blazer helped himself to at least 10 percent of *all* CONCACAF revenue, including money from vendor contracts, parking lot income, and even grants from FIFA. The four-year 1990-to-1994 contract was extended to 1998, but by then, Sportvertising had become Sportvertising Cayman Inc. and was incorporated offshore. In both contracts, Sportvertising was also to be paid a monthly fee to provide an employee, Blazer, though Chuck wasn't named in the agreement. The investigative committee determined that Sportvertising provided no actual service to CONCACAF, functioning solely as a cover for Blazer's income. All the company did was "supply an employee—Blazer—to serve as general secretary," the committee found.

Blazer's income showed up only as "commissions"—without any detail—on annual CONCACAF financial statements. That didn't really stand out because the statements were frequently riddled with obvious errors and contradictory information, and offered very few details, according to the report. Investigators also discovered what CONCACAF workers had long suspected: that accountant Kenny Rampersad often "audited" statements he had created himself when he was flown from Trinidad to New York each year to do so. He was hardly an impartial auditor. Not only did he work for Warner's Centre of Excellence, but he also cosigned bank loans for Warner as a representative of one of Jack's family companies, according to the integrity committee investigation. Concerns about Rampersad's apparent conflict of interest were raised by the CONCACAF executive committee as early as 1998, but nothing was ever done about it until after Warner resigned in disgrace thirteen years later.

"In no manner did these audits fulfill the legal requirements for an independent auditor, and he ignored international accounting standards," noted an accountant from one of the Big Four American firms who viewed CONCACAF financial statements and read the integrity committee report. In addition, American companies typically don't allow management to choose an auditor—in order to protect themselves from crooked managers and avoid exactly what happened at CONCACAF.

The CONCACAF statements have an astounding lack of detail. The 2008 CONCACAF financial statement, for example, reports a $1.5 million expenditure on "broadcasting" with no itemization, and $1.8 million in "commissions and fees," again with no detail about who received them (likely collected entirely by Chuck Blazer). One association asset is listed as $5 million worth of computer equipment and software, an incredible amount for such an organization. Lisle Austin questioned that report; Columbia University economics professor Sunil Gulati, who was also on the CONCACAF board that year, did not, according to board minutes obtained from the meeting when the statement was approved. In a 2015 interview with a reporters' roundtable, Gulati was asked why he wasn't more suspicious about the figures. He said he wasn't because they were audited. "You get financial reports that are audited," he said. "I'm not sure as one of thirty-five associations that gets those, what you're supposed to do with audited financials." The integrity committee report found that annual financial statements were questioned only three times in the executive committee meetings over some fifteen years, according to minutes that investigators were able to recover.

Probers also discovered what workers knew about CONCACAF's own drug-and-alcohol-addled controller: that he was in no condition to be in charge of the books. "The controller was plagued by persistent health issues, including issues that at times prevented him from properly performing his duties during the workday," the report stated. By the time the report was published, the controller was also grappling with cancer.

When Blazer's second contract expired in 1998, he kept on with business as usual for thirteen more years even though he had no authorization to do so, according to the report. Blazer collected at least

$20 million from 1990 to 2011, with $15 million of that branded by investigators as "misappropriated." Blazer's reported commissions soared from $195,000 in 1992 to $5 million in 2011. His genius in avoiding taxes lay in his commissions, which went directly to an off-shore shell corporation. Because his entire CONCACAF revenue came from commissions paid to his businesses and he was never a salaried employee of the association, Blazer never received a W-2 in his name from the organization nor a 1099, documents that likely would have alerted the IRS that he was dodging income taxes.

After CONCACAF's executive committee informed Blazer in October 2011 that he was out—and ordered him not to collect any more payment—he quickly called CONCACAF's bank, BAC Florida, requesting that a $1.4 million check be issued to his company Sportvertising Cayman for "payment of Gold Cup commissions." He made this final money grab just before stepping out the door as general secretary. He ignored CONCACAF's demand to repay the money, arguing that the association actually owed him millions more.

The integrity committee investigators were the first to determine that Blazer had lived virtually expense free—save for the cash he doled out to strippers. CONCACAF had covered nearly every penny of Blazer's living expenses for decades, including his astronomical Trump Tower rent, and was charged for an antique Mercedes and a Hummer he'd purchased for himself, the report found. The integrity committee also examined Blazer's $29 million in charged expenses over seven years, discovering that he paid off only $3 million in personal expenses in a kind of financial shell game by simply reducing the amounts he "claimed" CONCACAF owed him in commissions that he wasn't actually allowed to collect, according to the investigative report. Hundreds of thousands of dollars were also charged by other CONCACAF officials. Much of it likely covered legitimate tournament and travel expenses (though Italo Zanzi charged several lone Starbucks coffees, Subway and Taco Bell local lunches for himself, iTunes music, and a pair of Ferragamo shoes, according to his expenses), but the integrity committee was unable to locate documents backing up many of the expenditures.

Blazer also arranged other CONCACAF payments to third parties, including his housekeeper. The committee found "no evidence that the entities . . . provided any service to CONCACAF." Some of the entities, such as the Blazer shell corporation En Passant, existed to funnel more money to Blazer secretly. In late 2011 a BAC bank representative called Blazer to inquire about a $300,000 CONCACAF check to En Passant because he couldn't locate any information about the company. Blazer assured the rep that En Passant was a "broadcasting and sponsorship sales company," but nothing in reality backed that up. When payments were made to one of Blazer's shell corporations, amounts were usually broken down to avoid detection. A $100,000 payment, for example, would be made by Blazer from CONCACAF funds in five $20,000 payments in the course of a week, the committee discovered.

There was yet another perk: investigators discovered that Blazer also used $910,000 in CONCACAF funds as a down payment for two apartments costing a total of $4.5 million at the Atlantis Paradise Island Resort in the Bahamas. In 2009 Blazer used another $497,000 in CONCACAF money to buy a single Atlantis apartment. In both cases, he later personally assumed the debt for the properties to become the owner—at least on paper—by again covering the money owed with CONCACAF funds he claimed were commissions owed him. The properties were eventually purchased under the name of yet another one of Chuck's paper corporations, Sunset Lighthouse Ltd., and he collected thousands of dollars in rent on the real estate, according to Atlantis records.

In one final shocker, investigators also found that Blazer not only dodged paying his own taxes but also "willfully" failed to file federal tax returns for CONCACAF from 2006 to 2010, as required by law, and paid no taxes on the association's separate CMTV subsidiary from 2004 to 2010. CONCACAF lost its tax-exempt status temporarily as a result.

As Blazer's financial schemes were crumbling, so was his personal life. Blanks finally walked out on Blazer over Labor Day weekend 2012. She was convinced he was avidly romancing yet another woman in one of his Bahamas getaways, where he was extending his stay for another week. She informed him over the phone and then hung up. By the time Blanks settled in at a different address, there was an e-mail from Blazer calling her "crazy" and vowing to "straighten you out" when he returned.

One thing Blazer couldn't cheat was his health. The former heavy smoker had been battling the effects of obesity and borderline diabetes for years, yet avoided as many doctor visits as he could. In November 2012 he was rushed to the emergency room of St. Luke's–Roosevelt Hospital with a severe case of pneumonia. "The staff there was able to bring me back from a near-fatal disaster," Blazer would tell some thirty friends and relatives later in a surprisingly frank e-mail. "Following my extended stay, I returned home with a new set of limitations, including being on oxygen a great deal of the time."

DURING THE HOSPITAL STAY, BLAZER'S SON-IN-LAW, MARCI'S HUSBAND, STUART GOLD-farb, texted Blanks questions from Blazer's doctor. "Has he ever had pneumonia before?" "No," she responded. He asked about current medications, and Blanks recalled drugs for diabetes, high blood pressure, high cholesterol, sometimes various antibiotics. "Why do you think he's sick?" she was asked. "Maybe because he weighs four hundred fifty pounds?" she wondered.

The health news would get worse. Blazer was diagnosed in spring 2013 with colorectal cancer and had twenty-two weeks of chemotherapy and radiation before surgery in 2014. "During the pre-op visit with the surgeon, he said how unusual it was for a patient to go through 22 weeks of chemo and six weeks radiation and end up overall healthier than when treatment began," Blazer quipped in his e-mail to friends.

More seriously, he added: "It has been a very tough year. I am looking forward to good times to come."

Goldfarb would forward a follow-up e-mail from Chuck post surgery: "Hi everyone! Finished my first day of recovery—feeling great! Now, that might seem strange since I've just been cut wide open and stitched from my belly to stern, but, hearing from the doctor that the surgery was a total success was enough to make me smile."

Blazer, however, spent most of the following months in and out of hospitals due to surgery complications linked to his borderline diabetes and his compromised ability to heal.

In the late fall of 2014, as the New York *Daily News* team worked on its story about Blazer's cooperation with the federal investigation, he was in the midst of a long-term stay at Calvary Hospital on Eastchester Road in the Bronx. He was gracious and welcoming to a visiting *News* reporter four days before the story broke, appearing nearly as large as ever as he lay bare chested on the hospital bed in a ground-floor room of the Catholic facility, a big mound of belly spilling over his black boxers. He was connected to his BiPAP machine with a gray hose strapped over his face to aid his respiration. But the apparatus didn't impede his commanding ability to connect. He turned his great woolly head and piercing eyes to the reporter with a warm greeting and listened calmly to questions. When he was told that the reporter had heard much about him, he quipped, "All good, I hope." He explained that "now is not a good time for an interview," mentioning his surgery and "digestive problems" linked to his colostomy bag. "I've been very sick," he said sadly, "and in the hospital for six months."

When asked about his role as an FBI informant to ensnare FIFA crooks by secretly taping his colleagues, he responded: "I just can't talk about that." Then he added, searching for words, apparently worried that he had already confirmed too much: "I have lawyers. I can't say anything. As you probably know, I have a case against CONCACAF." Following CONCACAF's investigative report charging him with stealing millions of dollars, Blazer filed a lawsuit claiming that the federation still owed him $7 million in commissions.

Days after the *News* story was published, Blazer was back in his Trump Tower digs, leading to speculation that he might have been hiding out from enemies—and the press—at Calvary, though he spent most of the following months in New York and New Jersey health facilities. He would continue to battle serious health problems while still answering questions from the FBI. "Once you begin cooperating with the FBI, you're never really done," said one investigator.

All that was left now was to wait for the indictments to drop.

TWELVE

THE HAMMER FALLS

ON THE EVENING OF MAY 26, 2015, WORD BEGAN TO FILTER OUT OF THE FEDERAL COURT-house in Brooklyn that something seismic would be transpiring over-night and into the next day. High-ranking soccer officials, maybe even Sepp Blatter, would be arrested and brought to the Eastern District courthouse. There was also war, the constant threat of terrorism, and flailing European economies, but none of that mattered in the world press at that moment. The potential fall of FIFA eclipsed everything.

In New York, as the team of reporters at the *Daily News* began work on the story, their phones lit up with messages and texts from journal-ists in Europe and Britain. The *News* had revealed in November 2014 that a federal investigation of top FIFA bosses—aided by the coopera-tion of a US soccer official named Chuck Blazer—had been under way since at least 2011. The European media was desperate to know: Is something about to break on the Brooklyn front?

Just before midnight, the *News* outlined the massive criminal enterprise that would be the subject of the upcoming press conference led by the new US attorney general, Loretta Lynch. Moments earlier, the *New York Times* posted a story from Zurich describing the sensational early-morning arrests of FIFA officials. At around ten thirty eastern time that same morning, the Eastern District staff in Brooklyn began distributing the two-hundred-page bound notebooks that detailed an astonishing forty-seven counts of racketeering, wire fraud, and money laundering among fourteen defendants. They allegedly conspired to solicit more than $150 million in bribes and kickbacks over twenty-four years of greed and graft. An apartment for Chuck Blazer's cats was the least of it.

The defendants comprised a VIP list of international soccer: Jeffrey Webb and Jack Warner, the current and former presidents of CONCACAF; Eduardo Li, a FIFA Ex-Co member elect, CONCACAF executive committee member, and Costa Rican soccer federation president; Julio Rocha Lopez, FIFA development officer, former Central American Football Union president and Nicaraguan soccer federation president; Costas Takkas, attaché to the CONCACAF president; Eugenio Figueredo, FIFA vice president, Ex-Co member, former CONMEBOL president and Uruguayan soccer federation president; José Maria Marin, the former president of the Brazilian Football Confederation and head of the organizing committee for the 2014 World Cup in Brazil; Rafael Esquivel, CONMEBOL Ex-Co member and Venezuelan soccer federation president; Nicolás Leoz, former FIFA Ex-Co member and CONMEBOL president; Alejandro Burzaco, controlling principal of Torneos y Competencias, a sports marketing business based in Argentina; Aaron Davidson, president of Traffic Sports USA; Hugo and Mariano Jinkis, controlling principals of Full Play Group, another sports marketing business based in Argentina; and Jose Margulies, controlling principal of broadcasting businesses Valente Corp. and Somerton Ltd.

Listed beneath the names of those arrested were the men the

government had already flipped and convicted, including Darryl and Daryan Warner, the sons of Jack Warner. They copped to charges including wire fraud and money laundering. Daryan Warner paid a $1.1 million fine and agreed to pay more at sentencing. José Hawilla, owner and founder of Traffic Group, the Brazilian sports marketing conglomerate—and one of Blazer's erstwhile London dining partners—agreed to pay $151 million, $25 million of which was coughed up at the time of his plea. His affiliated companies, Traffic Sports USA and Traffic Sports International, pled guilty to wire fraud only days before the unsealing of the indictment.

And finally, there was Charles Gordon Blazer. Chuck waived indictment and pled guilty to a ten-count charge of racketeering, wire fraud, money laundering, tax evasion, and hiding an overseas bank account. He forfeited more than $1.9 million at the time of his plea and agreed to pay a second amount to be determined at sentencing.

In Zurich, the scene was almost surreal. Reporters had assembled at the Baur au Lac Hotel across the road from Lake Zurich, a half block away from the Bahnhofstrasse, where legend has it that the trolley running down the street rumbles atop the city's gold-filled bank vaults. It was within that fortress of Swiss security and privacy that members of the Ex-Co had gathered at the hotel for what was to have been the ritual reelection of Sepp Blatter to his fifth term as FIFA president. Instead, their longtime home away from home was the tumultuous backdrop to the arrests of numerous soccer mandarins ahead of the unsealing of the US indictment that would set off tremors around the world.

As FIFA officials slept in their elegantly appointed quarters, a dozen Swiss agents in plainclothes, working in conjunction with US law enforcement, barged into their rooms and led the suspects, shielded by white bedsheets held aloft by hotel valets, out of the Baur au Lac and into unmarked cars as their wives huddled in the lobby, crying.

The seven executives arrested in Zurich would be held in Swiss detention centers scattered around the area through much of the summer as they awaited extradition. Of the fourteen total arrests—nine current and former FIFA officials, and five sports marketing executives—all were from the Western Hemisphere. Critically, all had done some FIFA or CONCACAF business in the United States linked to the ceaseless machinations of Blazer and Warner. Once Blazer became an informant, American prosecutors had a way into the formerly impenetrable FIFA hierarchy.

Sepp Blatter was spared in the raid, but like those who faced extradition, he would hire one of the top legal minds in the United States to help navigate the minefields of American justice, costing FIFA untold legal fees as he fought off indictment. As one investigator said of Blatter's exposure: "You can't be absolutely sure he isn't already indicted under seal. If I'm the FBI, and I've spent this much time on this case, don't you think I'm going after the head of the crime family?"

It became clear quickly that more charges would come as US investigators continued to pressure informants and suspects. Meanwhile, Swiss officials seized records at FIFA headquarters as they opened their own wide-reaching corruption investigation into possible bribery surrounding the awarding of the 2018 and 2022 World Cups to Russia and Qatar.

Lynch had promised in May that the investigation was far from over, and on Thursday afternoon, December 3, six months after the original indictment, she dropped the hammer again. As the United States reeled from another mass shooting, this one in San Bernardino, California, Lynch convened a press conference in Washington to announce a ninety-two-count superseding indictment that would charge an additional sixteen defendants with the now-familiar counts of racketeering, wire fraud, and money laundering.

While this press conference wasn't as dramatic—especially with a domestic terrorist event unfolding in California—Lynch's tone regarding the FIFA scandal had evolved into one of indignation. "The betrayal of trust set forth here is outrageous," she said. She was particularly galled by Alfredo Hawit and Juan Ángel Napout, the current presidents of CONCACAF and CONMEBOL, who had replaced their indicted predecessors under the guise of reform. They were both collared at the Baur au Lac in another predawn raid led by Swiss and US authorities.

Lynch also singled out Rafael Callejas, a member of the FIFA television and marketing committee and the former president of Honduras; and Hector Trujillo, the Guatemalan soccer federation executive and a sitting judge on the Constitutional Court of Guatemala. She described Trujillo as a man "purportedly dispensing justice by day while allegedly soliciting bribes and selling his influence within FIFA." There was also Marco Polo del Nero and Ricardo Teixeira, the current and former presidents of the powerful Brazilian soccer federation.

All of the new defendants were from the CONCACAF and CONMEBOL regions, reflecting the deep-rooted corruption of those federations as well as the influence of the government's informants. In addition to Hawit and Callejas, five other CONCACAF officials were indicted, while six other CONMEBOL members joined del Nero and Teixeira on the dishonor roll.

LYNCH ALSO SENT A MESSAGE TO FIFA FUGITIVES: "YOU WILL NOT WAIT US OUT. YOU WILL not escape our focus." She said that officials were working to extradite Hawit and Napout, who would resign their positions in the days to come. That legal maneuver would not be necessary for Trujillo, who would face his charges after he was bundled off a cruise ship leaving Canaveral, Florida, at six in the morning the day after the press conference. Housed in an Oklahoma transfer center following his arrest and then in solitary confinement in a Brooklyn detention center for a week to assure his safety, he finally would be released on a $4 million bond on January 7.

Eight more defendants pled guilty, the feds announced, including Webb, Burzaco, and Marguilies, along with Ex-Co member Luis Bedoya and CONMEBOL vice president Sergio Jadue. Sports marketing executives Fabio Tordin, Roger Huguet, and Chuck Blazer's old friend and business associate Zorana Danis also admitted their guilt.

The superseding indictment recounted secret meetings in US cities where bribes were discussed openly, sham contracts drafted, plans for bank transfers set, and cover-ups hatched. It was a confounding display of arrogance, or stupidity, given that the defendants knew full well the scope of the ongoing DOJ investigation and the tactics being employed. Blazer had been revealed as an informant who had taped phone calls and meetings for four years; others were presumed to be cooperating. Yet about six weeks after the May indictment, Tordin met with Guatemalan soccer federation president Brayan Jiménez and Trujillo in Chicago, and the trio chatted about their preferred mode of bribe payments for the 2022 World Cup qualifying matches. "At the outset of the conversation," the complaint read, "Jiménez stated, 'Nothing should be said over the telephone. Nothing! . . . Nothing! Nothing!'"

Sepp Blatter was once again conspicuous by his absence on Lynch's indictment list. By then, however, he had fallen into the clutches of the Swiss side of the probe, under investigation by Attorney General Michael Lauber for underselling a World Cup television rights package to Warner in 2006 and for an undocumented 2011 payment of about $2 million to UEFA president Michel Platini. Blatter was provisionally suspended by his own ethics committee in early October. He would be joined on the suspended list by his second in command, General Secretary Valcke, who was implicated in a ticket-selling scandal; as well as the man whom most assumed would succeed Blatter: Platini. Four days before Christmas, the news for Blatter and Platini got even worse. Both were hit with eight-year suspensions, banned from all football-related activities by the same ethics committee that Blatter had created, deemed to have demonstrated an "abusive execution" of their positions. Blatter would vow to appeal to the Court of Arbitration for Sport, appearing at a press conference following the announcement of the long suspension unshaven and sporting a large Band-Aid across his face. "I will fight for me and for FIFA," he said. Platini, too, issued a statement, saying he was "extremely disappointed" in the decision.

"It has been rigged to tarnish my name by bodies I know well and who for me are bereft of all credibility and legitimacy."

Scattered throughout the original indictment were twenty-five unnamed coconspirators whose companies had done close business with the FIFA officials under arrest. Some of those coconspirators would be identified in the superseding indictment. One, listed as "Sports Marketing Company A," turned out to be a small firm based in Jersey City, New Jersey, International Soccer Marketing Inc., the "controlling principal" of which, as described in the indictment, was reported by the *Daily News* to be Serana Danis, originally referred to as "coconspirator number 5." She was close enough to Blazer to be invited to his sixtieth birthday celebration at Elaine's, Blazer's old watering hole.

Danis's company raised more than $100 million from Toyota, Bridgestone tires, and the Spanish bank Santander for sponsorship rights to South America's biggest soccer tournament, the Copa Libertadores. The corporations purchased the rights on behalf of the indicted Paraguayan Nicolás Leoz, one of Blazer's FIFA cronies. Danis's firm took a commission on every deal.

According to the original indictment, Leoz directed coconspirator number 5 to pay him millions in bribes and kickbacks over the years in order to retain "Sports Marketing Company A's" lucrative role as the exclusive marketing agent for CONMEBOL, which Leoz led from 1986 until his resignation in April 2013.

In late July 2015, the US government filed papers in Paraguay seeking the eighty-six-year-old Leoz's extradition, a move he then opposed, claiming that an extradition treaty between America and Paraguay was fraught with legal holes. "The defense is saying that you cannot extradite somebody if the law did not lay out the rules of the game," Leoz's attorney, Ricardo Preda, told reporters following a court hearing on the issue. "The treaty does not establish clear procedures to follow. There is a legislative void."

In September the Spanish newspaper *Diario AS* reported that Leoz had cut Danis in on a share of the $1.5 million payment he allegedly received in 2000 from the president of the Japan Football Federation to distribute among the ten South American federations in exchange for their votes for South Korea and Japan to host the 2002 World Cup. *Diario AS* revealed that Leoz put $1.2 million into his own account, gave $200,000 to CONMEBOL general secretary Eduardo Deluca, and, in what must have amounted to tip money, tossed $100,000 to Danis.

Danis secretly waived indictment in late May, pleading guilty to wire fraud and filing false tax returns to avoid the possibility of mandatory sentencing guidelines upon a conviction, while Deluca appeared as a new defendant. Presumably, Danis, herself a victim of Blazer's influence on the case, agreed to cooperate against Leoz and others. She also consented to forfeit $2 million.

Two months later, the man Blanks described as "a personable guy who was everyone's Cayman banker"—CONCACAF president Jeffrey Webb—got in line to meet Judge Dearie in the Cadman Plaza courthouse.

As recently as March 2015, *Sports Illustrated* described Webb, another putative reformer, as one of the "rising stars of global soccer politics, a guy who may someday be in the conversation to become FIFA president. Not only has the 50-year-old Cayman Islands banker become a power player in Zurich . . . but he has also made progress reviving CONCACAF after years of neglect and corruption under Jack Warner and Chuck Blazer."

SI quoted Webb as he spoke to reporters ahead of the announcement that the 2015 Gold Cup final would take place at Lincoln Financial Field in Philadelphia: "We started on a journey two and a half years ago of really reforming our confederation and becoming the catalyst for real transition. I believe when you look at the investment we've made in governance, we've made so much progress, but we have so much more work to do."

Two months later, Webb was alleged to have progressed deeply into accepting bribes negotiated by "coconspirator number 4," who was described in the original indictment as Webb's new general secretary—

once Blazer's role—and who had been closely aligned with Aaron Davidson at Traffic USA. That man was Colombia-born Enrique Sanz.

"Sanz will have a key role in the administration of CONCACAF," Webb said on the day he named Sanz to the post, a move that was approved unanimously by FIFA's Ex-Co. "I am certain that we have found a professional with competence and integrity to implement our roadmap to reform."

Sanz also would play a key role in the government's case. A former Traffic USA vice president and Davidson ally, he was not charged in either the original or superseding indictments but was named as an unindicted coconspirator in both and suspended by FIFA in June. Easily identified as coconspirator 4 in the main indictment and "coconspirator number 9" in additional court papers, he was said to be a bag man for Hawilla, delivering millions in bribes to CONMEBOL and CONCACAF officials, including Blazer, Warner, and the ubiquitous Leoz. According to a report in the Miami *New Times*, Sanz, who was being treated for leukemia in a Miami hospital over the summer, became a key informant implicating Hawilla, Davidson, and Webb. He fit the description of "coconspirator number 3" in the superseding indictment and appeared to be a strong link for the government to the newly charged as well.

Hawilla himself began cooperating as far back as March 2014, according to the terms of his secret December 2014 guilty plea. He described to the court the pressure he was under from a top CONMEBOL official—Leoz—to pay a bribe in exchange for his signature on Traffic's first Copa América contract in 1991. According to the charging document, "in a private meeting, Co-Conspirator #1 told Hawilla . . . that Hawilla would make a lot of money from the rights he was acquiring and that Co-Conspirator #1 did not think it was fair that he did not also make money. Co-Conspirator #1 told Hawilla that he would not sign the contract if Hawilla did not agree to pay him a bribe."

A repentant Hawilla told Judge Dearie, "I knew this conduct was wrong," and paid $25 million of the $151 million he agreed to forfeit.

He also signed off on a government plan to produce the remaining $126 million by selling the Traffic holdings and the Portuguese soccer team Estoril Praia—nicknamed the Canaries. "Everything's for sale," Traffic director Jochen Loesch told Bloomberg News in October at his São Paulo headquarters. Leoz, meanwhile, remained under house arrest in his Asunción estate, fighting extradition and being treated for high blood pressure in a private hospital.

THERE IS A SAYING IN LAW ENFORCEMENT: FIRST ONE IN, FIRST ONE OUT. OTHER THAN those who had already pled guilty, Davidson, the president of Traffic USA, was the first defendant to appear in Judge Dearie's courtroom and the first to open negotiations with prosecutors. That likely had much to do with information that Hawilla and Sanz had handed the government; Traffic Sports International and Traffic USA had pled guilty to wire fraud only days before the unsealing of the indictment, which described not only Davidson's heavy involvement in Traffic's dealings but also Webb's close relationship with the companies. In the court papers, Webb is alleged to have accepted bribes from Traffic executives "almost immediately after taking office" in 2012. Those schemes included media rights to soccer tournaments, and a $3 million bribe he allegedly sought and received in a complicated series of transactions through intermediary accounts—the kind of Byzantine transactions that Blazer had set up for the better part of two decades, pilfering CONCACAF's coffers.

Office insiders corroborated the government's account, saying the easy money was too tempting for Webb and Sanz to resist. "When Enrique and Jeff got there, they knew where the pot of gold was," one former employee said, describing Webb as a "rogue" who was "just hungry for the contracts. We all know about Chuck Blazer and Jack Warner, but Jeff Webb was the one who directed everyone to the Cayman banks. He was hungry for it all."

Another insider described the atmosphere that permeated

CONCACAF offices this way: "Webb and Sanz were raised in that business that way by their predecessors. They all saw how it worked—and it certainly worked to their benefit."

Webb's plane would touch down at John F. Kennedy International Airport in mid-July, a week after he agreed to extradition. Wearing a dark blue suit that hung on his lanky frame, he was led into an almost empty Brooklyn courthouse for a rare Saturday-afternoon bail hearing, escorted by US marshals and his lawyer, Ed O'Callaghan, a partner in the international law firm Clifford Chance and a former federal prosecutor in New York. Webb's wife, Atlanta-based physician Kendra Gamble-Webb, attended the hearing, along with her parents and grandmother.

There was no mention of a plea agreement as US magistrate judge Vera M. Scanlon explained the bail conditions carefully: $10 million, secured by an array of assets, including ten properties located from New York to Florida and owned by Webb and his family; the kind of expensive gifts that routinely found their way to the Ex-Co members and their wives, including eleven of Webb's watches—from Cartier to Rolex to Breitling to Hublot—and Kendra Gamble-Webb's diamond earrings, necklaces, and even her diamond engagement ring; a Ferrari, a Range Rover, and a Mercedes; and a 401(k) account.

Webb was taken to a Brooklyn jail, in far less cushy conditions than the Swiss detention center he had occupied for almost a month before arriving in the United States, until the bond details could be formalized a few days later. Judge Dearie had signed an order for "excusable delay," meaning the clock on Webb's right to a speedy trial was waived for thirty days, a tactic prosecutors often use when they are negotiating a plea deal. As one lawyer familiar with the case put it: his wife is in the US, his cohort is testifying against him, he can take down all of them: Warner, maybe even Blatter, and maybe save himself. Why wouldn't he cooperate instead of spending ten or fifteen years in jail?"

"He'll flip," said another investigator. "These people have no loyalty to each other. They don't even like each other."

It took Webb until November 23 to plead guilty to racketeering, wire fraud, and money laundering. He agreed to forfeit more than $6.7 million, coming to an agreement with the government from his home near Atlanta, where he had spent some of the bribe money on an elaborate swimming pool to complement his Loganville, Georgia, mansion. Webb, who in better days had been known to take a limousine from Atlanta to the CONCACAF offices in Miami, had asked Judge Dearie to allow him to live in Atlanta rather than New York, ostensibly to save money as he worked out his plea agreement. (Perhaps he was saving up for the Renaissance-themed party he would throw for his wife in February on the occasion of her fortieth birthday.)

Days after Webb's July surrender, Argentinian Alejandro Burzaco waved the white flag and was extradited from Italy, where he had fled upon hearing of the Baur au Lac raid. (He had been staying at a different hotel in Zurich.) As the controlling principal of Torneos y Competencias and a number of other companies, Burzaco often did business with the Traffic Group. He had joined with Traffic International and the marketing firm Full Play, owned by Hugo and Mariano Jinkis, to form a company called Datisa, which in turn entered into a $317.5 million contract with CONMEBOL in 2013 for four editions of the Copa América tournament.

The government alleged that Burzaco had conspired with "fellow executives and leaders of soccer confederations" in a series of kickback and bribery schemes that included the use of a numbered Swiss bank account, currency dealers, and trusted intermediaries "to affect bribe payments in a manner that obscured their true source and nature and promoted the corrupt schemes."

All told, Datisa allegedly agreed to pony up $100 million in bribes to CONMEBOL officials. The accounting went this way: $20 million a pop for the four editions of the Copa América contract, including the 2015, 2019, and 2023 Copa América tournaments and the 2016 Copa América Centenario. Out of each $20 million tranche, $3 million apiece went to the "top" three officials; $1.5 million apiece to seven other officials; and $500,000 to an eleventh official. Each bribe taker was a FIFA official.

There was never much subtlety involved, and Burzaco grasped the risks fully. "All can get hurt because of this subject. All of us go to prison," he said during a meeting in Florida on May 1, 2014, with his Datisa partners—which was apparently recorded by one of the participants.

The fifty-one-year-old Burzaco was led into the Brooklyn courthouse on Friday, July 31. Judge Scanlon set his bond at $20 million, twice as much as Webb's, and secured by cash and three US properties put up by two friends and his sister, who sat quietly in the courtroom, dabbing tears from her eyes. She was seated alongside Burzaco's ex-wife, who had flown in from Buenos Aires for the hearing. About a week before Webb pled guilty, Burzaco agreed to charges of racketeering, wire fraud, and money laundering. He forfeited $21.6 million.

Bail hearings in Brooklyn were destined to continue after the Swiss Federal Office of Justice (FoJ) approved the extraditions in September of three officials arrested in the May raid: eighty-three-year-old Uruguay native Eugenio Figueredo, charged with accepting millions from a Uruguayan sports marketing company for the sale of marketing rights to Copa América tournaments; Rafael Esquivel; and Eduardo Li. Figueredo appealed the September ruling and agreed to be extradited to Uruguay in November. The extradition of Costas Takkas, the Webb attaché at CONCACAF, was approved in October. Swiss authorities then chose the United States over Nicaragua's extradition request for that country's former soccer federation president, Julio Rocha Lopez, who also served as a FIFA development officer.

Possibly realizing that cooperation was the best avenue for leniency, a sixth defendant held in Zurich since May, José Maria Marin, agreed to end his extradition fight. Accompanied by two US police officers, he boarded a plane on November 3 bound for JFK. The eighty-three-year-old, accused of taking millions in bribes from sports marketing companies in connection with tournaments, arrived at the courthouse frail and shaking. Marin would sign a $15 million bond that secured his release as he awaited trial on the by now familiar charges of fraud, money laundering, and racketeering. He hadn't seen his wife, Neusa, since the Baur au Lac raid. When the hearing was over and she had signed the bail documents, they embraced, both in tears. Marin had spent five months in a Zurich jail, but in New York he would retreat to his Trump Tower apartment—under twenty-four-hour guard—just an elevator ride away from Blazer's digs.

Like Webb, Burzaco, and Davidson, he would wear the electronic monitoring device and was told not to interact with any other defendants or anyone associated with FIFA. He would hire retired FBI agents, who had carefully cased the swell neighborhood, to monitor his movements and escort him to court appearances or any medical appointments.

Li, facing similar charges, fought extradition until mid-December. "Li massively influenced the competitive situation and distorted the market for media rights in connection with the World Cup qualifying matches," the FoJ said in a statement. The later indictment described a series of bribes involving Li, including one negotiating session in which he asked coconspirator number 3—Sanz—for a six-figure bribe in exchange for awarding a contract to Traffic USA.

Meanwhile, in Port of Spain, Blazer's frenemy Jack Warner had toned down his outrageous denials and threats to take down Blatter and all of FIFA, along with the Trinidadian government, following his arrest and a night in jail. He was believed to be in hiding, surrounded by lawyers and advisers, including Edward Fitzgerald, a top British lawyer who had successfully fought the extradition of businessman Steve Ferguson—who was indicted in 2006 in connection with airport corruption—by tying up the defendant in local litigation. As one Trinidad insider said of the seventy-two-year-old Warner, "He figured if he could get caught up in the Trinidad courts, they couldn't extradite him. By the time that was settled, he'd be dead."

There's a home-field advantage in law, and Warner had even another trick up his sleeve. A few days after his jail stay, as dogs barked in the background and locals peddled snow cones to his constituents, Warner appeared before a crowd in a run-down Port of Spain neighborhood and compared himself to an Ebola victim as he proclaimed his innocence and touted his candidacy for reelection to Parliament. He was running on the Independent Liberal Party ticket he had created in July 2013 after he failed to be reelected as the candidate for the Chaguanas West seat by the United National Congress-Alliance. He surely figured a seat in Parliament couldn't hurt his fight to avoid extradition, a decision that would be made by a Trinidad judge after the US's extradition request was evaluated.

US prosecutors had moved slowly on a formal extradition request for Warner, but by July 22, five days before the deadline specified under the treaty between the two countries, Trinidadian officials had the paperwork in hand. Warner denied publicly that he would ever cooperate with US law enforcement, saying he had not been afforded due process, "and I have not even been questioned in this matter. I reiterate that I am innocent of any charges."

In late August, as Warner crisscrossed the island campaigning for the September 7 election, the general consensus was that he had cut a deal with the leader of another party also running for reelection that, should either of them win, Warner would not be extradited. "He is playing the game of wait-and-delay as much as he can," said one Trinidadian political insider, speaking on the condition of anonymity. "He is thumbing his nose at the US—a sort of Noriega approach. From my calculation, the US would have to come here with force for this guy and take him."

On the morning of September 21, Warner was back in a Port of Spain courtroom awaiting a ruling on extradition from Trinidad attorney general Faris Al-Rawi. He had assumed office on September 9 after voters ousted Prime Minister Kamla Persad-Bissessar's ruling party and slam-dunked Warner's Independent Liberal Party in the process. Warner lost his seat in Parliament and at least some of his political clout; but rumors circulated that he had cut a deal with the new prime minister, Keith Rowley, that saved him from the clutches of the US Justice Department. The deal was supposedly brokered by Warner's cousin, Winston "Gypsy" Peters, who resigned as a cabinet minister under the United National Congress coalition government and joined Rowley's party.

Flanked by television cameras and a flock of reporters, Warner emerged from the courtroom with another delay in hand. Warner's lawyers would eventually secure a judicial review of the extradition process itself, putting off their client's next court appearance until February 19, 2016.

As he left the courthouse, Warner's bodyguards lobbed insults at a French television reporter who tried to question him about the bribes and kickbacks. "Ask ISIS!" Warner's bodyguard shouted at the reporter, in an apparent reference to the November terrorist attacks on Paris. After the reporter asked a second question, Warner himself told the reporter, "Ask your mother."

IN SPITE OF THE OBVIOUS OBSTACLES, FOR THE FIRST TIME SINCE THE INDICTMENT WAS handed down, there seemed to be a belief in the Eastern District office that Warner would, like Blazer, ultimately find himself in Brooklyn before Judge Dearie, even in the face of all the delays.

The allegations in Warner's indictment revealed a trail of television rights contracts, bank records, e-mail, and the testimony of confidential witness number 1—Blazer—as well as that of Hawilla, the Traffic executive who admitted that his company paid Warner tens of millions in bribes. And, of course, Warner's sons, Daryll and Daryan, who had also pled guilty in October 2013 to a range of crimes in exchange for reduced jail time, and who remained in the family's Miami condo.

The indictment describes Jack Warner as a man engaged in a panoply of larceny, in the form of racketeering, bribery, wire fraud, and money laundering. That included millions in kickbacks via the various Traffic companies, as well as Gold Cup bribes. There was also the $10 million payoff from the South African government to support the African diaspora, along with the retrieval in the early 2000s from a Paris hotel room by Daryan Warner of a briefcase filled with bundles of cash in $10,000 stacks, allegedly provided by a South African bid official. There were even allegations that Jack Warner stole $750,000 in emergency aid intended for the desperately poor, earthquake-ravaged people of Haiti in 2010. The December indictment mentions that bit of grifting, too, saying that Warner and Webb "embezzled or otherwise personally appropriated funds provided by FIFA, including funds intended for natural disaster relief."

"The worst person I came across in football was Jack Warner," one person close to the investigations would say. "Just an absolute piece of shit."

The message from the US government was clear: the dominoes would fall. Attorney General Lynch held her now-historic press conference on May 27, signaling the beginning of the end of an unprecedented era of corruption in international sport, and the systematic dismantling of the cabal that ran the Fédération Internationale de Football Association. For those who had looted the global game, the long trek through the US criminal justice system was under way.

Even the banks weren't immune from scrutiny. On October 30, in a small paragraph slipped into its third-quarter financial report, Credit Suisse became the first bank to reveal that it, too, was being investigated.

"The US and Swiss authorities are investigating whether multiple institutions, including Credit Suisse, permitted the processing of suspicious or otherwise improper transactions, or failed to observe anti-money laundering laws or regulations, with respect to the accounts of certain persons and entities associated with FIFA. Credit Suisse is cooperating with the authorities on this matter," the bank said in its report.

According to a mid-December Reuters report, Michael Lauber's office confirmed that a financial unit called the Money Laundering Reporting Office Switzerland (MROS) was investigating suspicious activity around the awarding of the 2018 and 2022 World Cups to Russia and Qatar, and JPMorgan Chase & Co., Bank of America, Citigroup, HSBC, Credit Suisse, Standard Chartered, and UBS were reported to be holding discussions with US prosecutors about what they knew of transactions in question.

By late December, Swiss officials had handed US investigators documents relating to bank accounts allegedly used in the case, and Lynch's indictments identified several US banks that handled money from defendants.

Her superseding indictment pointed out ominously the "centrality of US financial systems" to various FIFA schemes, noting specifically the use of banks in New York and Florida. "The defendants and their coconspirators relied heavily on the United States financial system in connection with their activities with the enterprise," stated the document. By late February, Citibank had revealed in a regulatory filing that it had indeed received a subpoena from the Eastern District and said it was cooperating with authorities. "This reliance was significant and sustained and was one of the central methods and means through which they promoted and concealed their schemes." As 2015 came to a close, and the case continued to evolve on multiple levels, Lynch got the best award a prosecutor could hope for: Marvel Comics, the creators of super heroes like Spider-Man and Captain America, immortalized her as the FIFA Slayer, holding a soccer ball in one hand and a sword over her shoulder.

Her counterpart in Switzerland surely deserved his own salute. "This is not a ninety-minute game," Michael Lauber said. "It's like more or less not even at the half [time] break." Back in the United States, one soccer executive characterized the defendant's fate in starker terms. "They're all going to go away," he said. "We'll see them in some penitentiary."

Whether they'll meet Chuck Blazer there will be up to Judge Dearie—and Blazer's precarious health. Without Blazer's chameleon-like ability to transform himself from slick embezzler to slick undercover operative, the government would probably have no case against the FIFA bosses and their confederates. If there's time off for bad behavior, Blazer can argue that he earned it.

THIRTEEN

LA FIFA NOSTRA

LATE GAMBINO CRIME FAMILY BOSS JOHN GOTTI WAS RECORDED ON AN FBI WIRETAP touting "this thing of ours, La Cosa Nostra. We have some guys that can preserve it, and they'll be here forever. I'm gonna be in La Cosa till I die," the Queens crook told his crew in his hangout in Manhattan's Little Italy. He died in prison.

That mobster monologue is one of the highlights of the National Museum of Organized Crime and Law Enforcement (known as the Mob Museum), located, with almost perfect karma, in a converted federal courthouse in old downtown Las Vegas. Among the exhibits is a section of the bullet-riddled brick wall from the St. Valentine's Day Massacre where seven rival thugs were mowed down by Al Capone's gang in 1929.

In the summer of 2015, the roster of the notorious was joined by a couple of new mugs: Chuck Blazer and Sepp Blatter. Their stories and photos were featured in an exhibit of the latest chapter of organized crime: FIFA's Ex-Co. "Organized crime isn't about men in fedoras any longer," said Geoff Schumacher, the museum's director of content and the exhibit's curator. "The FIFA indictments reveal the face of a modern crime syndicate. The organization shares a number of similarities with the mob. It has been accused of international lawbreaking involving major institutions across the globe, and it has been run by a small group of men who have had no accountability, no oversight, for a very long time."

American law enforcement recognized the same parallels. The massive Justice Department case against FIFA leaders and sports marketing executives involved several violations of the Racketeer Influenced and Corrupt Organizations (RICO) Act, which was passed by Congress in 1970 specifically to nail the Mafia. In a US Senate subcommittee hearing on FIFA, Connecticut Democratic senator Richard Blumenthal called the organization a "Mafia-style crime syndicate," adding: "The only hesitation in using that term is that it is almost insulting to the Mafia because the Mafia would never have been so blatant, overt, and arrogant in its corruption."

The Ex-Co's version of La Cosa Nostra took thievery to a stratospheric new level within an intricate global network linking TV, major marketing companies, corporate sponsors, banks—and governments salivating over the chance to host the biggest sports events in human history. The crooked operations involved shakedowns and kickbacks, tax dodging, bank and wire fraud—and even death. The human rights organization Amnesty International has reported that hundreds of immigrant workers have died amid Qatar's frenzy of construction as that nation prepares to host the 2022 World Cup.

The Mob Museum is the brainchild of Oscar Goodman, former Vegas mayor and mob defense attorney. Goodman entertained one of the newest luminaries in the museum: Chuck Blazer. He met with Blazer during the CONCACAF general secretary's frequent trips to Vegas, where he attended electronics trade shows, gambled, and checked out the strip clubs, all on CONCACAF's tab. Blazer told associates that he urged Goodman to support a new stadium for a soccer team in Vegas. But the Sin City club was not to be. Major League Soccer turned down the city's bid for a franchise in mid-2015 (by then, Goodman's wife, Carolyn, was mayor), and a billionaire businessman instead filed papers in 2015 to move a National Hockey League team from Phoenix to Vegas. Other investors, however, are still fighting for a soccer team.

Despite his high profile in the Mob Museum, Blazer can't claim credit for organizing organized crime in FIFA and CONCACAF. But he was in the right place at the right time and took every opportunity to capitalize on an unprecedented era of FIFA graft—and played his part in speeding things along. Blazer stepped into his powerful position at CONCACAF, and later FIFA, just as television coverage of sports was surging and bringing an avalanche of media money to soccer. Ex-Co members were in a unique position to help themselves to dirty money from their safe perch in the mountains of Switzerland, protector of tax cheats and notoriously lax in regulating associations such as FIFA.

For most of a century, FIFA, founded in 1904 by the seven football nations of Belgium, Denmark, Sweden, Switzerland, Germany, France, and Spain, was viewed widely as a relatively honest—if stuffy, patriarchal, and even racist (the organization backed apartheid South Africa)—European men's club quietly managing global soccer. Leaders were driven by a missionary zeal to expand the gospel of the game and use the appeal of soccer to unify the world. They rolled out a confederation network that would later be vulnerable to graft and placed key decisions, such as choosing World Cup venues, in the hand of the elite Ex-Co. But they considered soccer the "Esperanto of sport," in the words of author and Brighton University professor Alan Tomlinson, who has studied FIFA for decades. "They viewed themselves as providing a public service on the global stage. They believed in the benefit of sport; there was a sense of idealism," he said. "But they were succeeded by a new generation of leaders: opportunistic wheeler-dealers."

The new leaders took over when the Eurocentric FIFA soccer world tipped momentously on its axis in 1974 with the election of the first president from outside of Europe: Olympic swimmer João Havelange of Brazil, who competed in the 1936 Berlin Games and in water polo in Helsinki in 1952. The matinee-idol-handsome Havelange was buoyed to victory by restless nations wanting in on the European power game, an aggressive presidential campaign—and financial support from Adidas.

Havelange, who had become a savvy businessman and lawyer as his athletic days waned, transformed FIFA during his twenty-four-year reign before handing it off to his handpicked successor, Sepp Blatter. For the first time in FIFA history, an association president cultivated soccer clout in South America, Asia, Africa, and the Caribbean, nurturing confederations in those regions with generous infusions of cash. The grateful organizations in turn repeatedly voted to back Havelange's presidency, fortifying his path to FIFA invincibility.

Like Blazer, Havelange was a quintessential salesman who could "convince you that a blue sky was red," a FIFA colleague once said. And much like Blazer would be, Havelange was a master politician who could appear to share power and lavish attention on a target even as he was maneuvering to get exactly what he wanted. People didn't mind because they were enjoying the riches like everyone else along for the ride. When Havelange took over, there were fewer than 100 national association members and a 16-nation World Cup. When he left in 1998, FIFA had 204 members, its first 32-nation Cup—and $1 billion in its coffers.

But even as Havelange grew soccer and broadened its power base, he also inaugurated FIFA's historic epoch of corruption. The era coincided with a revolutionary change that touched all major sports: the globalization of the broadcast industry and the growth of cable TV, which ignited a demand to fill hours of air time with popular content. During the 1990s, the number of television sets and people who could watch a single popular event expanded exponentially, from thousands, to millions, to billions around the world. This captive global audience of eager faces reflecting the flickering light of television was a gold mine for advertisers and corporate sponsors eager to display their wares. Playing to those fans also seduced nations lining up to take center stage in events such as the World Cup.

Television boosted sports, but sports also boosted television, in a mutually reinforcing cycle. When NBC first aired the baseball World Series in 1947, along with heavyweight fights and the Army-Navy football game, sales of television sets skyrocketed. As the price of TVs fell rapidly in the 1980s and 1990s, and as satellites made nearly every game available live, the cycle spiraled. Rupert Murdoch once called his strategy to scoop up television sports rights aggressively the "battering ram" for his planned expansion of his global pay TV network. "Sport absolutely overpowers film and everything else in the entertainment genre," he told the 1996 annual meeting of News Corporation stockholders. "Football [soccer], of all sports, is number one."

American soccer regularly played to crowds of just 4,000 in the first wave of its modern iteration in the 1970s. In a jaw-dropping contrast, by 2015, a record 26.7 million American viewers watched the 2015 Women's World Cup finals—the most watched soccer game in US history. At least 3.2 billion people, 46 percent of everyone on the planet, watched some of the 2014 World Cup in Brazil. Nearly a billion people—more than the entire population of Europe—watched the final match of the 2010 Cup. In 1972 Clive Toye purchased television rights for a US soccer tournament against Mexico and couldn't give them away. In 2014 Major League Soccer made an eight-year broadcasting deal with ESPN and Fox Sports for a combined $75 million per season, and with Univision for $15 million a season to present Spanish language broadcasts in America.

FIFA now collects $5.6 billion every four-year World Cup cycle, with 80 percent of the funds coming from television rights, sponsorships, and other marketing. Besides Adidas, 2015 sponsors included Coca-Cola, McDonald's, Budweiser brewer AB InBev, Hyundai Motor

Group, Gazprom, and Visa. (Emirates Airline pulled out to protest corruption; Sony, a longtime partner, declined to renew.) Though exact figures are secret, a four-year top-tier sponsorship is believed to cost the companies $100 million apiece.

But explosive exposure came at a price. "TV was the best and the worst thing that happened to soccer," said a source familiar with the FBI investigation of FIFA. TV spread the gospel of soccer, but it also helped tarnish the game it championed. The media market was chum to the circling sharks of sports marketing companies, and some would emerge as key villains in the FIFA scandal. Other than bribes related to specific World Cup bids, all of the corruption in the US indictments is linked to payoffs of FIFA or regional soccer confederation leaders by sports marketing firms. Of the fourteen men named in the original Eastern District indictment, five were executives of companies tied to millions of dollars in bribes; more would be named in the next round of indictments.

"FIFA was relatively unsophisticated when broadcast TV took off," said Michael Hershman, an accountability expert for the risk management firm the Fairfax Group, who served on FIFA's independent governance committee. "Sports marketing companies convinced FIFA officials that they had the connections and special knowledge to manage rights for the organization. I don't know why FIFA didn't—and still doesn't—handle that business entirely in-house. I sometimes think the major function of the sports marketing companies has been to serve as middle men to provide kickbacks to the executive committee."

Pay to play had become so ingrained in FIFA that honest businesses didn't bother to compete. "You just walk away," said Charlie Stillitano, cofounder and chairman of sports marketing company Relevent Sports in New York. "You're never going to be part of that club unless you play that game."

When FIFA and CONCACAF ostensibly brought TV and sponsorship rights deals "in-house"—after their early marketing partners floundered—in fact the soccer organizations become even closer bedfellows with their new marketing companies.

FIFA's very first major corporate brother was Adidas. The German company invented the cleated soccer boot and to this day supplies all the balls used in FIFA World Cup games. Company president Horst Dassler, the son of cofounder Adolf "Adi" Dassler, envisioned its popular triple-stripe logo on all things soccer. By 1970, he and Havelange had formed a partnership, and Dassler poured hundreds of thousands of dollars into FIFA bank accounts to make his dream a reality. FIFA's Web site lauds the company's "dedication to the sport and its close relationships with athletes and teams."

Adidas has a continuing sponsorship contract with FIFA until 2030 that grants it the sole right to sell FIFA merchandise. Its American rival Nike sponsored Brazil's national soccer team in the 2014 World Cup in Brazil, although Adidas still supplied the balls. Of the thirty-two teams that qualified for the Cup, a third—including the Americans—wore Nike uniforms, but neither Nike nor any other nonsponsorship brand was allowed to run ads with a World Cup theme. Nike, a relative newcomer to the game, might have learned the hard way how soccer is played. The federal indictments noted that "Sports Company B," headquartered in the United States, paid millions extra to an intermediary to win the rights to sponsor the Brazilian team, but Loretta Lynch refused to identify the company by name. "There is no allegation in court documents that any employee was aware of or knowingly participated in any bribery scheme," stated Nike.

The tight relationship between Adidas and FIFA raised early alarms, and a 1983 London investigation detailed in the Howell Report by the Committee of Enquiry into Sports Sponsorship criticized the company's too-close ties with the soccer federation. "We exist to sell boots and shirts, and wherever the action is, we need to be there," Dassler told the panel. Investigators didn't care if Adidas boots were on the ground at soccer games; what worried them more was that Dassler was too often at Havelange's side during governance meetings and influencing decisions. The panel was particularly troubled by Dassler's attendance with Havelange at World Cup draws and by the company's practice of keeping dossiers on various international sports officials, which it shared with favored leaders to keep them in power. "We are concerned at the close association of Mr. Dassler and Adidas," the panel concluded. Members called for the disclosure of all private companies' financial interests in international sports events and organizations.

Dassler, who died in 1987, is believed to have played as large a role as Havelange in choosing, and carefully grooming, Sepp Blatter to be the next FIFA president. Blatter, a former executive of the Swiss Tourist board and the Longines watch company, once referred to Dassler as a "father figure."

Dassler exited Adidas in 1980 to found the now-defunct International Sports and Leisure (ISL) corporation of Switzerland. ISL was the first sports marketing company to purchase event rights from FIFA or continental confederations, develop marketing concepts, and in turn resell the rights for a hefty profit to sponsors, TV networks, and other vendors, such as poster or apparel sellers. It was also the key marketing company for the Olympics. By 2000, ISL—along with its holding company, International Sports Media and Marketing—was one of the most powerful media and marketing enterprises in the world and an "appropriate business partner" for FIFA, according to an association official.

But in 2001, the company declared bankruptcy, with a staggering debt of $300 million, owing FIFA at least $130 million in expected income from ISL—though a chunk of that money had been siphoned off in bribes by members of its very own Ex-Co. Bankruptcy proceedings and a criminal case years later against ISL executives would reveal rampant corruption involving FIFA officials. Swiss prosecutors charged six former ISL executives with fraud, embezzlement, and falsifying documents.

Most damning was the discovery that ISL had paid millions of dollars in bribes to Ex-Co officials as early as 1989, including what was initially reported by journalist Andrew Jennings as a staggering $15 million to Havelange and his onetime son-in-law Ricardo Teixeira, a member of the Ex-Co and president of the Brazilian Football Federation. Also on the leaked list of FIFA administrators who paid hundreds of thousands of dollars in *schmiergeld*—translated roughly as "grease money," or bribes—were Ex-Co member from Camaroon Issa Hayatou and Paraguayan Ex-Co member and president of the South American association CONMEBOL Nicolás Leoz. Hayatou, accused later of accepting a $1.5 million bribe to vote for Qatar as the venue for the 2022 World Cup, stepped in as acting FIFA president when Blatter was suspended in October 2015.

Court documents released by Swiss authorities in 2012 would reveal that bribes paid to various FIFA and federation leaders from 1989 to ISL's bankruptcy totaled more than $100 million, with Havelange and Teixeira collecting $41 million for awarding rights to just the 2002 and 2006 World Cups. (Officials were only identified in code in the document; Blatter acknowledged that he was "P1," described as a FIFA leader who knew a $1 million payment from ISL was for Havelange.) FIFA would only admit that bribes paid were "not an inconsiderable amount."

After collecting the bribes, Havelange, Teixeira, and Leoz would continue in their soccer leadership roles for at least another twelve years and continue to vote on World Cup venues. The money was funneled to the men via bank accounts in offshore tax havens, according to prosecutors. Hayatou was reprimanded for bribe taking by the International Olympic Committee (IOC), where he also served at the time. But he wasn't fined, suspended, or ordered to return the payments. Jacques Rogge, the IOC president at the time, compared the reprimand to receiving a yellow card on the soccer field, which would allow Hayatou to continue in the game.

FIFA launched its own investigation led by former US federal attorney Michael Garcia in 2010 after Swiss criminal cases against the men were dropped because bribes weren't illegal in that nation at the time. FIFA's ethics committee chief, Hans-Joachim Eckert, ruled in 2013 that bribes had indeed been paid to Havelange, Teixeira, and Leoz. He chastised the men, but because FIFA had "no ethics rules whatsoever" until 2004, noted Eckert, there were no penalties—not even suspensions—nor a demand to repay the funds. Nevertheless, Eckert stated that the men "should not have accepted any bribe money," and should have had to pay it back, since it involved selling off media rights that belonged to FIFA. He called their actions "morally and ethically reproachable." True to its laissez-faire pattern, FIFA took no further "superfluous" action—in the words of Eckert. Havelange did, however, give up his post as honorary FIFA president, and Leoz and Teixeira resigned from the Ex-Co after the findings. Leoz and Teixeira would be home free until 2015. Leoz was indicted by the feds in May, and Teixeira in the second round of charges in December, both for bribery, racketeering, wire fraud, and money laundering linked to several other deals.

ISL's liquidator went to Swiss courts in a bid to claw back the bribe money on behalf of the company's stiffed investors and creditors—which, ironically, included FIFA. Leoz and Havelange, however, used FIFA lawyers against the association's own interests to negotiate their own advantageous settlements. They agreed to return just $3 million of their bribes; in exchange, FIFA agreed to drop the organization's efforts to recover the $130 million it was owed by ISL. Garcia branded the deal a brazen conflict of interest by the bribe takers. Eckert agreed, though, again, he took no action against the men.

The ethics committee found "no indication" that boss Blatter had taken bribes in the ISL case, though he did sign off on a mysterious $1.4 million check to Havelange and Teixeira from ISL that was channeled through FIFA accounts. The report cleared Blatter of "criminal and ethical misconduct," but he was chided for being "clumsy." It "must be questioned whether President Blatter knew or should have known over the years . . . that ISL made payments (bribes) to other FIFA officials," Eckert noted.

But Havelange did implicate Blatter, according to a letter uncovered later by Andrew Jennings and reported in a BBC *Panorama* episode in late 2015. In the letter, obtained by the FBI and forwarded to Swiss authorities with a request for help with the US investigation, Havelange discusses the payments he received from ISL and says that Blatter had "full knowledge of all activities" and was "always apprised" of them:

"During the period of time in which I was FIFA president, Mr. Joseph Blatter was the general secretary, I maintained commercial relationships with sports marketing companies which were under my economic control, and, as a result of these relationships, I received remuneration, in accordance with FIFA regulations," Havelange acknowledged in the letter, which he believed exonerated him of wrongdoing. He also admitted using FIFA attorneys to defend him during the investigations into his "remuneration."

Eckert believed that ISL set up a process right from the start to hide bribes to Ex-Co officials using a network of misleading "front" operations and bank accounts, including a trust registered in the tax haven of Lichtenstein. This was how ISL mixed legal payments with "deliberately fraudulent and disloyal conduct" as Havelange, Leoz, and Teixeira collected "not inconsiderable amounts" of payola, Eckert determined.

Other jolting revelations of corruption followed the ISL debacle—and again were linked to rights deals. In 2001 FIFA's general secretary, Michel Zen-Ruffinen, accused Blatter of gross financial mismanagement by giving away some $500 million worth of FIFA media rights to regional soccer leaders to solidify his support so that he would remain president election after election.

The Caribbean, Zen-Ruffinen underscored, was key to that strategy. Blatter granted Caribbean media rights to two World Cups for $1 each to kingmaker and Blazer buddy Jack Warner, Zen-Ruffinen revealed in the report, an accusation that was admitted to later by Warner. The millions Warner made reselling the rights to broadcast

companies was ostensibly to be used to strengthen soccer organizations in the Caribbean. But, as with many FIFA expenditures, there
was absolutely no follow-up to determine how the money was spent.
FIFA's finance committee approved a $4.5 million budget for an under-
twenty-one tournament in Trinidad in 2001. When charges came in
at $8.2 million, no one asked questions, according to Zen-Ruffinen's
report.

Zen-Ruffinen also accused Blatter of simply writing off a $9.75
million debt that CONCACAF owed to FIFA without offering any ra-
tionale. An entire section in the report was devoted to Warner. "The
president has constantly taken decisions which are favorable to the
economic interests of Jack Warner and some of his family members
and are contrary to the financial interests of FIFA," Zen-Ruffinen declared.

The report prompted eleven Ex-Co members to file a criminal complaint against Blatter with Swiss authorities. The general secretary was
attacked immediately by Blatter, who denigrated him as "Mr. Clean,"
as if that was the worst insult imaginable. (Zen-Ruffinen protested
bizarrely that he wasn't Mr. Clean.) For his part, Blatter admitted, "I
have made mistakes now and then, but there have been no criminal
actions." Zen-Ruffinen was drummed out of FIFA by 2002 by Blatter,
and neither the boss nor Warner was punished for the media rights
giveaway after Swiss authorities dropped their investigation. Ten years
later, Blatter would be suspended by FIFA's ethics committee for offering a nearly identical discounted media deal: this time selling World
Cup media rights for $600,000 to Warner, who resold them for mil-
lions. (Zen-Ruffinen would later be embarrassed in a 2010 sting by
London *Times* journalists who claimed he offered to be a "fixer" for the
Russia and Qatar World Cup votes, noting that many Ex-Co members
could be bought with cash or "the ladies.")

Just as the ISL bribes and Zen-Ruffinen's damning findings were
coming to light, Blazer became enmeshed in his own messy deal with

another media marketing company linked to FIFA. In 2000 a new Blazer venture called Global Interactive Gaming Ltd., headquartered in London, was setting up what he touted as the world's first live-action interactive betting service. It was owned jointly by Blazer's shell company MultiSport Games Development, registered in Delaware, and Prisma iVentures of the German Kirch media group—which had obtained global TV rights to the 2002 and 2006 World Cups after ISL imploded. While sports wagering is legal in many countries through authorized betting parlors and Web sites, the endeavor would have used technology newly licensed by MultiSport that would allow real-time sports betting directly through television sets. Blazer invested some $7 million from his CONCACAF fees and from other investors in the operation.

The London papers got wind of the venture and questioned the obvious conflict of interest concerning a member of the Ex-Co entering into a business deal with a company that had been granted World Cup rights by the same committee. Adding live gambling via TV to sports events also exponentially increased the likelihood of match fixing, which was already plaguing FIFA events, particularly in Asia.

Initially, Blazer insisted nothing was amiss and that there would be an unbreachable boundary between gambling profits on matches and one of the most powerful soccer administrators in the world. Blatter defended him. But as press outrage mounted, Blatter conceded that perhaps FIFA needed to "establish a code of conduct" to eliminate such situations for Ex-Co members. The operation never got off the ground; the Kirch Group declared bankruptcy in 2002, with losses of some $5.5 billion. Blazer's budding enterprise collapsed.

Blazer would later take center stage in yet another major FIFA controversy, this time involving a big sponsorship deal for the World Cup. FIFA was caught by a US judge double-dealing as it negotiated to sell a single sponsorship to credit card rivals MasterCard and Visa. MasterCard forged a deal in 2002 with FIFA to be a key sponsor for all FIFA competitions from 2003 to 2006, including that year's World Cup, at a cost of some $100 million. In addition, the judge found that it was granted the right of first refusal for the 2007 to 2011 tournament cycle and reached a tentative agreement in 2006 for the next round. Despite the agreement, FIFA ended up signing an eight-year deal with Visa that was supposed to begin at the start of 2007. MasterCard sued, and Blatter, who has long feared the US justice system, asked Blazer to represent FIFA in the court case in the Southern District of New York.

Blazer was initially flattered to be asked to fill in for his boss—then he realized he might have been tagged as a sacrificial lamb by the cunning FIFA chief. US District Judge Loretta Preska found in MasterCard's favor. FIFA officials, who later pushed for arbitration in Zurich after a US appellate court sent the decision back to Preska for clarification, ended up settling with MasterCard for $90 million.

The lower court decision stunned Blazer, who had been proud of his performance on the witness stand and assumed he had successfully beguiled the judge as he denied that MasterCard's deal had been terminated illegally by FIFA. Preska, however, characterized Blazer's testimony as "generally without credibility based on his attitude and demeanor and on his evasive answers on cross-examination." In fact no one in FIFA had much credibility, as far as the judge was concerned. Preska found that FIFA officials had lied relentlessly to both companies about every aspect of their sponsorship deals. "While the FIFA witnesses at trial boldly characterized their breaches as 'white lies,' 'commercial lies,' 'bluffs,' and, ironically, 'the game,' their internal e-mails discuss the 'different excuses to give to MasterCard as to why the deal wasn't done with them,' how we (as FIFA) can still be seen as having at least some business ethics,' and how to 'make the whole f***-up look better for FIFA,'" Preska noted in her ruling.

Despite the litany of revelations of corruption at FIFA over twenty years that sullied its reputation, Ex-Co members nimbly dodged any major penalties—until the federal indictments. A key aspect of the problem has been FIFA's protection under Swiss law. The organization is registered as an association and thus sheltered by extremely lax regulations, though that is now beginning to change. But as of late 2015, FIFA had yet to make public basic financial information about the organization, including the salaries of its Ex-Co officials. FIFA is not required to pay taxes or to file basic information accessible to the public. But with billions of dollars in income, "it should be treated like what it is: a major corporation," Hershman testified before a US Senate committee hearing on the FIFA scandal in July 2015.

Hershman found his work on the FIFA independence panel increasingly frustrating. Few of its recommendations were enacted, including none of the suggestions he believes are most crucial to safeguarding any organization's integrity, such as term and age limits, and financial transparency. "I went in with my eyes open," Hershman said. "But it was disillusioning. You don't find many organizations like FIFA. I underestimated how protected it is. Most organizations want to change to create a positive public image, or they recognize a need for reform because they're vulnerable to civil or criminal consequences. FIFA has never had to worry about that. Until now, it has been a completely insular organization. It's been run by a group of personalities who grew in power and arrogance."

Sports organizations often get a free ride—they pay no taxes and are exempt from antitrust laws in the United States—because they can highlight the noble side of humanity while providing a thrilling, unifying distraction in a world wracked by war and poverty. Professor Tomlinson calls FIFA a "para-state parasite" for its thieving and tax-dodging superstatus, but acknowledges that soccer, regardless of news about crimes linked to sport administrators, continues to provide "glorious minutes." Former US secretary of state Condoleezza Rice, speaking at a New York City conference in November 2015, said that sports "presents the world as we want it to be, not as it is"—one where people play by the rules and meet on a level playing field.

"Sports has values we appreciate: integrity, teamwork, fair play," said Hershman. "Sports used to have a degree of purity. I don't know if we can ever get that back."

FOURTEEN

INJURY TIME

THE BANKER BEGAN TO SWEAT AS HE PORED OVER THE DETAILS IN A PRINTOUT OF THE Eastern District indictments. Chuck Blazer had been his customer, and he was worried that he could be implicated in the crimes. He had transferred money between Blazer's offshore and Manhattan accounts, and monitored a line of credit that the former CONCACAF general secretary used to buy resort property in the Bahamas. As the banker turned a page, he read about a Caribbean courier who had flown into New York's Kennedy Airport to collect a check made out to Blazer and deposit it in the Bahamas. He blanched. That courier was him.

Weeks after the arrests at the Baur au Lac in Zurich, the banker was fired. His legal status remains perilous. Unemployed and fruitlessly seeking work elsewhere, he called Blazer's son-in-law, Stuart Goldfarb, to get this message to Chuck: "You have destroyed my life."

There are flesh-and-blood victims in the FIFA scandals. Most were further from the scenes of the crimes than the courier. They include thousands of innocent workers tainted by Ex-Co and CONCACAF schemes, as well as players, fans, honest business managers, and people of nations that don't pay bribes—if any exist. To many, especially Americans more attuned to the controversies plaguing the National Football League, Ex-Co corruption seems to be a planet removed from sport—a place where soccer officials already fat on graft accept bribes with impunity, and sports marketing companies squeeze extra millions from rich media corporations or sponsors.

But any nonchalant attitudes about FIFA corruption disintegrated in late 2010. The choice of Qatar to host the World Cup drew a line in the desert sand in FIFA's decades-long dirty history. The decision was so absurd on its face that many believed there could be no explanation other than bribes to locate the event in a nation with no soccer tradition and temperatures that could kill an athlete. "You can't air-condition an entire country," Blazer quipped famously after America lost out to Qatar to host the event. "It was a dirty decision to put a World Cup on a strip of sand that was broiling," Andrew Jennings testified before the US Senate Consumer Protection Subcommittee in July 2015. Qatar's searing summer heat prompted an Ex-Co decision to switch the 2022 World Cup to November and December from June and July for the first time in FIFA history, upending long-established soccer schedules. "If you want to die young, come to England and [say], 'Hey, we're going to stop you from having football for seven weeks because Jack Warner took the money,'" said Jennings. "You can't walk into somebody else's sports culture and just take it away."

The most immediate victims of Ex-Co's corruption have been honest rank-and-file workers in FIFA and its member federations. Several officials and employees did know what was going on and might have colluded in the crimes. Other leaders should have known; some had suspicions. Major League Soccer Commissioner Don Garber said he unknowingly trusted people "who lied." But he was disturbed by the "largesse" of CONCACAF. "There was so much money being spent, and so much focus on pomp and circumstance," Garber said.

"I was aware of some level of discomfort; a general feeling," testified US Soccer Federation CEO Dan Flynn, who substituted for his boss, Sunil Gulati, when he declined an invitation to appear before the Senate subcommittee hearing on the FIFA scandal. "I had no hard evidence." Despite concerns, US Soccer continued to participate in CONCACAF, to "try to influence the organization," he added. When pressed about what made him uncomfortable, he offered only this: "How Mr. Warner ran a meeting, and went through an agenda, and how he had hand votes versus sealed votes." He never confronted Warner or Blazer about his concerns, because if he had, he might have "felt discomfort in a different way," said Flynn.

Employees of CONCACAF's New York office suspected the Federation's financial statements were crooked but felt powerless to act. "What do you do in that situation? We couldn't very well report it to our bosses Chuck Blazer or Jack Warner, who seemed to be orchestrating everything," said one. "So then what? Do we call FIFA? Pick up the phone and talk to the FBI?"

Whistle-blowers and their supporters have traditionally been forced out of FIFA and its federations. Now reputations are being tainted among the the armies of people who get things done in the world of soccer and haven't taken bribes. Panicked, innocent FIFA employees have been sending out a "flurry of resumes," said Michel Carrard, the head of FIFA's 2016 reform committee, who credited the honest workers with keeping the global soccer system moving. "There are still millions of reputable people in the world of soccer."

Jill Fracisco gets it. While Chuck Blazer was secretly pocketing his Gold Cup bribes, she was doing the yeoman's work of running the complicated tournaments. She was in charge of an overwhelming array of details, from arranging venues and team travel, to scheduling practice times, field access, and games years ahead. Once Blazer launched the tournaments with Fracisco, in 1991, she ran them largely on her own, while the general secretary was sequestered in his office playing the stock market. "There were times when Chuck was completely out of touch, with his door closed doing his day trades, and we were under orders not to bother him," recalled Clive Toye.

Fracisco is one of the most experienced soccer tournament directors in the United States. Yet because she was linked to CONCACAF, she has struggled since losing her job with the association to piece together work projects. Potential employers are suspicious of anyone with ties to Blazer and Warner. "I worked long days, I sacrificed a lot of my personal life for CONCACAF, but it was my choice. I loved my work," she said. Fracisco was one of the candidates in line to become CONCACAF's next general secretary after Blazer left under a cloud in 2011, and would have been the first woman ever to hold that post. But instead, she was forced out by incoming president and Cayman Island banker Jeffrey Webb and his new general secretary Enrique Sanz, who swept into CONCACAF offices at Trump Tower, seizing records and computers.

They jettisoned Fracisco to make way for friends and relatives and another round of corruption. Webb, who was busted at the Baur au Lac by Swiss police, was charged with laundering millions of dollars in bribes. Sanz, who appears in the charging document as the unnamed coconspirator number 4, is linked to kickbacks arranged through Traffic Sports. He was fired by CONCACAF after the indictments and faces a lifetime ban from FIFA. He is believed to be cooperating with the feds.

After Fracisco was pushed out of the job she had held for nearly twenty years, she called Blazer to ask if he could recommend her to some other sports organizations. "'I don't think my word counts for much now,'" she recalled Blazer telling her. "He didn't apologize. He isn't the kind of man who apologizes, but he did say, 'I thought you'd be safe.' I respected Chuck when we worked together, but he betrayed everyone's trust."

US Attorney General Lynch made a clear distinction between leaders charged with crimes and the associations she said they "exploited," characterizing CONCACAF and FIFA as victims in the case. That marked a dramatically different approach in the Justice Department's typical crackdown on illegal operations. Rather than charging entire organizations, such as banks in the subprime mortgage debacle, this time only individuals were named. Lynch called Warner and Blazer's CONCACAF an "organization in crisis," adding: "We have already reached out to its representatives to ensure that the people of integrity who work there know that we stand ready to work with them to reform their practices."

The workers most critical to the global soccer system—the athletes who play the game—have suffered a particularly appalling history in Jack Warner territory. At least twice, he took money out of the pockets of Trinidad and Tobago players; the first time was in 1989, after they lost to the United States in a critical playoff game. Then, after the Soca Warriors won a spot in the 2006 World Cup in Germany, making Trinidad and Tobago the smallest nation ever to compete, Warner engineered an even more brazen rip-off.

In a deal brokered by Warner, who was special adviser at the time to the Trinidad and Tobago Football Confederation (TTFC), all profits from the 2006 World Cup were to be split equally between the team and the association. Warner would say later that in a "moment of euphoria," he agreed to share the wealth, but that it was to be only 30 percent of the take. It was moot anyway, he said, because he never signed an agreement. And given that Warner was in charge of the accounting, the players would never have known what the true income was.

The association initially reported having earned $3 million for the event in sponsorship and media deals against costs of $2.8 million, leaving almost nothing for the athletes. It offered the sixteen players who went to Germany a whopping $830 each. (By contrast, the American men's team collected $9 million after finishing eleventh in the 2014 World Cup; US women collected $2 million after winning the 2015 Women's World Cup.) Later examination of the TTFC's income indicated that revenue was at least $27 million, likely much more. By Warner's own admission, he had paid a single dollar for Caribbean media rights to the 2006 Cup, turned over to him by FIFA president Blatter, ostensibly so that Warner could resell them for millions to help build soccer in the region.

"It was astonishing," said Soca Warrior Kelvin Jack, the team's goalkeeper. "We knew about Jack Warner, and knew he probably wouldn't pay us our fair share, but what he did was absolutely shocking, particularly hard to imagine because we were at our best moment as a country then." When players took action to recover their money, some were blacklisted and forced out of the sport in their prime by Warner and his cronies.

Players denied their World Cup bonus appealed for help to the London-based Sport Dispute Resolution Panel—now known as Sport Resolutions. The panel ruled that Warner's agreement was a binding contract and ordered a $1.5 million initial payment to the players. The TTFC ignored the panel, and players headed next to Trinidad's high court. "Lucky or unlucky for you, I have some experience in the accounting field," said Justice Devindra Rampersad, alerting Warner and the TTFC. What his sharp accounting eye noticed was that there was no accounting. No one had records tracking income related to the Cup, and Warner ignored an order from the judge to produce the documents. TTFC had never requested an accounting of the income, which Rampersad called "quite astounding." The justice ordered the association to pay the players $3 million.

TTFC turned over half the money. When the next installment languished, players and police swept through association headquarters and removed computers and furniture to sell in an attempt to recover some value. They finally received a second check in 2014 for $1.1 million—from the government. It was handed over by Prime Minister Kamla Persad-Bissessar. The first female prime minister rose to power in 2010 with the help of a political coalition including the United National Congress, headed then by Warner. Some players believe she climbed the ladder on contributions from Warner that came from World Cup media profits that should have gone to the athletes. Persad-Bissessar lost the 2015 election amid accusations of corruption.

"We are not unmindful of the long and protracted legal battles waged by these football heroes of ours," said Persad-Bissessar as she presented the check in a public ceremony to former player and activist Brent Sancho and pointed out that the government was under no obligation to cover the debt. Players were "still owed and entitled to a payment from the TTFF," she added, but noted that the now financially struggling association was "unlikely to be in a position to pay." A local editorial writer complained that taxpayers got stuck with the World Cup bill twice: first in subsidies to develop the team, and then covering player payments that had ended up in Warner's bank accounts.

Sancho was moved to tears by the gift, but railed against island soccer administrators and Warner, for trying to intimidate the members of the team who spoke out against corruption. Persad-Bissessar soon named Sancho her sports minister, and the fight against the TTFF faded, though a court case continues.

The FIFA corruption trail also revealed that players elsewhere had been systematically shortchanged by their association bosses. In September 2015 a Bolivian team refused to take part in a national training camp leading up to World Cup qualifying matches, in a protest over unpaid wages to two top club teams. The action followed the arrest of the president of the Bolivian Football Federation (FBF) and CONMEBOL treasurer Carlos Chávez on charges that he had misappropriated $400,000 in proceeds from a competition that were supposed to go to the family of a fan who had died at a match. The investigation into Chávez was triggered by the arrest of former CONMEBOL president Rafael Esquivel in the FIFA indictments.

IN QATAR, A VERY DIFFERENT CATEGORY OF VICTIMS—AN ARMY OF POWERLESS IMMI-grant workers—has become the most wrenching casualty linked to the controversial pick for the World Cup. The nation's economy functions on human arbitrage. Qatar has the highest ratio of migrants to citizens in the world. There are only 278,000 citizens in the oil-rich nation, less than the population of Anchorage, Alaska. But 1.5 million immigrant workers from Bangladesh, India, Nepal, and the Philippines keep the country running. The low-paid labor force is hard at work constructing stadiums for the World Cup—not one regulation stadium existed when Ex-Co members sized up the nation for the event—as well as thousands of hotel rooms and a light-rail transit system, and renovating the airport to prepare for the expected hordes of soccer fans.

Workers are brought to Qatar under an oppressive *kefala* system, which Human Rights Watch compares to slavery. Employers must sponsor workers before they can enter Qatar, and they need permission from a boss to leave the country. They serve at their employers' convenience—and pay rates. Passports are often held by bosses, marooning some workers with starvation wages and no way out.

In addition, laborers desperate to find jobs often agree to pay astronomical rates to employment agencies that arrange work and travel. Debts are so high that workers are trapped in an indentured servitude to pay the bills.

"In the most extreme examples, foreign migrant workers have become suicidal after being trapped without pay by employers in Qatar," Sunjeev Bery of Amnesty International testified at the Senate subcommittee hearing on the FIFA scandal. "They have been forced to depend on charity from others simply to eat. It's FIFA's responsibility under UN principles to ensure that its operations do not turn a blind eye to or directly involve serious human rights abuses, and it's pretty clear that human rights abuses and labor exploitation are rampant in Qatar today."

Indian and Nepalese officials have charged that four hundred nationals died of various health and safety problems in a single year, and a study by the *Guardian* and a labor council found that the toll could be in the thousands.

FIFA has trumpeted the World Cup as a "catalyst" for change, but so far that hasn't happened. Qatari government officials vowed in 2014 to enact reforms to the *kefala* system, but few significant improvements have been implemented. The government even denies that working conditions are unsafe. In December 2015, four years after Qatar was chosen to host, Amnesty International said labor abuses were still rampant. "Despite massive public exposure of the appalling conditions faced by most migrant construction workers, the Qatari authorities have done almost nothing effective to end chronic labor exploitation," said organization researcher Mustafa Qadri. "Unless action is taken—and soon—then every football fan who visits Qatar in 2022 should ask themselves how they can be sure they are not benefiting from the blood, sweat, and tears of migrant workers."

American companies operating in the nation—and hoovering up some of the World Cup dollars—are also linked to the *kefala* system. Several companies based in the United States, such as CH2M Hill, Aecom, and Bechtel, are involved in building either World Cup–related sites in Qatar or other projects in Gulf States that rely on migrant labor. US companies usually entrust subcontractors to provide workers. But just as the United States has policed banking and soccer, American companies might have a chance to do the same in labor. CH2M, the overall project manager for the planned main World Cup stadium, recently introduced a set of global worker welfare policies. The company, headquartered in Colorado, has also met with human rights groups for advice on how to address the labor concerns.

Qatar isn't just desperately short of native labor: the nation is also woefully lacking in top-of-the-line citizen soccer players. Those, too, can be imported, if somewhat more expensively. Qatar launched a strategy in the 1990s to quickly grant citizenship to foreign athletes so they could compete as nationals. In 2000 Qatar spent $1 million on an entire eight-man Bulgarian weight-lifting team and granted instant citizenship for the 2000 Olympics. (Other countries have shopped for athletes, too.) As for soccer, Qatar is nurturing young local players and many from Africa in its intense Aspire Football Dreams system of training, recruiting boys as young as six, but the program has been criticized as another aspect of a kind of Qatari human trafficking.

Qatar's hunt for women to play the game is less enthusiastic. Female athletes struggle to find a role at home even as their nation avidly pursues hosting international sports events as part of a national economic strategy to highlight Qatar's wealth and increasing media might in the Mideast. It hosted the 2010 debut track meet for the Diamond League of the International Association of Athletic Federations (IAAF), the 2006 Asian Games, the 2010 World Indoor Track and Field Championships, and was tapped for the 2019 IAAF Track and Field championships—a ten-day event that draws the third-largest TV audience behind the Summer Olympics and the World Cup.

To help give women some role in the events that Qatar is hosting, in 2000 the country launched the Qatar Women's Sports Committee to encourage female athletes. The change hasn't been easy. Women often struggle with religious and cultural clothing restriction in sports—and biases that see such physical activity as unseemly for women. Female athletes are often forced to sweat in head-to-toe workout clothing to protect their modesty. Parents are concerned about their teenage daughters' chances of finding a husband when they wear "immodest curve-hugging" uniforms to train on soccer fields.

Qatari women are subject to legal discrimination, and they live under rules that would shock many foreigners. Qatar remains one of only three Arab countries—along with the United Arab Emirates and Oman—that did not ratify the Convention on the Elimination of All Forms of Discrimination Against Women. The treaty, often described as an international bill of rights for women, was passed by the United Nations in 1979. Just over half of Qatari women have jobs, but sex outside of marriage is illegal (which might give tourists traveling to see the World Cup pause), and close to a hundred immigrants are jailed each year for having children out of wedlock. Women's behavior is ruled by the Muslim code of Sharia, which is the basis of Qatar's legal system.

As Qatar tries to bolster its image as a modern, sophisticated Arab country that welcomes people from all cultures, Sharia is less obliging. Drunken fans and women baring midriffs or cleavage at World Cup competitions could be more than Qatari officials will tolerate. As for other fans who aren't straight and conservative, there are strict laws against gay sex (Blatter urged gays to "refrain from any sexual activity" while attending the Cup). In early 2016 the nation banned the film *The Danish Girl*, based on transsexual painter Lili Elbe, for its "depraved content."

In another early sign of cultural dysmorphia that bodes ill for the World Cup, two crews of Western journalists were arrested in the summer of 2015. Qatar's prime minister had invited BBC reporters in July, to show off a new housing complex for laborers. But when they deviated from the specified tour and returned with a worker to another neighborhood, they were busted. "Our arrest was dramatic," recounted reporter Mark Lobel, who said the journalists wanted to "see for ourselves" housing conditions. "Suddenly eight white cars surrounded our vehicle and directed us on to a side road. A dozen security officers frisked us in the street, shouting at us when we tried to talk." Their equipment was seized, and they were whisked to security headquarters, where the cameraman, translator, driver, and Lobel were grilled separately. "The questioning was hostile," said Lobel, who discovered during the interrogation that security agents had been photographing the team's every move from the moment it landed in Qatar. "We were never accused of anything directly. Instead, they asked over and over what we had done and who we had met," Lobel recounted.

The team spent the night in prison and was questioned again the following day. "This is not Disneyland," one interrogator told Lobel. "You can't stick your camera anywhere"—a warning that 2022 fans might heed. The journalists were finally released from custody after forty-eight hours—and from the country within four days. Government officials were unapologetic and accused the crew of "trespassing on private property"—even though they were invited by a resident.

Two months earlier, journalists from West German Broadcasting, also investigating labor abuses, were arrested, interrogated for fourteen hours, and not allowed to leave the country for five days. Officials said they had failed to obtain a film permit, as if detention and interrogation were reasonable responses in such a case. Equipment was returned four weeks later, and all data had been erased and some of the equipment damaged.

No matter who ends up staging World Cups, the price of prestige is becoming increasingly steep, though it might not matter much to Qatar. Host nations have built multiple stadiums and hotel rooms that are often underused and even abandoned once the event is over. Taxpayers foot the bill for staging yet another magnificent sports event within a fascinating new travelogue backdrop, while media companies swoop in to telecast the spectacle and collect advertising fees, and FIFA crooks collect their bribes. Cities are beginning to dodge the "honor" of hosting massive sports events because of the crushing cost of providing facilities, transportation, and security. Increasingly, countries with command economies controlled by the government instead of the market, such as China and Russia, find themselves in favored positions for events such as the Olympics.

After South Africa won the venue for 2010 World Cup—following a bid campaign that cost $150 million before bribes—a group of excited young men in a Johannesburg ghetto celebrated in the streets, chanting, "Money! Money! Money!" In fact, while the nation gained an "intangible legacy," in the words of a government report, the event cost an estimated $4 billion, with at least a quarter of the money used to build and upgrade stadiums, some of which were abandoned six months after the Cup. Though huge TV audiences watched the games on TV, only three hundred thousand spectators traveled to the country, 30 percent less than expected. The billions in investment resulted in only $540 million in foreign spending; some had hoped for spending and economic spinoff worth as much as $6 billion. South African citizens, already struggling with unemployment and a lackluster economy, were delighted that the Cup showed Africa in a good light but angry that they still lacked for basics such as sanitation. "The World Cup made FIFA and the corporate sponsors a lot of money, but it left the state floundering," said Johannesburg-based writer and researcher Dale McKinley. "It was an event funded by taxpayers that benefitted very few."

The disappointment was similar years later in Brazil. In the months leading up to the 2014 World Cup in Brazil, what was supposed to be a celebration of *o jogo bonito*—"the beautiful game"—instead turned into a massive political protest against President Dilma Rousseff. Brazilians adore their soccer, but they were furious about the flagging economy and the billions spent for stadiums at the expense of schools, roads, and health care.

That argument came home recently when in 2015 Boston turned down consideration to be a possible Olympic host for the 2024 Summer Games. A campaign against the Olympics was launched by a tough crew of Bostonians who "think there are better ways to spend public resources than on a three-week party," according to the No Boston Olympics organization's Web site. The average price tag for hosting a Summer Olympics is $15 billion—more than all of Massachusetts collects annually in income taxes. Critics were concerned that the dollars spent on sports facilities and housing and food for athletes and spectators would mean far fewer funds for schools, hiring police officers, and fixing potholes. They were also annoyed by what they saw as Boston 2024's lack of transparency and the belief that a small cabal of business leaders who stood to profit were running the show in secrecy. Los Angeles replaced Boston as the potential host city.

CHUCK BLAZER CAN'T BE HELD ACCOUNTABLE FOR THE QATAR VOTE. HE DESPERATELY wanted America to stage the World Cup, regardless of the cost. It would have made him a bigger deal maker than ever before. He would have reaped yet another clandestine fortune, again no doubt plumped with under-the-table payoffs. And just as CONCACAF always did for Blazer, those who pay their taxes would have picked up the tab for the event. He would have simply banked his commissions—and bribes.

FIFTEEN

GAME OVER

YOU'D HARDLY CALL IT A DEN OF THIEVES. YET WHEN A FRAIL EIGHTY-THREE-YEAR-OLD José Maria Marin entered Trump Tower on the evening of November 3, 2015, he repaired to his $3.5 million apartment in the same luxe Fifth Avenue high-rise that Chuck Blazer had occupied for twenty-five years. Marin agreed to extradition in late October, paying a $15 million bond for the privilege of residing in his own quarters—shackled by an ankle bracelet, and monitored by a security force—while preparing to join Blazer and the growing list of other informants on the flipped list. Co-operation was likely the best option, if he didn't want to die in jail.

Blazer himself hadn't stepped foot in 49J for the better part of a year, moving from the Bronx rehab facility to New York Presbyterian/ Weill Cornell Hospital on the East Side of Manhattan, and finally to a bed in the Hackensack University Medical Center's hospice unit in New Jersey at one point, "hooked up to tubes," according to one visitor. "I think one thing was better, and two things were worse. He's a complete mess, sick as hell."

Blazer's doctors and lawyers had managed to keep journalists and private investigators at bay, citing health issues, but the feds were a different matter. No doctor's note could fend them off. Blazer was the centerpiece of the US investigation and had provided the government with much of the evidence for the indictments, but he was by no means the sole perpetrator of the corruption that permeated the sport. Blazer had met with Marin and the other South American and Central American defendants and unindicted coconspirators countless times over the years, huddling in Le Hall at the Baur au Lac, or at tournaments, or on Ex-Co extravaganzas. In one November trip in 2006, they dined together at Ricardo Teixeira's Rio apartment before heading to Carnivale as the guests of the Brahma beer company—almost always conversing in Spanish as they discussed their deals.

Those cozy meetings were history for the Ex-Co gang and their marketing pals, but overarching questions remained as the case headed into winter with a new round of indictments and the February FIFA presidential election looming: Who would replace Sepp Blatter? And would the federation manage to survive following the December roundup of sixteen more current or former FIFA officials and their marketing company accomplices? Several of Blatter's would-be successors had their own problems, many of which played out in the daily dispatches from the world's press, each more damning than the last. As one investigator said, "The sad part is the people who'll replace him are even worse."

In the months following the May indictment, Michel Platini—a spectacular player in his time—had been the overwhelming favorite to replace Blatter. But that was before Blatter and the UEFA president were hit with provisional ninety-day suspensions over the dubious $2 million payment that Platini had received from Blatter in 2011— based on a verbal contract, said Sepp. Platini had been expected to drop from the race but got a reprieve when Domenico Scala, the head of FIFA's ad hoc electoral committee, confirmed that the suspension would not automatically rule him out of the running for the February 26 vote. Scala declined, though, to perform an ethics review of Platini as long as the suspension was in place.

By mid-November, the man who had replaced Platini as the favorite, Sheikh Salman bin Ebrahim al-Khalifa of the kingdom of Bahrain, once again came under heavy fire for what activists termed "crimes against humanity." In an early November letter to Issa Hayatou, Blatter's stand-in during the suspension—and himself accused by the *Sunday Times* in 2011 of having taken a bribe to support Qatar's World Cup bid—the organization Americans for Democracy & Human Rights in Bahrain reminded Hayatou that it had informed Blatter in 2013 of its "deep concern" over allegations of human rights violations involving Sheikh Salman in the Arab Spring of 2011. The group repeated claims that Sheikh Salman had identified athletes who had participated in prodemocracy protests in Bahrain. The group says that Salman's security forces then used the information to "arrest, detain, torture, and publicly defame these athletes."

Sheikh Salman staunchly defended himself, telling the Associated Press that he had been "used as a tool just for a purpose, which is a political one." He continued: "All I can say to them is that they either got the wrong guy and the wrong name, or I'm sorry to say they are creating nasty lies about something they want to use for their purpose."

There were fears among investigators, officials, and reformers about the unlikelihood of actual reform among such a fractured, chaotic group, and even the chilling possibility that another presidency could be bought and paid for. "Salman is the guy I would worry about," said one source. "Look at his record on women, on human rights. He's much worse [than Blatter]. And he could win. He has Asia, and he'll buy Africa. Once again, it'll come down to CONCACAF." Nicholas McGeehan, a Gulf researcher for Human Rights Watch, put it more bluntly. "If a member of Bahrain's royal family is the cleanest pair of hands that FIFA can find, then the organization would appear to have the shallowest and least ethical pool of talent in world sport," he said.

FIFA watchdog Michael Hershman, wasn't expressing much hope, either. In an interview following the November 2015 New York conference organized by the Qatar-based International Center for Sports Security, the stated global mission of which is to promote and protect the integrity and security of sport, Hershman said he had no faith that the twelve-member FIFA reform committee set up in August and led by former IOC general director Michel Carrard would have significant impact in curtailing corruption. There had been talk that only half of the proposed reforms would ultimately pass, and the committee itself was waffling on what Hershman considered the most important: term limits. "The only way things will change is if there's a top-to-bottom, complete reorganization of FIFA, with a change in leadership and in the top staff," Hershman said. "Aren't they the guardians at the gate?"

The guardians gathered, appropriately enough, on the same day that the presidents of CONCACAF and CONMEBOL were hauled out of the Baur au Lac and Lynch announced her new raft of indictments. Maybe seeing two more of their number jailed spurred the executive committee to approve unanimously the reform committee's proposals, which included term limits for the president and Ex-Co members, transparency on the pay of top officials, integrity checks, a statute protecting human rights, and perhaps most controversial: replacing the Ex-Co with a thirty-six-member FIFA Council. That new council would also include at least one woman from each federation. The proposals awaited approval by the entire 209-member FIFA Congress on February 26, the same day as the presidential election—no sure bet.

Carrard, the Swiss lawyer who led the IOC through its own crisis during the 2002 Salt Lake City Winter Olympics payola scandal (but refused to divulge his own compensation for chairing the reform committee), had spoken at the same ICSS conference and expressed doubts about term limits. "There are situations in some countries where you have strong leaders who could be useful for more than eight or twelve years," Carrard said. "We have to be very careful and refrain from over-simplistic, Western ideas about corporate governance." He went on to characterize the DOJ investigation as having put FIFA "in a crisis which was triggered by the rather violent intrusion of police forces," and disagreed with the idea that the "Ex-Co needs to be fixed by out-siders. Being some kind of an insider I believe is a necessity . . . at some point, you need insiders to get reforms through. I sense the will to change."

Sure enough, nine days after Carrard's comments, Sheikh Salman's candidacy was approved by Scala's ethics committee along with four others who made the cut: Prince Ali bin al-Hussein of Jordan, Jérôme Champagne of France, Gianni Infantino of Switzerland, and Blazer's and Blanks's old traveling companion from the 2004 South Africa bid trip, Tokyo Sexwale. The electoral committee rejected the candidacy of Musa Bility of Liberia "in view of the content of the integrity check report relating to him," but declined to be more specific.

Of the candidates, Prince Ali emerged the least tainted by scandal, but whether he could ever round up enough votes to win was another matter: he had already lost to Blatter in the election held barely two days after the first US indictment dropped, despite the obvious impli-cations for Blatter. In a mid-November interview with the AP, Prince Ali said he supported adding four more teams to the 2026 World Cup, increasing the lineup to thirty-six, and advocated a return of the Cup to the CONCACAF region, thirty-two years after America hosted the tournament. The 2026 bidding was stalled in the wake of the Ex-Co upheaval and will be a priority for the next president, with Canada, the United States, and Mexico set to enter the fray.

By late fall, Hershman had joined the chorus of skeptics and critics who were asking not only if FIFA would survive the scandal but also whether it should survive at all—a question that became even more pressing in the wake of the December indictments. "The time has al-most come for a rival FIFA," Hershman said. "I wouldn't have said that was possible five years ago. And it will depend on the next leader. If a new president comes in with a tarnished past, it's very possible federations will join together to start again with a completely new organization, with a clean sheet of paper."

Even some of the sports marketers themselves questioned the value of an organization so rife with corruption that it had basically destroyed itself, managing even to put into question its shop window: the World Cup. "Will FIFA exist in my lifetime?" asked one executive. "Probably not. And who cares? The leagues themselves have risen to such power, why do I need FIFA? The leagues and teams are the engine of the sports economy. The World Cup is increasingly marginalized. The Champions League draws as well as the World Cup."

For now, the World Cup remains the single most valuable piece of sports programming extant. Its rising value, in fact, helped prompt the seismic shift in the media landscape that played out in the background of the criminal cases and raised issues of television's complicity in the scandal. "Deregulation of the media hugely influenced all this," said one executive. "Follow the trajectory of ESPN, and that'll answer all your questions."

Blazer's rejection of NBC's $350 million bid in 2006 in favor of a $425 million deal with ESPN and Univision that would include MLS broadcasts helped the fledgling league attract stars such as David Beckham and Thierry Henry to the United States. It also helped line the pockets of the men controlling the rights. The agreement that Chuck Blazer crafted was emblematic of a FIFA culture with far-reaching tentacles.

The deal that FIFA announced in February 2015, extending US media rights with Fox and NBCUniversal's Telemundo through the 2026 World Cup, roiled the television landscape, leaving Fox's competitors crying foul after FIFA failed to open the bidding process. Was Fox, which also holds the North American rights for the 2022 Cup, afforded favored treatment as compensation for switching the 2022 Qatar tournament to winter, a season already overflowing with sporting events? ESPN's Bob Ley, the veteran anchor of ESPN's soccer coverage, tweeted immediately what everybody else was thinking: "Did FIFA just grant rights to WC2026 without opening it up to bidding? #typicalFIFA." Reports surfaced of the US Justice Department's interest in the relationship between the media companies, including Fox, and sports marketing firms after the December 3 indictments, which didn't name the company. Blazer's deal with ESPN and Univision might seem paltry compared with the potential value of World Cup contracts in an open bidding atmosphere, but whether the television industry will continue to spend extravagantly in an on-demand world is questionable, even on a level playing field. While live sports events still drive ratings and allow advertisers to spread their messages without the filters of on-demand content, the foundations of over-the-air networks and cable entities are by no means on solid ground as the terrain shifts with technology. The same forces that disrupted the music industry and print media are now affecting television as well.

The idea that an event like the World Cup would have to be reimagined seems apocryphal to almost anyone who professes to love the sport.

But after the events of the past year, nothing is off the table, certainly not as the self-described guardians of the game continued their slow parade through the Brooklyn courthouse. Former US secretary of state Condoleezza Rice spoke at the ICSS conference, too, defending the US crackdown and stressing the necessity of guaranteeing some semblance of fair play in the country that some view as potentially the most valuable soccer market in the world. "It is certainly the government's role to make certain corruption isn't taking place using US institutions," she said. "I believe fully in the right of the US, even extraterritorially if necessary, to make sure that US laws are not being violated and that US institutions and decision-making processes and practices are not being used to shield corruption. Corruption is the greatest tax on human development in almost any country in the world that you can think of."

Both Rice and Donna de Varona, the Olympic gold medal swimmer, broadcaster, former president of the Women's Sports Foundation, and longtime Title IX advocate, joined the call for immediate and significant change. "There is no argument that for FIFA to earn back credibility, a culture shift must take place," de Varona wrote. "For decades its leadership has been drawn almost exclusively from the ranks of rich and powerful men who serve without term limits or transparency. If FIFA is to have any chance at persuading the world that it's serious about reform and rehabilitating its brand, the organization needs to embrace new leadership and consider recruiting outside the football fraternity."

One thing was certain: the Ex-Co and its enablers had been decimated by the American Boy Scouts, its old guard rendered powerless, indicted, or cowering; several of them checking themselves into hospitals; others remaining prisoners in their own mansions, wandering the halls like aging Mafia dons, receiving medical care or meeting with the feds. Even Sepp Blatter, seventy-nine, was taken ill, spending about a week in a Zurich hospital in November for what his personal adviser, Klaus Stoehlker, described as a "small emotional breakdown."

Blatter's ailments paled in comparison to those of the seventy-two-year-old José Hawilla, who described a litany of maladies to Judge Dearie during his plea hearing on December 12, 2014.

"How is your health?" asked the judge.

"I had some health problems, during the course of this investigation I had—prior to this I had a lung problem which got worse here, which became an illness called pulmonary hypertension," Hawilla said. "I had a cancer underneath my tongue," he continued, "which was treated with radiotherapy and chemotherapy for some months . . . And now I finished, and I'm in recuperation. The doctors say that I am free of the illness. But I have to do follow-up, which I am doing twice a month, and I'm doing tests at the same time that I am doing treatment for my lung. I take medication. I do physiotherapy one hour a day, and I sleep with an oxygen apparatus.

"Apart from that, when I finish what I have to do—I have to put a stent in one of my coronary arteries. Those are my problems. And I take several medications a day."

"Well," replied Judge Dearie, "that's certainly enough for one man."

Upon learning of the arrests in Zurich and that he, too, was among the indicted officials, Nicolás Leoz checked into the private hospital he owns in Asunción for treatment of high blood pressure and other ailments. He remained under house arrest in Paraguay, fighting extradition.

As he prepared for an early December Ex-Co meeting, Issa Hayatou, Blatter's stand-in during his suspension, had his own health problems, undergoing a kidney transplant in November, according to a FIFA statement. Sergio Jadue, the president of the Chilean football federation (ANFP), escaped the DOJ's original indictment, but he ended up pleading guilty in the second one, taking a faux thirty-day medical leave in November, shortly before the country's police said they wanted to question him as part of an investigation into financial misappropriation at the Chilean federation. Jadue's illness wasn't disclosed, although his leave was announced on the ANFP Web site hours after he had returned from a trip to Brazil. He denied he had gone there to cooperate with the US authorities, but days later, Jadue resigned from his ANFP post and was reported to be doing just that. Surely no coincidence, Lynch announced in her December 3 press conference that Jadue had pled guilty on November 23 to racketeering and wire fraud. He agreed to forfeit all funds in his US bank account.

Enrique Sanz, an unindicted coconspirator, had managed to avoid arrest, but he was in and out of a Miami hospital through the fall, being treated for leukemia and presumably continuing to cooperate. "Very sick," said one source.

Long before he himself fell ill, Chuck Blazer seemed to have premonitions of doom. One CONCACAF employee described the "frantic summer of 2011" and suspected that Blazer knew the feds were on the doorstep. "There were many closed-door meetings; he was lawyered up," said the employee. "This was about Chuck knowing something big was going down."

Whatever Blazer knew couldn't save him: he would go quietly into the grip of the US government. As the men of the Ex-Co and the sports marketers were rounded up, Blazer's part in the DOJ's relentless mission had come into sharper focus. His cooperation helped lead to the dismantling of a RICO enterprise that had seemed far beyond the reach of any country's laws. The information he provided, the recordings he made, the schemes he unwound, led not only to the corrupt Western Hemisphere officials named in the indictment but also to the heart of old-Europe FIFA itself.

Sepp Blatter, unindicted but blacklisted, was suspended by his own organization, under investigation by his government, and fearing eventual extradition to the United States. "If the US is happy with what the Swiss do with him, that'll be that," said one source close to the investigation. "If not, they can try to extradite him . . . They've achieved what they wanted to achieve. His whole life was taken away."

For Blazer, the dizzying power, the money, the nights at Elaine's, the private jets, and the Bahamian paradise—even the woman he called the "love of his life"—were long gone. As he lay in the New Jersey hospice in November 2015, the ravages of disease seemed to be taking their toll on his mind, too. The government's star witness was talking gibberish and hallucinating. Maybe it was the medication. Only a few weeks later, he was said to be coming off the ventilator, possibly even moving to a subacute care facility. Maybe he would somehow recover from the long stay in hospice care, as safe from the reaches of enemies that the government could keep him. As the New Year broke, he was sending messages to friends, hopeful that 2016 would be better than 2015. Or maybe the end really was finally near.

It was a journey that warped the American rags-to-riches storybook: the boy who diligently flipped burgers and ran the cash register in Blazer's Spa Luncheonette on Queens Boulevard, the young hustler who worked the trade shows at Manhattan's old Coliseum and coached his kids' soccer teams at the New Rochelle Soccer Club; the slick marketer who helped shepherd a "foreign" sport into the age of mind-blowing TV rights fees; but finally the swindler who couldn't resist dipping into the pot of gold he helped create.

Chuck Blazer had come into US soccer at just the right moment, scheming his way through a frontier as wide open as any on the American landscape. The letter that Mary Lynn Blanks found in her mailbox on the occasion of her fiftieth birthday was, perhaps, the perfect description of how far Blazer had come. "I now, as the only American in history, have a key leadership role on the world body of soccer, FIFA, and the World Cup," he wrote. "I have dined with kings and presidents while averaging over 200,000 miles a year globetrotting and having fun. It has been a great ride."

Whether he believed his own con is hard to say. The man who once described himself to Blanks as "just a crook from Queens" also saw himself as a shrewd businessman who deserved his "commissions," as he called them. Blazer's moral dualism allowed him to claim the role of righteous whistle-blower horrified by the blatant greed of a grifter like Jack Warner. It wouldn't be a stretch to say that Blazer believed his work as a government informant would somehow help save soccer. Maybe it has. Maybe he was more, in the end, than an American huckster, forever hawking his goods.

EPILOGUE

DELEGATES FROM ALL BUT TWO OF FIFA'S 209-MEMBER NATIONAL ASSOCIATIONS (Kuwait and Indonesia were suspended) crammed into the Hallenstadion hockey arena in Zurich on February 26, 2016, to elect a new president. Four miles away, Sepp Blatter watched on television at his daughter's apartment as his replacement, UEFA general secretary Gianni Infantino, took the reins of the federation Blatter had ruled for 18 years.

Blatter had been banned from the FIFA House headquarters he had occupied for nearly two decades and is said to have set up office at the posh Sonnenberg, a nearby restaurant where the chef's whites bear the FIFA logo. As the proceedings unfolded, he was sharing a bottle of white wine with Corinna Blatter, according to the Associated Press, and quickly issued a statement praising Infantino's "experience, expertise, strategic and diplomatic skills," before adding a somewhat cringe-worthy kicker: "He has all the qualities to continue my work and to stabilize FIFA again."

It wasn't Blatter's opinion that led the voters to choose a mild-mannered bureaucrat over Sheikh Salman of Bahrain, Prince Ali of Jordan and Jérôme Champagne of France (Tokyo Sexwale of South Africa withdrew spectacularly before the voting, telling the candidates, "It's your problem now."), to replace their disgraced president. Nor did Blatter have any input in implementing the sweeping changes members approved hours before the election. Almost 4,000 miles away in Brooklyn, the real audience the voters were playing to—prosecutors from the U.S. Attorney's Office in the Eastern District of New York—surely felt some measure of satisfaction. Blatter was out and under investigation in Switzerland. His cohort, and Infantino's boss, Michel Platini, was out as well, linked to Blatter and a suspicious $2 million payment. Forty-one soccer officials and marketing officials had been indicted by the Department of Justice, 12 of them from FIFA's notorious Executive Committee. Reforms that included term limits for FIFA presidents—a maximum of 12 years, in four-year increments—were passed, along with revealing his or her salary. The reforms also stripped power from the Ex-Co and included a mandate that six women occupy top jobs. It had been made clear to the members that an acceptable replacement for Blatter, and substantial reforms, were vital to retaining the organization's one remaining trump card: its status with the DOJ as a victim of corruption rather than its perpetrator. Blatter said it best:

"I do hope our friends in the United States will accept that FIFA has promised these reforms, is doing these reforms, and that they will let us work in peace," he said after the measures were passed.

That may or may not happen. Blatter himself is still at risk of indictment. And even as the election took place, one of South Africa's top officials, Port Elizabeth Mayor Danny Jordaan—who is also the South African Football Association president—was conspicuously absent. Jordaan led the South African bid for the 2010 World Cup, which DOJ officials say was secured with a $10 million bribe shared by Jack Warner, Chuck Blazer and another unidentified Ex-Co member. Jordaan has not been indicted, but his absence prompted South African political opponents to question why he avoided Zurich, the site of a raid that nabbed seven officials in May 2015 and two others in December.

In the meantime, Infantino, described by one acquaintance as "humble and hard-working, usually near Michel at events. I know most people will think he's Platini's puppet, but he's his own man, and he loves football."

Perhaps, but Infantino also promised to double cash grants to the member federations, a campaign tactic Blatter had utilized over the years. As a longtime FIFA observer familiar with all the candidates put it: "He is the most suitable for what was being offered."

CHUCK BLAZER'S
TEAM OF CRONIES

SOCCER'S CROOKED DEAL MAKER COULDN'T DO IT BY HIMSELF. HE NEEDED HELP, NOT just from coconspirators but also indirectly from the top ranks of the Fédération Internationale de Football Association (FIFA), where fair play is left on the field, and doesn't extend to smoke-filled back rooms. Blazer's web of corruption and his cooperation with the federal government eventually entangled more than forty of soccer's international movers and shakers. Here's the roster of rogues.

SEPP BLATTER: There's no proof (so far) that FIFA's imperious president since 1998 ever took a bribe—but none that he ever stopped one from being taken, either. Reelected two days after police hauled away top FIFA officials in a May 2015 raid, Blatter subsequently announced in June that he would step aside once a suitable replacement was found. Suspended provisionally in October (by the FIFA ethics committee he'd established) pending a Swiss criminal investigation and hit with an eight-year ban in December, his sentence was reduced to six years in late February, two days before his successor was elected.

JÉRÔME VALCKE: The general secretary and Sepp's number two authorized a $10 million bank transfer central to the US federal case. The feds say it's a bribe paid to Jack Warner, Chuck Blazer, and a third, unnamed member of FIFA's executive committee (known as Ex-Co) in exchange for their votes in favor of South Africa's hosting the 2010 World Cup. Placed on leave by FIFA in September 2015, Valcke says the transfer was legit. Was found in 2006 to have violated FIFA ethics rules by negotiating with Visa when MasterCard already had an agreement, costing FIFA a $90 million settlement. Returned to FIFA in 2007. In February 2016, the FIFA ethics committee found Valcke guilty of wide-ranging misconduct including abuse of travel expenses, destroying evidence, and granting TV rights to the 2018 and 2027 World Cups far below their market value. He was banned for twelve years, four years longer than his Boss Blatter.

MICHEL PLATINI: A former French soccer star, Ex-Co member, and onetime president-in-waiting, Platini was suspended while Swiss authorities investigated claims against him and Blatter over a $2 million payment for work done by Platini years ago but not paid until 2011—possibly as a payoff for him not to run against Blatter. Banned by FIFA's ethics committee from all soccer-related activity for eight years, he officially withdrew his candidacy for the federation's presidency a month later. Like Blatter's, his ban was reduced to six years in late February, at which time he vowed an immediate appeal to the Court of Arbitration for Sport and claimed to be the victim of a system he was about to expose.

JOÃO HAVELANGE: As president of FIFA from 1974 to 1998, Havelange expanded the World Cup and broadened membership. He also laid the groundwork for epic and endemic corruption. With his former son-in-law, Ricardo Teixeira, he accepted millions from the sports marketing company International Sports and Leisure (ISL) in exchange for World Cup marketing rights—a conflict of interest, albeit one that was permitted at the time.

BRAZIL'S PAYOLA HAT TRICK

Years ago, the great Pelé railed against corruption in the Brazilian game, even tangling with Havelange and Teixeira over what he perceived as a corrupt television rights deal. He suffered for it both politically and publicly. But the striker was on target.

RICARDO TEIXEIRA: Corruption is part of the family. The ex-son-in-law of ex-FIFA president Havelange served as president of the Brazilian Football Confederation (CBF) and was a FIFA Ex-Co member. During his Ex-Co run, he and Havelange siphoned more than $41 million in bribes linked to the 2002 and 2006 World Cup marketing rights, according to a Swiss prosecutor's report in 2012. While those payments were not considered a crime at the time, Teixeira was among those indicted in December in the US on charges of conspiracy and money laundering. He has been charged separately in Brazil with tax evasion, forgery, and money laundering.

JOSÉ MARIA MARIN: A member of FIFA's club committee, which deals with developments and proposals involving teams and makes recommendations for changes to the FIFA Ex-Co, and Teixeira's successor at CBF. Marin agreed to extradition in November 2015 and is currently under house arrest at his Trump Tower apartment. "He's one of the rats I've been denouncing for a long time," said Romário, the former star Brazilian player, now a senator from Rio de Janeiro.

MARCO POLO DEL NERO: Del Nero, the third CBF boss to be charged with corruption, fled Zurich, Switzerland, in the wake of his indictment. He resigned from the FIFA Ex-Co on November 26, 2015. Returned to his job as head of the Brazilian Football Confederation in early January 2016 following a forty-five-day suspension to plan his legal defense.

THE CONCACAF CABAL

For the Confederation of North Central American and Caribbean Association Football—the main source of the Western Hemisphere's corruption infection—no deal was too small to steal from, and even charities were ripped off.

CHUCK BLAZER: The former CONCACAF general secretary, FIFA Ex-Co member, and all-around soccer scam artist became the key informant against fellow execs in November 2011. He secretly pled guilty in 2013 to racketeering, money laundering, income tax evasion, and bank wire fraud. As this book went to press, Blazer was ill with cancer and in hospice care in New Jersey, awaiting sentencing.

JACK WARNER: "The biggest piece of shit of all of them," one investigator called Warner, Blazer's partner in crime for two decades. The former head of CONCACAF, FIFA vice president, and Ex-Co member is accused of looting millions in FIFA and CONCACAF funds, accepting bribes for World Cup votes, and even stealing from Haiti's earthquake relief fund. Fighting extradition in Trinidad.

DARYLL AND DARYAN WARNER: Jack Warner's two sons pled guilty in July and October 2013 to wire fraud and money laundering. They traversed the country to make deposits in various banks in order to bypass reporting laws. Daryan Warner forfeited more than $1.1 million and agreed to a second forfeiture at his sentencing.

JEFFREY WEBB: The Ex-Co's favorite Cayman Islands banker, Webb set up accounts for his friends to stash cash. A former FIFA vice president who became president of CONCACAF in 2012—pledging reform—he took up Blazer's corruption habit immediately. The onetime president of the Cayman Islands Football Association pled guilty on November 23, 2015, to racketeering, wire fraud, and money laundering, and had to forfeit more than $6.7 million.

ALFREDO HAWIT: Following Jeffrey Webb's indictment in May 2015, Hawit replaced him as president of CONCACAF—only to be busted in Switzerland seven months later and charged with racketeering, fraud, and money laundering. In January 2016 Hawit agreed to extradition to the United States and entered a not guilty plea in Brooklyn in January.

RAFAEL ESQUIVEL: The Venezuelan Football Federation president allegedly solicited some $1 million in 2007 from Brazilian marketing company Traffic Sports, which organizes and manages the commercialization of soccer events throughout the Americas, including TV rights and sponsorships, for continued support as the exclusive holder of marketing rights to South America's soccer competition, the Copa América. Indicted in May 2015.

ARIEL ALVARADO: This member of the FIFA disciplinary committee is a former CONCACAF Ex-Co member and president of the Panamanian Football Federation. Indicted in December 2015.

RAFAEL CALLEJAS: Member of the FIFA television and marketing committee. Former Honduran soccer federation president and president of the Republic of Honduras. Indicted. Appeared before Judge Raymond J. Dearie on December 15, 2015, released on $4 million bond.

BRAYAN JIMÉNEZ: Guatemalan soccer federation president and member of FIFA committee for fair play and social responsibility. Indicted.

EDUARDO LI: Costa Rica's national football chief was due to join FIFA's Ex-Co two days after the May raid when he was indicted. Alleged to have accepted massive bribes. Waged a hard-fought extradition battle before finally dropping his appeal in mid-December.

JULIO ROCHA LOPEZ: FIFA development officer from Nicaragua.

RAFAEL SALGUERO: Former FIFA Ex-Co member and Guatemalan soccer federation president. In September, according to court documents, Salguero met with Hawit and Alvarado and told them in reference to the US investigation: "The three of us are in the same shit." Indicted in December.

COSTAS TAKKAS: An attaché to Jeffrey Webb, the ex–CONCACAF president. From Great Britain. Former general secretary of the Cayman Islands Football Association (CIFA). Indicted in May.

HECTOR TRUJILLO: Current Guatemalan soccer federation general secretary. He was a judge on the Constitutional Court of Guatemala prior to his indictment. Released on $4 million bond on January 7.

REYNALDO VASQUEZ: Former Salvadoran soccer federation president. Indicted in December.

MANUEL BURGA: Former member of FIFA development committee and former Peruvian soccer federation president. Indicted in December.

THE CONMEBOL CLIQUE

They ran South America's soccer associations to benefit themselves.

JUAN ÁNGEL NAPOUT: The president of the South American football governing body CONMEBOL, from Paraguay, was arrested in a second predawn raid in Switzerland. Charged with racketeering, wire fraud, and money laundering. Agreed to extradition on December 7, 2015. Resigned days later and appeared before Judge Dearie on December 15. Called "an embezzling, filthy rat bastard" in 2012 by Marcelo Recanate, president of Paraguay's Club Olimpia.

JOSÉ LUIS MEISZNER: The CONMEBOL general secretary turned himself in on December 10, 2015, in Quilmes, Argentina; former president of Quilmes AC soccer club. Accused of bribing officials for exclusive broadcast rights to Argentine national team's tournament matches.

NICOLÁS LEOZ: The former FIFA Ex-Co member and CONMEBOL president, arrested in Paraguay, allegedly took bribes over two decades for awarding companies marketing and media rights to Copa América. Under house arrest in Asunción, Paraguay; extradition to the US approved by Paraguayan courts in December 2015.

LUIS BEDOYA: Member of the Ex-Co, a CONMEBOL vice president, and, until November 2015, president of the Colombian soccer federation.

Pled guilty to racketeering and wire fraud. Forfeited all funds in his Swiss bank account.

EUGENIO FIGUEREDO: CONMEBOL president accused of taking millions from a Uruguayan sports marketing company tied to marketing rights for the Copa América in 2015, 2016, 2019, and 2023.

CARLOS CHÁVEZ: CONMEBOL treasurer. Former Bolivian soccer federation president. Arrested and jailed in Bolivia in July and accused of "alleged corruption in the management of resources," according to Bolivia's public prosecutor. Indicted by US authorities in December.

LUIS CHIRIBOGA: Ecuadorian soccer federation president and member of CONMEBOL Ex-Co. Four days after his indictment, Ecuador ordered his arrest.

EDUARDO DELUCA: Former CONMEBOL general secretary, deputy to Nicolas Leoz, resigned in 2011, citing health reasons. Indicted in December 2015.

ROMER OSUNA: Former member of the FIFA audit and compliance committee. Former CONMEBOL treasurer. Indicted in December 2015.

SERGIO JADUE, CONMEBOL vice president and president of the Chilean soccer federation. Pled guilty to racketeering and wire fraud. Forfeited all funds in US bank account.

SPORTS MARKETERS—THE GRAFT KINGS

As the value of sports programming rose, those who owned a piece of it stood to make millions. Marketing firms lined up to hand out bribes to soccer officials, whose lust for payoffs seemed unquenchable.

JOSE HAWILLA: Founder of Traffic Group, the Brazilian sports marketing conglomerate at the heart of bribery allegations facing top officials at CONCACAF and CONMEBOL. Pled guilty on December 12, 2014, to racketeering, wire fraud, money laundering, and obstruction of justice.

Agreed to forfeit more than $151 million. His companies, Traffic Sports International and Traffic Sports USA, pled guilty on May 14, 2015, to wire fraud conspiracy. In the United States, awaiting sentencing.

HUGO AND MARIANO JINKIS: Controlling principals of Full Play Group SA, a sports marketing business based in Argentina, where the father-son duo surrendered in June after May indictment. Won release from house arrest in Buenos Aires but were ordered to remain within thirty-seven miles of the courthouse. The indictment says that Full Play paid millions in bribes to gain the TV rights to the South American World Cup qualifying matches.

ALEJANDRO BURZACO: Controlling principal of Torneos y Competencias SA, a sports marketing company based in Argentina. Indicted in May and pled guilty on November 16, 2015, to racketeering, wire fraud, and money laundering. Agreed to forfeit more than $21.6 million.

ZORANA DANIS: Close friend of Blazer's who dined with him frequently at Elaine's. Feasted on bribes related to the Copa Libertadores, a famous South American club tournament. Founder of International Soccer Marketing, a Jersey City, New Jersey, company. Pled guilty May 26, 2105, to wire fraud and filing false tax returns. Forfeited $2 million.

ROGER HUGUET: CEO of Media World, a Miami-based sports marketing company. Pled guilty to wire fraud conspiracy, one count of money laundering. Forfeited more than $600,000.

JOSÉ MARGULIES: Controlling principal of the soccer broadcasting companies Valente Corp. and Somerton Ltd. Bagman for illicit payments between sports marketing executives and soccer officials. Pled guilty on November 25, 2015, to racketeering, wire fraud, and money laundering. Agreed to forfeit more than $9.2 million.

FABIO TORDIN: Former CEO of Traffic Sports USA and an executive with Media World. Pled guilty to wire fraud and tax evasion. Forfeited more than $600,000.

ACKNOWLEDGMENTS

MARY PAPENFUSS: This is how it started.

"I've found myself in the soccer mafia, but if I tell you about it, they'll have to kill me."

That comment launched this book. It was told to me by an old friend who had come to one of my readings for an earlier book in Barnes & Noble on Manhattan's Upper West Side the summer of 2014. Mary Lynn Blanks happened to see my photo in the window and took the opportunity to reconnect after so many years. We had been young moms together when our children attended the same New York elementary school in the neighborhood, PS 9. I eventually moved to California and she stepped into a very different lifestyle. When she approached me in the bookstore, I was surrounded by people and didn't have time to talk to her then, but her remark stuck in my mind. I reached out to her the next time I was in New York.

We spent hours the day I returned walking in Central Park and she told me of her years of incredible experiences: having tea with the Queen of England, jetting to the Caribbean from Africa with Nelson Mandela next to her in a private jet, chatting with Mick Jagger. She traveled regularly to Zurich, and visited London and Marrakech, Johannesburg, Singapore, Doha, and Berlin. I was agog. Most fascinating of all were the accounts about her ex-lover, Chuck Blazer, a larger-than-life Svengali who spent $290,000 a year on Trump Tower rent in Manhattan and ran American soccer. Who knew? I told her he sounded like drug dealers who spend fortunes on rents, refusing to buy property for fear that big-ticket, recorded purchases would pique the interest of the IRS—and alert agents to millions of dollars in unpaid taxes. "Wait," she said. "I'm getting to that."

That's when she told me that Blazer was a tax cheat and the FBI and IRS had used the crime to force his cooperation in an extensive investigation into the Fédération Internationale de Football Association. Blazer had been secretly recording his soccer colleagues for three years.

I immediately worried that the probe was nearing the end of its shelf life and indictments could be issued any day; there was no time like the present to tell the story. I called Ellen Tumposky, an editor friend at the New York *Daily News*, where I used to work on the city desk. I told her to walk into the sports editor's office and say: "Chuck Blazer has been cooperating with the FBI for three years to take down FIFA." I had no idea who the sports editor was. Ellen delivered my message. Teri Thompson phoned me within minutes.

TERI THOMPSON: As Ellen walked into my office I was meeting with Nate Vinton, a member of our Sports Investigative Team, about the same topic—the Eastern District of New York's investigation into corruption in the highest ranks of international soccer. We had begun looking for a New York angle in the spring of 2014 in the wake of the very fine reporting on FIFA corruption coming out of Britain and had pressed our best sources for help. By June, we had solid, exclusive information about the Eastern District's investigation and Blazer's possible involvement, a bombshell for sure, but I wasn't comfortable going to press without additional confirmation and more detail on Blazer. Throughout the summer, Nate and another member of our team, Christian Red, and I began poring over the various reports and documents commissioned by FIFA and CONCACAF, contacting every name we came across, from lawyers to judges to politicians to administrators to accountants and law enforcement agents. We carefully mined the news reports and outlined our story. We were confident in our reporting, but having produced years of game-changing sports investigations, I knew that something was missing. And then Ellen Tumposky stepped into my office.

MARY AND TERI: During the heady days of preparations for the first story for the *Daily News*, we continued to pore over thousands of pages of documents. We scrutinized tax forms, emails, credit card bills, and internal investigation reports. We spent hours quizzing Mary Lynn, people she connected us with, and a burgeoning pool of investigative sources. We continued to contact lawyers, auditors, and officials and staff working for soccer organizations; armed with more information, we sought comment from numerous federal law enforcement officers. We approached Blazer himself, first through his attorneys and friends, and then directly at the medical facility where he was residing (limited by a gag order by the feds, he declined to be interviewed).

Mary Lynn was nervous. She had walked out on Blazer almost a year after he began cooperating with the FBI, and had left her high life far behind. But she knew the FBI was monitoring everyone linked to Blazer. She also worried about the physical danger of a story baring a worldwide scam and retaliation from people who she suspected were stealing millions; some of them frightened her. We code-named her "George" in our conversations and emails to protect her identity.

Our first *Daily News* story hit the front page on November 1. It revealed the massive Eastern District investigation into FIFA and detailed Blazer's role in it. The piece was picked up around the world from the *Guardian* and the BBC to the *Sydney Morning Herald* and the *New York Times*.

But then, silence. We continued to work the story, and published updates, but there was a disquieting lull from investigators, and no follow-ups from the media on the Eastern District's probe. Had the undercover operation been a bust, we wondered. Was there a grand jury? Had the feds somehow pulled the plug? We had information that the crackdown was targeting top FIFA executives, including vice president Jack Warner of Trinidad and several others, and could include warrants and even arrests in Zurich, but was that really possible? We began to worry as the months dragged on.

Suddenly, the story broke larger than anything we had imagined. The long arm of American law indeed reached across the ocean on May 27, 2015, to pluck FIFA officials from the very bosom of their outlandish privilege at the plush digs of Zurich's Baur au Lac Hotel, where they were gathered for an annual FIFA meeting. The number of names linked to the indictments burgeoned in the following months. Even governments were swept up in influencing World Cup decisions. FIFA president Sepp Blatter would report near the end of 2015 that both France and Germany pushed for the controversial choice of Qatar to host the 2022 World Cup because both countries had economic interests in the nation and stood to profit from a major sports event there. The world began to look like one giant soccer crime syndicate.

We pressed on with the story for this book. We developed more sources, uncovered new documents, delved deeper into the drama and the personalities behind the crimes. Mary Lynn was absolutely essential. Her access to intimate details about Chuck Blazer and their shared FIFA and CONCACAF life, as well as her attention to detail, honesty, and endless curiosity about everything she had seen and experienced, was critical. She graciously shared with us an exploration of a past that was both splendiferous and painful for her. She believed in that journey and that the story was important to tell.

We are also indebted to others in the creation of this book. Longtime CONCACAF workers Jill Fracisco, Tim Longo, and Mel Brennan shared their experiences and key observations about Chuck Blazer, the way he ran his office, and their suspicions. Ted Howard provided valuable information about CONCACAF history. Clive Toye, straight from the old glory days of New York City's "Pelé Cosmos," was as entertaining and provocative as ever—and incredibly gracious and generous with his time—as he walked us through the history of American soccer and shared his insights into Chuck Blazer as well as into the evolution of soccer and its twisted administration.

Simon Strong of Tenacitas International in Miami helped unravel the net that later fell on Chuck Blazer, and guided us through some of the intricacies of his critically important investigation into CONCACAF. Lisle Austin was open and frank about his long, sometimes dramatic, history on the board of CONCACAF and, briefly, as its president.

Lasana Liburd, reporter extraordinaire for Wired868 in Trinidad, has been shouting a warning for years through his journalism about Jack Warner. He provided a wealth of information about Warner and his schemes, and a fascinating perspective from Warner's island nation. Kelvin Jack, a member of the Soca Warriors, the Trinidad soccer team that went to the 2006 World Cup, and one of the players who sued Warner when they were cheated out their pay, shared his insights into Warner and what's it's like to be a flesh-and-blood victim of the CONCACAF and FIFA scandals.

Jon. Krabbenschmidt explained some of the intricacies of financial statements and accounting and auditing procedures, and the law, and pointed out the most obvious flaws in CONCACAF records. Watchdog Michael Hershman of the Foxcroft Group has a wealth of experience up close and personal with FIFA and shared his surprises and disappointments. University of Brighton professor and author Alan Tomlinson provided intriguing historical details and analysis of FIFA's evolution through the years. Johannesburg-based researcher and writer Dale McKinley had the perspective and the numbers to demonstrate that South Africa's World Cup was far from the bonanza everyone had expected. Charlie Stillitano's insight into the world of sports marketing was invaluable.

Chuck Blazer's pals from Elaine's offered an intriguing portrait of the man at play. Some of them included friends of ours, who were reluctant to have their names used because they're loyal to Blazer to this day, which was an education in itself. Photographer Neil Leifer perfectly articulated the impression Blazer made at Elaine's.

ACKNOWLEDGMENTS

Woody Salvan, Murray Vale, and Kirby Sales helped us travel through time for a glimpse at the young Chuck. Sax man Lonnie Youngblood shared his experiences with the party-loving Blazer. Bernard Spain told the intriguing history of the smiley face button and his not-so-happy business relationship with Blazer.

Thanks to our agent Rachel Sussman for championing our proposal and seeing us over the speed bumps, and ICM film agent Josie Freedman for selling the film rights in record time to Red Wagon and Broad Green, whose executives were so infectiously enthusiastic. We owe a debt of gratitude to Harper-Collins executive editor David Hirshey for believing that this book is the one people will want to read and for editing it along with Bill Saporito. Thanks, too, to Kate Lyons, for shepherding the manuscript through the byzantine production process.

We also owe huge thanks to the best lawyer anyone could find, the incomparable Tom Harvey, who not only guided us through the contractual process of producing a book but provided invaluable help on the manuscript itself. Thank you, Matthew Hiltzik, for your invaluable counsel.

MARY: This has been an incredible journey guided by a thoughtful, insightful witness to history, Mary Lynn. Thanks, ML. Big thanks go to Teri, who made the task of writing this book in short order not only possible but also fun. I'm grateful to my California friends, particularly Bryan and Nancy Kemnitzer, Shaila and Madhav Misra, and Kipp Delbyck, who put up with countless, breathless tales about Chuck Blazer, CONCACAF, and FIFA. Thanks, too, to my earliest story cheerleader, Maralyn Matlick.

My long-suffering kids, Leda and Luke, who are always excited about what I'm doing, didn't complain—too much—when I was curled up with my computer instead of them. Not making me feel guilty is golden, guys. And finally, to my eternally supportive husband, Roland Cline, who has generously shared me over a lifetime with my other paramours: my laptop, my phone, and the next story, which he always wants to hear about. I love you, Rol.

TERI: Thanks to Mary for including me in this project and for your patience, diligence, and good humor, and of course to Mary Lynn Blanks for her courage and willingness to share her life with Chuck Blazer with us. I can't imagine two better collaborators. Thanks to Ellen Tumposky, a gift to the craft. My eternal gratitude to my husband, Jim Herre, the best editor I've ever worked with and the most supportive partner I could hope for. Thanks for loving this project and encouraging me every step of the way. Couldn't do it without you. Thanks to my always supportive family, my mom, Nettie Thompson, the best role model a girl could have, and Nancy and Cheryl, the best sisters a girl could

ACKNOWLEDGMENTS

have, and the kids, John Sears and Erin Heim, and the brothers-in-law, Jeff Sears and David Heim. My dad, Jess Thompson, is always with me. Thanks to Mary Jo Kinser and Greg Hawkins, and Marie McGovern and Martin Dunn, the best editor I ever worked for, and to Bill Madden and Mike Lupica, for your unfailing support and friendship. Thanks to Frankie Saponaro, Joe Tito, Jerry Balch, and the guys and gals at the clubhouse. Thanks to *Daily News* court reporter John Marzulli, a tremendous help to us in the Eastern District, and managing editor Rob Moore, who made our story better. Nate, Christian, and Mike O'Keeffe, thank you for all you've done for me, not only on this project, but in our years of difficult, game-changing work. You are the best sports investigative team out there. Last but certainly not least, thanks to the faithful, dependable, informed sources who stay in the background, willing to take the risks to help tell a story.

BIBLIOGRAPHY

Allison, Lincoln. *The Global Politics of Sport: The Role of Global Institutions in Sport*. London: Routledge, 2005.

Blake, Heidi, and Jonathan Calvert. *The Ugly Game: The Qatari Plot to Buy the World Cup*. London: Simon & Schuster, 2015.

Bondy, Filip. *Chasing the Game*. Cambridge, MA: Da Capo Press, 2010.

Doyle, John. *The World Is a Ball: The Joy, Madness, and Meaning of Soccer*. Emmaus, PA: Rodale, 2010.

Foer, Franklin. *How Soccer Explains the World: An Unlikely Theory of Globalization*. New York: HarperCollins, 2004.

Forrest, Brett. *The Big Fix: The Hunt for the Match-Fixers Bringing Down Soccer*. New York: William Morrow Paperbacks, 2015.

Goldblatt, David. *The Ball Is Round: A Global History of Soccer*. New York: Riverhead, 2008.

Haner, Jim. *Soccerhead: An Accidental Journey into the Heart of the American Game*. New York: North Point Press, 2007.

Hill, Declan. *The Fix: Soccer and Organized Crime*. Toronto: McClelland & Stewart, 2008.

Hopkins, Gary. *Star-Spangled Soccer: The Selling, Marketing and Management of Soccer in the USA*. Basingstoke, UK: Palgrave Macmillan, 2010.

Hornby, Nick. *Fever Pitch*. New York: Riverhead, 1998.

Jennings, Andrew. *The Dirty Game: Uncovering the Scandal at FIFA*. London: Century, 2015.

———. *Foul! The Secret World of FIFA: Bribes, Vote Rigging and Ticket Scandals.* London: HarperSport, 2006.

———. *Omertà: La FIFA di Seep Blatter, una famiglia criminale organizzata.* Rome: Rizzoli, 2015.

Korr, Charles P., and Marvin Close. *More Than Just a Game: Soccer vs. Apartheid: The Most Important Soccer Story Ever Told.* New York: Thomas Dunne Books, 2010.

Kuhn, Gabriel. *Soccer vs. the State: Tackling Football and Radical Politics.* Oakland, CA: PM Press, 2011.

Kuper, Simon. *Football Against the Enemy.* London: Orion, 2003.

Kuper, Simon, and Stefan Szymanski. *Soccernomics: Why England Loses, Why Germany and Brazil Win, and Why the US, Japan, Australia, Turkey and Even Iraq Are Destined to Become the Kings of the World's Most Popular Sport.* New York: Nation, 2009.

La Grange, Zelda. *Good Morning, Mr. Mandela: A Memoir.* New York: Plume, 2015.

Messing, Shep, and David Hirshey. *The Education of an American Soccer Player.* New York: Dodd, Mead, 1978.

Newsham, Gavin. *Once in a Lifetime: The Incredible Story of the New York Cosmos.* New York: Grove, 2006.

Once in a Lifetime: The Extraordinary Story of the New York Cosmos. DVD. Directed by Paul Crowder and John Dower. Santa Monica, CA: Miramax: July 7, 2006.

Pelé, and Brian Winter. *Why Soccer Matters.* London: Celebra, 2014.

Plenderleith, Ian. *Rock 'n' Roll Soccer: The Short Life and Fast Times of the North American Soccer League.* New York: Thomas Dunne Books, 2015.

Romano, Christiano. *FIFA's Corruption Scandal—Everything You Need to Know: A World Cup of Money.* New York: Rounders, 2015.

Seese, Dennis J. *The Rebirth of Professional Soccer in America: The Strange Days of the United Soccer Association.* Lanham, MD: Rowman & Littlefield, 2015.

Singh, Valentino. *Upwards Through the Night: The Biography of Austin Jack Warner.* Port of Spain: Lexicon Trinidad, 1998.

Spurling, Jon. *Death or Glory: The Dark History of the World Cup.* London: VSP, 2010.

Sudgen, John, and Alan Tomlinson. *Badfellas: FIFA Family at War.* London: Mainstream, 2003.

Szymanski, Stefan. *Playbooks and Checkbooks: An Introduction to the Economics of Modern Sports.* Princeton, NJ: Princeton University Press, 2009.

Tomlinson, Alan. *FIFA: The Men, the Myths and the Money*. London: Routledge, 2014.

Toye, Clive. *Anywhere in the World*. Haworth, NJ: St. Johann Press, 2015.

———. *A Kick in the Grass: The Slow Rise and Quick Demise of the NASL*. Haworth, NJ: St. Johann Press, 2006.

Vecsey, George. *Eight World Cups: My Journey Through the Beauty and Dark Side of Soccer*. New York: Times Books, 2014.

Wangerin, David. *Soccer in a Football World: The Story of America's Forgotten Game*. Philadelphia: Temple University Press, 2008.

Warner, Jack, with Valentino Singh, *Zero to Hero: Jack Austin Warner, the Man Who Inspired Trinidad and Tobago to Its First World Cup*. San Juan: Lexicon Trinidad, 2006.

Winner, David. *Brilliant Orange: The Neurotic Genius of Dutch Soccer*. Woodstock, NY: Overlook Press, 2008.

NOTES

INTRODUCTION

ix *Early on a November evening in 2011*: Descriptions of Blazer's agreement with federal agents to cooperate in the Eastern District investigation from eyewitness Mary Lynn Blanks.

x *As general secretary of CONCACAF . . . Blazer and Trinidad and Tobago's Jack Warner . . . had helped themselves to millions in kickbacks and bribes*: United States of America against Jeffrey Webb, Eduardo Li, Julio Rocca et al., May 20, 2015 (May Eastern District indictment).

x *He often carried bundles of cash through airports*: Mary Lynn Blanks, Eastern District changes of Willful Failure to File Report of Foreign Bank and Financial Accounts.

x *The agents needed less than an hour to flip him*: Blazer's account to Blanks following meeting with federal agents.

xi *"They've got me for RICO . . . Racketeering, embezzlement, fraud income tax"*: Blanks, May Eastern District indictment.

xi *There was his $29 million in American Express charges*: The Confederation of North, Central and Caribbean Association Football Integrity Committee Report of Investigation Presented to the Executive Committee of CONCACAF, April 18, 2013; copies of Amex bills.

xiv *Blazer lay ill with cancer in a New Jersey medical facility*: From accounts of friends and associates.

CHAPTER ONE: TEETERING AT THE TOP

1 *Chuck Blazer was pale, breathing hard*: Descriptions of Blazer in his apartment during the bin Hammam cash-for-votes scandal, May 10–13, 2011, from eyewitness Mary Lynn Blanks.

1 *his address was also a reassuringly sublime perch*: Blazer spoke several times to Blanks, coworkers, and friends about what living in Trump Tower meant to him, and often repeated the story about his grandfather Max washing windows in Midtown Manhattan (page 2).

2 *spotty phone call he had just concluded*: Content and chronology of phone calls between Anton Sealey, president of the Bahamas Football Association (BFA), and Blazer revealed in affidavits from Sealey, Blazer, and whistle-blower Fred Lunn, vice president of the BFA, all gathered by former US Attorney for the Northern District of Illinois John Collins, of the Chicago law firm Collins & Collins, who was hired by Blazer on May 15, 2011, to investigate the cash-for-votes scandal.

2 *on his block on 193rd Street in Flushing*: Address of his childhood family home provided by Chuck Blazer to Blanks.

4 *brown envelopes stuffed with $40,000 in cash*: The Port of Spain meeting and cash exchange are described in detail by Fred Lunn in a May 14, 2011, memo to Blazer and in his affidavit, as well as in the investigative report prepared by attorney John Collins, and in a probe for FIFA by Freeh Group International Solutions conducted by former FBI director Louis Freeh (report June 29, 2011). Events were also recounted in the FIFA ethics committee decision suspending Mohamed bin Hammam (May 29, 2011) and by the Court of Arbitration for Sport ruling lifting the suspension (July 19, 2012). Details also revealed in the Eastern District superseding indictment December 3, 2015.

5 *"Dear Brother," bin Hammam wrote*: From an e-mail exchange between Mohamed bin Hammam and Jack Warner on April 1, 2011.

5 *"I hope this is an April Fool's joke"*: First line of an e-mail from Blazer to Warner April 1, 2011; first Warner e-mail response to Blazer, April 1.

6 *his reading of the North and Central American members of CONCACAF*: E-mail from Blazer to Warner, April 3, 2011.

7 *bin Hammam did not want to attend the Miami congress*: From an e-mail written by Warner to Blazer, April 4, 2011.

8 *"This isn't going to end well"*: From a conversation between Blazer and Blanks in their Trump Tower apartment, May 13, 2011.

CHAPTER TWO: ON THE HUSTLE

9 *stunned to receive a letter out of the clear blue*: Letter written by Chuck Blazer to Mary Lynn Blanks, October 15, 2002.

9 *She was left trembling and spattered with her own blood*: Account of confrontation by Mary Lynn Blanks; injuries corroborated by her friend Cynthia Georgeson, who arrived on the scene shortly after.

11 *met while she was modeling for a print ad for the Seagram's liquor company*: Account of first meeting with Chuck Blazer from Blanks.

11 *Blazer was there plugging products*: Blazer's history of his incentives and promotional marketing businesses through corporations registered in Delaware based on his own accounts to several friends, colleagues, and business associates, including Bernard Spain, and Delaware corporation records. Blanks visited the Wham-O and Kentucky Fried Chicken headquarters with Blazer while he was on business calls, and attended Frisbee "fly-in" events.

12 *"Chuck could sell ice in Alaska"*: Blazer's sales skills based on interview with a longtime CONCACAF worker as well as with Blazer's friends and colleagues, including his CONCACAF deputy Ted Howard and colleague Clive Toye.

12 *Blazer's Spa Luncheonette*: Name, location, and work described by Blazer to Mary Lynn Blanks and his friends and employees. He provided the address to Blanks. His parents took out an ad Blazer's senior year in his 1961 high school yearbook confirming the name and the address of the business.

12 *"He was incredibly personable"*: Blazer's early aptitude for sales success based on interviews with Queens neighbors and classmates, including Sherwood "Woody" Salvan and Kirby Sales.

12 *treasured spot in the Bronx High School of Science*: From Blazer's Forest Hills High School transcripts.

13 *checking hall passes*: Based on interviews with Blazer's high school classmates Murray Vale, Rhoda Berke, and Woody Salvan, and information from Blazer's 1961 Forest Hills High yearbook.

13 *graduated in January*: From Blazer's Forest Hills High School transcripts.

13 *The invisible student would win sweet revenge*: Account of fiftieth high school reunion party by Blazer in his blog, and by Blanks, members of Blazer's graduating class, his friends, and bandleader Lonnie Youngblood.

15 *"a half century of memories and accomplishment"*: "50th High School Reunion," from Chuck Blazer, *Travels with Chuck Blazer and His Friends* (blog), September 18, 2011, http://chuckblazer.blogspot.com/2011/09/it-seemed-quite-impossible-but-here-it.html.

15 *earned a degree in accounting at New York University*: NYU transcripts.

16 *usually registering them in Delaware*: From Chuck Blazer's accounts to Mary Lynn Blanks, confirmed by registration documents in Delaware.

17 *Remember the Smiley Face button?*: History of the Smiley Face icon from the Harvey Ball World Smile Foundation in Worchester, Massachusetts, and from Jimmy Stamp, "Who Really Invented the Smiley Face?," *Smithsonian*, March 13, 2013; and interview with Bernard Spain.

18 *when he responded to a lawsuit by Singer in 1984*: From a hearing transcript from the lawsuit *Fred Singer Direct Marketing, Inc., v. Charles Blazer, Susan Blazer and Windmill Promotions, Inc.*, Supreme Court of the State of New York, County of Westchester, filed November 13, 1984.

19 *volunteered to coach his children's teams*: Account of Blazer's work in Westchester youth soccer from Blazer, in press accounts, and from fellow members of the New Rochelle Soccer Club, the Westchester Youth Soccer League, and the Eastern New York Youth Soccer Association (ENYSSA).

20 *one of the first sponsors of a children's soccer team in the nation*: Tripp Mickle, "Trail Blazer," *Sports Business Journal*, June 7, 2010.

20 *"most powerful American in the world of soccer"*: From profiles in ENYYSA's Hall of Fame, www.enyssa.com/docs/2011%20ENYSHOF.pdf.

23 *He told her, again, that she was the love of his life*: Blanks's account of the encounter in Blazer's Trump Tower apartment.

CHAPTER THREE: BIRTH OF A SOCCER FIEFDOM

25 *hadn't made much headway in the twenty-three years*: Account of CONCACAF history by association general secretary and Blazer's former deputy, Ted Howard; from Clive Toye; and from *CONCACAF Integrity Committee Report of Investigation*.

26 *in frigid upstate New York*: Account of planned CONCACAF game involving Rochester Lancers from interview with Clive Toye and in Toye, *A Kick in the Grass* (Haworth, NJ: St. Johann Press, 2006). 42; information about 1971 CONCACAF Champions Cup tournament also available in Rochester Lancers history online, www.rochesterlancers.com/lancers.php.

26 *tens of millions of dollars*: CONCACAF Integrity Committee Report of Investigation, 5.

27 *Toye was in on the pulse-quickening first wave of US soccer*: Account of American soccer history beginning in the late 1960s based on interviews with several soccer officials, including Toye and Howard, and on details in various press reports and magazine articles, as well as in Ian Plenderleith, *Rock 'n' Roll Soccer: The Short Life and Fast Times of the North American*

Soccer League (New York: Thomas Dunne Books, 2015); Toye, *Kick in the Grass*; and *Anywhere in the* World (Haworth, NJ: St. Johann Press, 2015); and Gary Hopkins, *Star-Spangled Soccer: The Selling, Marketing and Management of Soccer in the USA* (Basingstoke, UK: Palgrave Macmillan, 2010).

28 *stumped by a game that didn't have built-in breaks for commercials*: Toye, *Kick in the Grass*, 8.

28 *referee Peter Rhodes admitted after the game that he had pressured players to milk after the game*: Milton Richman, "League in Panic," *Ottawa (Canada) Journal*, May 16, 1967, www.newspapers.com/newspage/44396509.

28 *Few elite American athletes played soccer*: Details of teams and crowd attendance on the comprehensive online site the American Soccer History Archives, http://homepages.sover.net/~spectrum; also Toye, *Kick in the Grass* and *Anywhere in the World*, and Plenderleith, *Rock 'n' Roll Soccer*.

28 *The NPSL also had to battle for fans*: Dennis J. Seese, *The Rebirth of Professional Soccer in America: The Strange Days of the United Soccer Association* (Lanham, MD: Rowman & Littlefield, 2015).

29 *"the hostility of the baseball people"*: Toye, *Anywhere in the World*, 13.

29 *Ahmet and Nesuhi Ertegun, soccer-obsessed Turkish American brothers*: Cosmos history in Gavin Newsham, *Once in a Lifetime: The Incredible Story of the New York Cosmos* (New York: Grove, 2006), as well as accounts by Clive Toye.

30 *pulled off the soccer coup of the century*: Based on Toye's account of recruiting the soccer superstar and on Pelé's memoir, Pelé and Brian Winter, chaps. 6–8 in *Why Soccer Matters* (London: Celebra, 2014).

31 *"It was hard not to be in awe—every day"*: *Once in a Lifetime: The Extraordinary Story of the New York Cosmos*, directed by Paul Crowder and John Dower (Santa Monica, CA: Miramax: July 7, 2006), DVD.

33 *He wrangled an endorsement from Pelé*: Account of campaign by Pelé that helped Blazer win a position on the board of the US Soccer Federation in *Why Soccer Matters*; and Blazer's own account in Mickle, "Trail Blazer."

34 *Warner also recognized that he could be a kingmaker in FIFA*: Warner's early life and rise to soccer power are described in Valentino Singh, *Upwards Through the Night: The Biography of Austin Jack Warner* (Port of Spain: Lexicon Trinidad, 1998).

34 *Blazer joined forces with his neighbor and youth-coach nemesis Toye*: Interview with Toye.

35 *draining the franchise's dwindling income for pricey dinners*: Ken Bensinger, "Mr. Ten Percent: The Man Who Built—and Bilked—American Soccer," BuzzFeed, June 6, 2014.

35 *"I was able to see past the officialdom"*: Singh, *Upwards Through the Night*, 30.

36 *"One cannot imagine"*: Ibid., 31.

36 *Warner was accused*: Ibid., 35.

36 *"The place was packed like sardines"*: George Vecsey, *Eight World Cups, My Journey Through the Beauty and Dark Side of Soccer* (New York: Times Books, 2014), 67.

37 *The event was so chaotic*: Based on interviews with Lasana Liburd, reporter, reporter, editor of Wired868.

37 *He had lied earlier*: Singh, *Upwards Through the Night*, 40–43.

37 *"Did Warner believe he was God?"*: Andrew Jennings, *Even More Foul: The Story of FIFA Corruption* (Andrew Jennings, self-published, 2014), 92.

38 *"man behind the man"*: Blazer's account of helping Warner win the presidency of CONCACAF, as told to Mary Lynn Blanks.

38 *provided fees and a 10 percent commission*: From Chuck Blazer 1990 contract signed by Blazer and Jack Warner.

38 *Sportvertising, which was eventually registered in the tax haven of the Cayman Islands*: CONCACAF Integrity Committee Report of Investigation, 42.

39 *After 1991, the two were off to the races*: Blazer pled guilty to ten counts of racketeering, wire fraud, money laundering, and tax evasion, confessing to Judge Raymond Dearie in court November 25, 2013 (transcript unsealed by Dearie, June 3, 2015) that he and Jack Warner took bribes for every Gold Cup after 1991 until he left CONCACAF in 2011.

CHAPTER FOUR: PLAYBOY OF WESTERN CONCACAF

41 *In the summer of 2001*: Blazer often discussed his 2001 vacation in the Hamptons with friends, coworkers, and Blanks, and frequently showed off a photo of a female friend posing nude on the grill at the rental; accounts confirmed by C.T.

42 *a longtime girlfriend*: Accounts by Blazer, friends, and CONCACAF employees who knew C.T. and were aware that she had an office in the CONCACAF headquarters and lived with Blazer in Trump Tower; confirmed by C.T.

44 *a mini-iteration of the World Cup*: History and success of the Gold Cup based on CONCACAF income records and details from Jill Fracisco, who ran the tournaments for twenty years, and Blazer's deputy, Ted Howard.

44 *Traffic Sports International of South America and its American affiliate, Traffic Sports USA*: from United States of America against Jeffrey Webb, Eduardo Li, Julio Rocca et al., May 20, 2015 (May Eastern District indictment).

45 *By 2009, the Gold Cup had helped boost CONCACAF revenues to $35 million*: CONCACAF Integrity Committee Report of Investigation, 5.

45 *With an initial "six-figure" bribe*: Bribe details revealed in account in the May and December Eastern District indictments. Blazer admitted accepting the bribes in United States District Court in Brooklyn in a November 23, 2013, appearance before Justice Raymond Dearie.

46 *worked out a deal*: CONCACAF rent arrangement and "barter system," allowing some to use offices for free, based on reports from CONCACAF staff members.

47 *A key Blazer coup*: Based on several press accounts and a statement from FIFA and Blazer.

48 *FIFA's annual Ex-Co pay*: Estimates based on investigators, press accounts, CONCACAF employees, and Blazer's FIFA pension documents.

49 *he rang up $29 million in expenses on his black Amex card*: Details from copies of Blazer's American Express bills; *CONCACAF Integrity Committee Report of Investigation*, 63–65.

49 *ascended to what he considered restaurant heaven*: Blazer's Manhattan high life described by several friends, including Elaine's regulars, CONCACAF staff members Jill Fracisco, Mel Brennan, Tim Longo, and Ted Howard, and by Mary Lynn Blanks.

51 *"it's just an ethnic sport for girls in schools"*: Juliet Macur, "Reform Chief Questions United States Involvement in FIFA, Defends Sepp Blatter," *New York Times*, August 24, 2015.

52 *Blazer celebrated his sixtieth birthday*: Information on birthday party from friends, colleagues and employees; guest list obtained from employee.

53 *In one conversation, he boasted to an apparently young "Oh Kissa"*: From screenshot of chat from Chuck Blazer's computer.

55 *Blazer's obesity complicated daily living*: Account of daily routine from Mary Lynn Blanks and CONCACAF workers.

57 *a Blazer account registered to MultiSport Games Development Inc.*: Details from obtained copies of the 2007, 2008, 2009 and 2011 annual reports for Blazer's MultiSport Games Development Merrill Lynch account.

57 *guarded access to most of CONCACAF's accounts*: Reports from CONCACAF staffers, including Jill Fracisco and Tim Longo.

61 *I am very grateful for all the bills you have paid*: From exchange of e-mails between Mary Lynn Blanks and Chuck Blazer.

CHAPTER FIVE: MAD PARROTS AND CRAZY IDEAS

63 *hated by many*: CONCACAF staffers Jill Fracisco, Tim Longo, Clive Toye, and Ted Howard all complained about Max's incessant squawking in the office.

64 *Max finally struck it rich*: Deal to build the TV studio, Blazer's $300,000 "commission" from FIFA funds to construct it, and the creation of the association subsidiary CONCACAF Marketing and TV in Miami Beach described in *CONCACAF Integrity Committee Report of Investigation*, 45–48.

66 *"We did long checks beforehand"*: Associated Press, "Roma CEO Passed Club Checkup into Past Work at CONCACAF," September 15, 2015, appeared in *USA Today* among other publications.

66 *Zanzi was paid a $250,000 salary and a $250,000 annual bonus*: From Blazer's CONCACAF salary records for his staff.

66 *Zanzi shared the cats' quarters*: Account by Mary Lynn Blanks.

66 *a man with "tremendous potential"*: "Newsday Endorses," *Newsday* (Long Island, NY), October 31, 2006.

66 *with 38 percent of the vote*: Room Eight, "NY-01: A Perfect Politician of the Worst Kind," *Huffington Post*, June 6, 2010.

67 *The association had to spend hundreds of thousands*: TV studio building project details from CONCACAF staffers and *CONCACAF Integrity Committee Report of Investigation*. 48.

67 *The subsidiary bought Florida real estate*: Described in *CONCACAF Integrity Committee Report of Investigation*. 60.

CHAPTER SIX: UNCLE JACK

72 *But the CONCACAF board didn't discover until 2012*: Details about the Centre of Excellence in *CONCACAF Integrity Committee Report of Investigation*, 21–38.

73 *"blossomed into a multipurpose facility"*: Centre of Excellence Web site, www.coetnt.com.

73 *scene of concerts by popular Bollywood singers*: Sonu Nigam, performance, 2012, available on YouTube, www.youtube.com/watch?v=yRd9ljiusa0.

73 *gospel music recitals*: Point Fortin Youth Music Ministry, June 1, 2015, available on YouTube, www.youtube.com/watch?v=eUvKjPcRVbo.

73 *Barely Legal Pimp My Ride car show*: Available on YouTube www.youtube.com/watch?v=wjbXdF9h7zI.

73 *"Firing Your Wedding Planner"*: "Firing Your Wedding Planner," Centre of Excellence blog, January 26, 2015, www.coetnt.com/blog.php.

73 *at an association executive committee meeting*: Minutes of CONCACAF executive committee meeting, July 28, 1995.

74 *praised Warner for his "vision"*: *CONCACAF Integrity Committee Report of Investigation*, 22.

76 *"if we do get a World Cup, it would continue"*: "Beckham wins hearts at Macoya," *Daily Express*, September 26, 2010.

77 *"There is no ambiguity"*: "Warner: FIFA Gave Me £4M in Deal," ESPN April 26, 2013.

79 *Warner was a bright, industrious student*: Warner's early life and career described in detail in Singh, *Upwards Through the Night*; and Jack Warner with Valentino Singh, *Zero to Hero: Jack Austin Warner, the Man Who Inspired Trinidad and Tobago to Its First World Cup* (San Juan, Trinidad: Lexicon Trinidad, 2006).

80 *"I know that it would have caused some anxiety"*: Warner with Singh, *Zero to Hero*, 88

81 *cooperated with US investigators*: Lasana Liburd, "US Justice Department Confirms: Warner Charged, Daryan, Daryll Pleaded Guilty," Wired868, May 27, 2015, http://wired868.com/2015/05/27/us-justice-dept-confirms-warner-charged-daryan-daryll-pleaded-guilty.

81 *Simpaul Travel spun Jack's 1989 playoff ticket operation*: Doug McIntyre, "Jack Warner: Five Things to Know About Executive at Heart of FIFA Scandal," ESPN FC, June 5, 2015; Andrew Jennings, "FIFA Chief's World Cup Ticket Scam," *Independent* (UK), September 12, 2006.

81 *Simpaul made at least a $1.7 million profit selling $30,000 ticket-and-trip packages*: Nick Harris, "FIFA Executive in World Cup Ticket Scandal," *Independent* (UK), January 16, 2006.

81 *charges filed against Daryan Warner*: Teri Thomson and Nathaniel Vinton, "FIFA VP Jack Warner's Ticket-Scalping Son Sang to Federal Investigators," *Daily News* (New York), June 2, 2015.

82 *"sold" Caribbean broadcast rights*: "Warner Got FIFA World Cup Rights for $1," *Trinidad and Tobago Newsday*, December 30, 2011.

82 *Blatter sold Caribbean broadcast rights for the 2010 and 2014 World Cups to Warner*: Reuters, Mark Hosenball and David Ingram, "Swiss to Probe Contract Signed by FIFA's Blatter: Officials," September 13, 2015.

82 *accused Warner in 2011 of soliciting almost $4 million in return for votes*: Owen Gibson, "FIFA Executives Accused by Former FA Chairman Triesman of Seeking Bribes," *Guardian* (UK), May 10, 2011.

82 *"laughed like hell"*: Marco Giacomelli, "Jack Warner 'Laughed Like Hell' at Claims," *Evening Standard* (London), May 11, 2011.

83 *landed in an account controlled by Warner*: Cindy Boren, "FIFA's Jack Warner allegedly diverted Haiti earthquake money," *Washington Post*, June 9, 2015.

83 *In 2004 Scottish Football Association president John McBeth accused Warner*: "FIFA and Coe," *Panorama*, BBC One, October 29, 2007.

83 *McBeth was forced to step down in 2007 from a new position as vice president of FIFA after he was accused of racism by Warner*: "McBeth Accused of Racism," *Irish Times* (Dublin), May 29, 2007.

88 *bursting columns of flame*: "FIFA Scandal: John Oliver 'Fires' Back at Jack Warner," Sports Illustrated Wire, June 16, 2015, www.si.com/planet -futbol/2015/06/16/fifa-scandal-jack-warner-john-oliver-response-video -fire#.

CHAPTER SEVEN: LIFE WAS GOOD

89 *According to his indictment, Blazer admitted to a vast array of crimes*: May Eastern District indictment.

91 *Sepp Blatter rarely made an appearance at Le Hall*: Firsthand account by an attendee.

92 *As the old joke goes*: Blazer, *Travels with Chuck Blazer and his Friends. http:// chuckblazer.blogspot.com/.*

95 *$3,000 pearl necklace*: Firsthand account by Blanks.

95 *UEFA president Michel Platini*: Press accounts, FIFA ethics committee.

96 *Russia's World Cup bid*: Firsthand account, Blanks; Blazer: *Travels with Chuck Blazer* (blog). http://chuckblazer.blogspot.com/.

96 *Putin charmed Blazer, noting his remarkable resemblance to Karl Marx*: Firsthand account, Blanks.

97 *given pearl cuff links*: Press accounts, including quotes from Bonita Mersiades, former head of corporate and public affairs at the Football Federation Australia and FIFA whistle-blower.

98 *Ladies Day Program*: Firsthand account, Blanks.

CHAPTER EIGHT: PAY TO PLAY

101 *Chuck Blazer and Jack Warner extracted from Morocco, Egypt, and South Africa*: May Eastern District indictment; Stephen Grootes, "The Day FIFA Stole a Part of US," *Daily Maverick* (Johannesburg, SA), May 27, 2015.

102 *Marrakech was just the first stop on the 2004 bribe-a-thon*: Firsthand account, Blanks.

103 *In Cairo a week later, the $10 million South African bribe had already been settled*: May Eastern District indictment.

104 *No one was more acutely aware of Mandela's worldwide influence than Jack Warner*: Irvin Khoza, chairman, South Africa organizing committee, to a university forum in 2009.

105 *Jordaan pressed Mandela to go*: Robyn Dixon, "South Africa Is Shaken by FIFA Corruption Probe," *Los Angeles Times*, May 28, 2015, www.latimes.com/world/africa/la-fg-fifa-south-africa-20150529-story.html.

105 *On April 28, 2004, Mandela boarded a Gulfstream V for the twenty-two-hour flight to Port of Spain*: Firsthand account, Blanks.

105 *Mandela had barely slept on the flight, and La Grange, his assistant, was upset that he was seated in the front of the plane*: Firsthand account, Blanks; Zelda La Grange, *Good Morning, Mr. Mandela: A Memoir* (New York: Plume, 2015).

106 *In 2015, as the FIFA scandal deepened, Sexwale announced his candidacy . . . Sexwale received an endorsement from the German great Franz Beckenbauer*: Franz Beckenbauer speaking at the anuual Beckenbauer Camp in Kitzbuehel, Austria, October 6, 2015.

106 *a part that led to his December 17 appearance as a witness before the Eastern District grand jury*: Richard Conway, "Tokyo Sexwale: Fifa candidate questioned over World Cup bribes," BBC, December 21, 2015.

107 *Dr. João Havelange Centre of Excellence*: Multiple media reports; firsthand account, Blanks.

CHAPTER NINE: A HUNDRED AND FIVE IN THE SHADE

109 *As dusk fell on the evening of December 2, 2010*: Multiple media reports; firsthand account, Blanks.

110 *The second announcement, however, would truly raise hell*: Ibid.

111 *"requires precautions to be taken"*: 2022 FIFA World Cup Bid Evaluation Report: Qatar (Zurich, Switzerland, FIFA Evaluation Group for the 2018 and 2022 FIFA World Cup Bids).

111 *At the time of the dual bid announcements*: 2018–2022 FIFA World Cup Host Candidate Assessment Final Report to Executive Committee, FIFA Evaluation Group, Zurich, Switzerland, October 2010.

112 *was based on spec*: Multiple media accounts, including *Sunday Times* (London), *Telegraph* (UK), and *Guardian* (UK), June 2014; Heidi Blake and Jonathan Calvert, *The Ugly Game: The Corruption of FIFA and the Qatari Plot to Buy the World Cup* (London: Simon & Schuster, 2015).

112 *There were nine dog-and-pony shows*: Firsthand account, Blanks; media accounts.

113 *There were media reports that the former president returned to the Savoy Baur en Ville Hotel*: Holly Watt, Claire Newell, and Ben Bryant, "Qatar World Cup 2022 Scandal: Bill Clinton's Fury at Vote Triggered Global Search for Truth," *Telegraph* (UK), June 3, 2014.

116 *Russia in 2018 and the United States in 2022*: "Blatter: FIFA scandal provoked by Michel Platini," Tass, October 28, 2015.

117 *The only one Qatar hadn't tried to bribe*: Firsthand account, Blanks.

118 *shown up at the party*: Ibid.

CHAPTER TEN: PIRATES OF THE CARIBBEAN

119 *"Clean up FIFA" platform*: Matt Scott, "Mohamed bin Hammam Set to Run Against Sepp Blatter for FIFA Presidency," *Guardian* (UK), March 10, 2011.

120 *specially called, all-expenses-paid meeting*: E-mailed invitation to members of the Caribbean Football Union (and select other members of CONCACAF) from Warner.

120 *were allowed to skip standard immigration*: "Hammam Took Suitcase Full of Bribe \$\$ to Trinidad," *Stabroek News* (Georgetown, Guyana), June 22, 2014.

121 *"more say, more support, and more pay"*: Paul Kelso, "Revealed: FIFA's Top Secret Bribery Files on Mohamed bin Hammam and Jack Warner," *Telegraph* (UK), May 28, 2011.

121 *instructed them to go to one of the hotel conference rooms and collect their "gift"*: Account of payments following bin Hammam's speech in an affidavit by Fred Lunn as well as in investigative reports by attorney John Collins, the Freeh Group, and the FIFA ethics committee, and in a decision lifting bin Hammam's suspension from soccer activities by the Court of Arbitration for Sport.

122 *"It hurt to give it back"*: From screenshots of text messages between Fred Lunn and Anton Sealey, collected by Chuck Blazer for evidence in the investigation of the cash-for-votes scandal.

122 *"were doing some damage"*: E-mail from Blazer to Warner dated May 11, 2011.

123 *"I saw a few of you rush to the office in New York"*: Warner's comments to CFU members at the Port of Spain Hyatt, May 12, 2011, recorded by his assistant, Angenie Kanhai. Recording available on YouTube, www.youtube.com/watch?v=dfFcgOfcOqs.

124 *"worse than witchcraft"*: "Jack Warner Responds to London Telegraph Video: Ingratitude Worse than Witchcraft," *Trinidad and Tobago Guardian*, October 8, 2011.

127 *he had absolutely no knowledge of any payments*: *Mohamed bin Hammam v. FIFA*, Arbitral Award ruling by the Court of Arbitration for Sport, July 19, 2012.

128 *"as a token of appreciation"*: Ruling by the Court of Arbitration for Sport, 52.

128 *"I cannot believe the CAS decision"*: From e-mail exchanges between attorney John Collins and Chuck Blazer, July 21, 2012.

129 *raised questions about bin Hammam's role*: "AFC Process Improvement Review," PricewaterhouseCoopers, July 13, 2012.

CHAPTER ELEVEN: WHISTLE-BLOWING PAST THE GRAVEYARD

131 *man of the hour*: Associated Press, Nancy Armour, "Blazer Is Witty, Gregarious, and a Whistle-Blower," ESPN, June 4, 2011.

132 *"Do what I did. Expose it where it exists"*: Interview on Sky News with Blazer in Zurich, June 1, 2011.

133 *"cease all contractual arrangements"*: Letter from Lisle Austin sent to Chuck Blazer, May 30, 2011.

133 *complaint with FIFA's ethics committee*:

135 *characterizing the probe as part of the CONCACAF coup orchestrated by Americans*: Tariq Paja, "Jack Warner Says He'd Rather Die than Meet FIFA Investigator," Bloomberg, June 21, 2011.

135 *"claim that Louis Freeh and I are somehow close because we are Americans is laughable"*: Ibid.

136 *"we have zero tolerance"*: Matt Scott, "Chuck Blazer Welcomes Lifetime Ban for Mohamed bin Hammam," *Guardian* (UK), July 24, 2011.

137 *the FBI was examining mysterious payments*: Andrew Jennings, "FBI Investigates Secret Payments to FIFA Whistle-Blower," *Independent* (UK), August 13, 2011.

141 *Forty-four names made the initial list*: Copy of the list of names targeted for recording, as well as names off-limits, provided to Blazer and his attorneys by federal authorities.

142 *"Tex-Mex Costa Rican Jew"*: Michelle Kaufman, "Miami Soccer Broker's Fall Shocks Those Around Him," *Miami Herald*, May 29, 2015.

145 *Blazer capitalized on his attendance at the 2012 London Summer Olympics*: Invitations in series of e-mails dated July 12–23, 2012.

147 *One blog post the FBI refused to allow*: Undated draft blog Blazer submitted for approval to FBI handlers.

148 *All the company did was "supply an employee—Blazer"*: CONCACAF Integrity Committee Report of Investigation, 43.

148 *Not only did he work for Warner's Centre of Excellence*: Ibid., 82.

149 *"what you're supposed to do with audited financials"*: Jeff Carlisle, "USSF President Sunil Gulati: FIFA Needs a Culture Change," ESPN FC, November 13, 2015.

149 *"The controller was plagued by persistent health issues"*: CONCACAF Integrity Committee Report of Investigation, 71–72.

151 *documents backing up many of the expenditures*: Ibid., 65.

151 *"willfully" failed to file federal tax returns*: Ibid., 107.

153 *as the New York* Daily News *team worked on its story*: Teri Thompson, Mary Papenfuss, Christian Red, and Nathaniel Vinton, "Soccer Rat! The Inside Story of How Chuck Blazer, Ex-US Soccer Executive and FIFA Bigwig, Became a Confidential Informant for the FBI," *Daily News* (New York), November 1, 2015.

CHAPTER TWELVE: THE HAMMER FALLS

155 *and into the next day*: Teri Thompson, Mary Papenfuss, Christian Red, and Nathaniel Vinton, "Soccer Rat! The Inside Story of How Chuck Blazer, Ex-US Soccer Executive and FIFA Bigwig, Became a Confidential Informant for the FBI," *Daily News* (New York), November 1, 2015.

156 *Just before midnight, the* News: Ibid; Matt Apuzzo, Stephanie Clifford, and William K. Rashbaum, "FIFA Officials Arrested on Corruption Charges," *New York Times*, May 26, 2015.

156 *The defendants comprised*: May Eastern District indictment.

156 *Listed beneath the names of those arrested were the men the government had already flipped*: Ibid.

157 *In Zurich, the scene was almost surreal*: Michael S. Schmidt, and Sam Borden, "In a Five-Star Setting, FIFA Officials Are Arrested," *New York Times*, May 27, 2015.

158 *minefields of American justice*: David Ingram, "FIFA's Blatter Hires US Lawyer for Corruption Probe," Reuters, June 17, 2015.

158 *Lynch had promised in May that the investigation was far from over*: December Eastern District superseding indictment.

159 *That legal maneuver would not be necessary for Trujillo*: Evan Perez, "FIFA Executive Arrested on Cruise Ship," CNN, December 4, 2015.

159 *Eight more defendants pled guilty*: December Eastern District superseding indictment.

160 *Four days before Christmas, the news for Blatter and Platini got even worse*: "Fifa: Sepp Blatter and Michel Platini get eight-year bans." BBC Sport, December 21, 2015.

162 *Danis secretly waived indictment in late May*: Ibid.

162 *Two months later, the man Blanks described as "a personable guy who was everyone's Cayman banker"—CONCACAF president Jeffrey Webb*: First-person account, Blanks; Webb appearance before Judge Raymond J. Dearie, Eastern District of New York, Brooklyn.

163 *"Sanz will have a key role in the administration of CONCACAF," Webb said on the day he named Sanz to the post*: CONCACAF, "CONCACAF Appoints

Sanz General Secretary," news release, July 13, 2012. www.concacaf.com /article/concacaf-appoints-sanz-general-secretary.

163 *in additional court papers*: May Eastern District indictment; December superseding indictment; *US v. José Hawilla Traffic Sports USA Inc. and Traffic Sports International Inc.*, December 12, 2014.

163 *Hawilla himself began cooperating*: Ibid.

164 *appear in Judge Dearie's courtroom*: Appeared before Judge Raymond J. Dearie, Eastern District of New York, Brooklyn.

164 *accepted bribes from Traffic executives*: May Eastern District indictment.

164 *Office insiders corroborated the government's account*: CONCACAF employees; Teri Thompson and Nathaniel Vinton, "Wise Guys: Jeffrey Webb and Enrique Sanz Took Over CONCACAF with Same Mafia Ways as Predecessors," *Daily News* (New York), July 25, 2015; May Eastern District indictment.

165 *There was no mention of a plea agreement*: Webb appeared before US Magistrate Judge Vera M. Scanlon, July 18, 2015; Michael O'Keeffe, Teri Thompson, and Nathaniel Vinton, "Jeffrey Webb Enters Not Guilty Plea to 17 Felony Charges in FIFA Scandal, Released on $10 Million Bail," *Daily News* (New York), July 18, 2015.

166 *racketeering, wire fraud, and money laundering*: December superseding Eastern District indictment.

166 *his home near Atlanta*: December superseding indictment; CONCACAF office source.

166 *Argentinian Alejandro Burzaco waved the white flag*: Teri Thompson and Nathaniel Vinton, "FIFA Defendant Alejandro Burzaco to Be Extradited to US to Face Charges," *Daily News* (New York), July 23, 2015.

166 *The accounting went this way*: May Eastern District indictment.

167 *Bail hearings in Brooklyn were destined to continue*: Swiss Federal Office of Justice approved extraditions, September 2015.

168 *plane on November 3 bound for JFK*: Swiss Federal Office of Justice; appeared in the Eastern District courthouse November 3, 2015; Nathaniel Vinton, "Extradited FIFA Defendant Pleads Not Guilty in U.S. Court," *Daily News* (New York), November 3, 2015.

168 *Li, facing similar charges*: Swiss Federal Office of Justice.

168 *Meanwhile, in Port of Spain, Blazer's frenemy Jack Warner*: Michael O'Keeffe, Christian Red, Nathaniel Vinton, and Teri Thompson, "Feds Outline Ex-FIFA Vice President Jack Warner's Alleged Bribery Schemes," *Daily News* (New York), May 29, 2015.

169 *A few days after his jail stay*: Nathaniel Vinton, Mary Papenfuss, and Teri

Thompson, "King of Thieves! Called Robin Hood by Some, Jack Warner's Corruption & Abuse of Power in FIFA Ran Deep," *Daily News* (New York), June 6, 2015; AP and media reports.

169 *September 7 election*: Multiple media reports; confidential source account.

170 *about the bribes and kickbacks*: Nathaniel Vinton, "Former FIFA Vice President Jack Warner's Extradition Hearing to US Delayed," *Daily News* (New York), December 2, 2015.

171 *it, too, was being investigated*: Credit Suisse report; Jeffrey Voegeli, "Credit Suisse Probed by US, Switzerland in FIFA Case," Bloomberg, October 29, 2015.

172 *According to a mid-December Reuters report*: "Swiss examine 133 suspicious transactions linked to 2018 and 2022 World Cups," December 14, 2015.

CHAPTER THIRTEEN: LA FIFA NOSTRA

176 *immigrant workers have died*: "279 Migrant Indian Workers Died in Qatar Last Year: Amnesty International," *Economic Times*, May 31, 2015.

177 *But the Sin City club was not to be*: Alan Snel and James Dehaven, "Major League Soccer Takes a Pass on Las Vegas, Ending Downtown Stadium Dreams," *Review-Journal* (Las Vegas), February 12, 2015; Steve Carp, "Las Vegas' Bill Foley Not Fazed by Report of NHL Looking at Seattle Franchise," *Review-Journal* (Las Vegas), November 24, 2015; Alan Snel, "Development Partners Push to Get Las Vegas on MLS Short List," *Review-Journal* (Las Vegas), December 11, 2015.

177 *they considered soccer the "Esperanto of Sport"*: Alan Tomlinson, *FIFA: The Men, the Myths and the Money* (Abingdon, UK: Routledge, 2014).

178 *could "convince you that a blue sky was red"*: Ibid., 62.

179 *"Sport absolutely overpowers film"*: Robert Milliken, "Sport Is Murdoch's 'Battering Ram' for Pay TV," *Independent* (UK), October 15, 1996.

179 *2015 Women's World Cup finals*: Richard Sandomir, "Women's World Cup Was Most-Watched Soccer Game in United States History," *New York Times*, July 6, 2015.

179 *eight-year broadcasting deal with ESPN and Fox Sports*: Jonathan Tannewald, "MLS, US Soccer Officially Announce New TV Deal with ESPN, Fox, Univision," Philly.com, December 13, 2015.

179 *FIFA now collects $5.6 billion every four-year World Cup cycle*: "What Is FIFA and What's This Corruption Scandal All About?," William Troop, Public Radio International, May 28, 2015.

181 *paid millions extra to an intermediary*: From the Eastern District superseding indictment, December 3, 2015.

181 *The tight relationship between Adidas and FIFA raised early alarms*: The Howell Report: Committee of Enquiry into Sports Sponsorship (London: Central Council of Physical Recreation, 1983), 89.

182 *Bankruptcy proceedings and a criminal case years later against ISL*: David Bond, "The £66M 'Bribe' Shadow Hanging Over FIFA," *Telegraph* (UK), March 13, 2008.

182 *Most arresting was the discovery that ISL had paid millions of dollars in bribes*: "Three FIFA World Cup Officials Took Bribes," *Panorama*, BBC, November 29, 2010.

183 *Court documents*: Translation of the Order on the Dismissal of the Criminal Proceedings of May 11, 2010, Prosecutor's Office, Canton of Zug.

183 *Blatter acknowledged that he was "P1"*: David Conn, "Sepp Blatter faces calls to step down at FIFA over 'bribery cover-up,'" *Guardian*, July 12, 2012.

183 *Hayatou was reprimanded for bribe taking*: Owen Gibson, "Lamine Diack and Issa Hayatou Disciplined by IOC over Kickbacks," *Guardian* (UK), December 8, 2011.

184 *bribes had indeed been paid to Havelange, Teixeira, and Leoz*: FIFA, "Statement of the Chairman of the FIFA Adjudicatory Chamber, Hans-Joachim Eckert, on the Examination of the Case," report of findings, April 29, 2013, 3.

184 *"should not have accepted any bribe money"*: Ibid., 3.

184 *was chided for being "clumsy"*: Ibid., 5.

185 *But Havelange did implicate Blatter*: Matt Bonesteel, "The FBI Is Now Investigating Sepp Blatter over FIFA Bribes," *Washington Post*, December 7, 2015.

185 *Michel Zen-Ruffinen, accused Blatter of gross financial mismanagement*: Michel Zen-Ruffinen, presentation by the General Secretary at FIFA Ex-Co meeting May 3, 2002, Zurich.

186 *Zen-Ruffinen would later be embarrassed in a 2010 sting*: Richard Bright, "World Cup 2018: Former FIFA Official Michel Zen-Ruffinen Offers Himself as '£210K' Fixer," *Telegraph* (UK), October 23, 2010.

187 *a new Blazer venture called Global Interactive Gaming Ltd.*: Andrew Jennings, "FIFA Bigwig Sets Up Gambling Site," ESPN Soccernet, December 18, 2001.

187 *with losses of some $5.5 billion*: "Kirch Declares Itself Insolvent," BBC, April 8, 2002.

188 *Blazer's testimony as "generally without credibility"*: MasterCard International v. FIFA, United States Court, Southern District of New York, December 7, 2006.

CHAPTER FOURTEEN: INJURY TIME

193 *"so much focus on pomp and circumstance"*: Ives Galarcep, Goal USA, December 4, 2015, www.goal.com/en-us/news/1110/major-league-soccer/2015/12/04/18015572/one-on-one-with-garber-miami-fifa-corruption-promotionrelegation-

195 *marked a dramatically different approach*: Rebecca C. Ruiz, "US Sees FIFA as Victims and Its Leaders as Wrongdoers," *New York Times*, October 9, 2015.

196 *players headed next to Trinidad's high court*: Matt Scott, "Court Ruling Exposes Broken Promises Made by Jack Warner," *Guardian* (UK), November 29, 2010.

196 *They finally received a second check*: "State Picks Up $1.3M Tab for Footballers," *Trinidad and Tobago Guardian*, July 8, 2014.

198 *a Bolivian team refused to take part*: Reuters, "Soccer-Bolivian Player Strike Threatens World Cup Qualifiers," September 15, 2015.

198 *which Human Rights Watch compares to slavery*: Human Rights Watch, "Qatar: New Reforms Won't Protect Migrant Workers," news release, November 8, 2015.

198 *a study by the* Guardian *and a labor council found that the toll could be in the thousands*: Owen Gibson and Pete Patisson, "Death Toll among Qatar's 2022 World Cup Workers Revealed," *Guardian* (UK), December 23, 2014.

200 *Female athletes struggle*: Mai Akkad, "Women's Football in Qatar Making Strides, but More Young Talent Needed," *Doha (Qatar) News*, February 25, 2014.

201 *"Our arrest was dramatic"*: Mark Lobel, "Arrested for Reporting on Qatar's World Cup Labourers," BBC, May 18, 2015.

202 *the event cost an estimated $4 billion*: Matt Egan, "South Africa's World Cup Warning to Brazil," CNNMoney, June 10, 2014; Wolfgang Maennig and Andrew S. Zimbalist, eds., *International Handbook on the Economics of Mega Sporting Events* (Northampton, MA: Edward Elgar, 2013), 387.

203 *instead turned into a massive political protest*: Juliet Macur, "The Dazzle and the Desolation of Stadiums in World Cup Cities," *New York Times*, June 28, 2014.

203 *"think there are better ways to spend public resources"*: From the Web site of No Boston Olympics, accessed December 30, 2015, www.nobostonolympics.org.

CHAPTER FIFTEEN: GAME OVER

205 *occupied for twenty-five years*: Hugo Miller, "FIFA's Marin Swaps Jail for Trump Tower as Legal Strategy Shifts," Bloomberg, November 17, 2015; confidential sources.

205 *New York Presbyterian/Weill Cornell Hospital*: Confidential sources; Thompson et al., "Soccer Rat!"

206 *Teixeira's Rio apartment*: Firsthand account, Blanks.

206 *received from Blatter in 2011*: Rebecca R. Ruiz, "FIFA Ethics Review Clears 5 Candidates to Succeed Sepp Blatter," *New York Times*, November 12, 2015; multiple media reports.

207 *"crimes against humanity"*: Letter to acting FIFA president Issa Hayatou from Husain Abdulla, executive director, Americans for Democracy & Human Rights in Bahrain, October 19, 2015; multiple media reports.

207 *Sheikh Salman staunchly defended himself*: "Fifa Candidate Sheikh Salman: Torture Claims Are 'Nasty Lies,'" Sheikh Salman bin Ebrahim al-Khalifa, interview by BBC, October 27, 2015, www.bbc.com/sport/0/football/34 644191.

207 *he had been "used as a tool"*: Rob Harris, "Cleared to Run in FIFA Election, Sheikh Slams 'Dirty Tricks,'" Associated Press, November 14, 2015.

209 *Scala's ethics committee*. Ibid.

210 *open the bidding process*: Richard Deitsch, "FIFA Grants Fox, Telemundo US TV Rights for World Cup," *Sports Illustrated*, February 12, 2015.

211 *media companies, including Fox, and sports marketing firms*: Mica Rosenberg and David Ingram, "Exclusive—US Investigates Broadcasters in Widening FIFA Case," Reuters, December 13, 2015.

212 *immediate and significant change*: Donna de Varona, "Donna de Varona: A Message to FIFA Leadership," Inside the Games, November, 22, 2015.

213 *high blood pressure and other ailments*: Associated Press, "Former Head of South American Soccer under House Arrest," *San Diego Union Tribune*, June 1, 2015.

213 *misappropriation at the Chilean federation*: Luis Andres Henao, "Chilean Soccer Association President Takes Medical Leave," Associated Press, November 13, 2015.

214 *toll on his mind, too*: Confidential sources.

214 *subacute care facility*. Ibid.

AUTHOR BIOS

MARY PAPENFUSS

Mary Papenfuss has been an editor at the New York *Daily News*, the Associated Press, and *Salon*, and currently writes for Reuters and the *International Business Times*. She's written extensively on issues of criminal psychology and domestic violence. This is her third nonfiction book. She divides her time between New York and Mill Valley, California.

TERI THOMPSON

Teri Thompson is a former top editor at the New York *Daily News*, where she created the newspaper's award-winning sports investigative team that broke the Chuck Blazer story in 2014. Before coming to the *News*, she was a sports columnist at the *Rocky Mountain News* and an editor at ESPN. She has co-authored two books, including the critically acclaimed *"American Icon: The Fall of Rogers Clemens and the Rise of Steroids in America"* and is also a member of the Connecticut bar.